RESULTS BASED FACILITATION

MOVING FROM TALK » TO ACTION

2ND EDITION

ADVANCED SKILLS

BOOK 2

IN MEETINGS

IN NEIGHBORHOODS AND ORGANIZATIONS

IN COMMUNITIES

BY JOLIE BAIN PILLSBURY, Ph.D. A PUBLICATION OF SHERBROOKE CONSULTING, INC. ARLINGTON, VA

Results Based Facilitation: Book Two - Advanced Skills - 2nd Edition
ISBN: 9780989017749 (Print Version)

ISBN: 9780989017770 (Kindle)

Sherbrooke Consulting, Inc.
1500 22nd Street North
Arlington, VA 22209
www. sherbrookeconsulting.com
www.rbl-apps.com

PREFACE

> THE FIRST PROPERTY OF MIRACLES IS THAT THEY SHOULD NOT OCCUR.
>
> -DAVID HUME

I am always awed by mastery and by what people can do when they dedicate themselves to the relentless practice necessary to achieve it. Over the years, I have been inspired and informed by the artists of the Cirque du Soleil, Gary Bokovnik's watercolors, and Yo-Yo Ma playing Bach and have always wondered how they were able to achieve mastery. To the novice, mastery seems like a miracle of inborn talent. To the practitioner, mastery appears as the product of hard, skilled labor.

In my 30-year career I have been privileged to contribute to the measurable improvement of community well-being — tangible changes in life circumstances for children, adults, and families. Without these efforts, these children might not have been born healthy, had homes, or entered school ready to learn, and adults might not have returned to settle safely and productively in their communities after serving a prison sentence.

In all these instances, my contribution was not to work with the families and children directly but to deploy a set of skills that facilitated the work of the many gifted, talented, and passionate people working to make whole communities healthier, wiser, and in so many ways better off. Over the years, I have become very good at what I do, learning through constant trial and error to practice and help others practice a particular kind of facilitation — Results Based Facilitation (RBF) — at a mastery level.

"I THINK YOU SHOULD BE MORE EXPLICIT HERE IN STEP TWO."

Evidence is emerging that using RBF skills increases the odds that problems will be solved, conflicts resolved, decisions made, and actions taken that over time contribute to improving lives. Yet most people are unaware of the skill set, may not recognize it when it is practiced, and may not have the opportunity or interest to learn and practice these skills at a level of mastery that can make a difference for themselves and others.

This manual, *Results Based Facilitation: Book Two — Advanced Skills,* is the outgrowth of those years of discovering through experience what it takes for people to work together in service to their communities with the same discipline, skill focus, and mastery that they use in any creative and constructive endeavor. At an advanced level, RBF invites people to engage in the quality of community life game with the same intensity, metrics, training methods, and energy with which they play sports.

I believe we all have in us the will and spirit that, if ignited, can grow the skills that nurture our humanity and, against all odds, can substitute peace for war, action for inaction, and positive, desired results for negative and often unintended consequences. In every community, right now, there are children, families, and adults at risk. For every person who goes a day without good food, good health care, or a loving and stimulating environment, there are consequences. The lack of action matters for that person and for the community.

Often the media reports on a child being lost, and heroically, the whole community comes forward to help with the search. People come from far away to help with the search. Every hour that goes by is precious. People have come forward in a crisis and responded together.

Crises of this type give a sharp, clear signal to us all. However, it is easy to miss the many people in a community who are just as urgently in need. It is easy to overlook those who on a daily basis do not have what they need to survive and thrive. The consequences for the invisible can be just as devastating as the consequences for those whose plight is easy to see.

But this daily toll on the lives of children, families, and adults creates an opportunity for a community to figure out together how to make a contribution to improving the quality of life for *all.*

Results Based Facilitation: Book Two — Advanced Skills reflects many years of partnership with colleagues who have greatly contributed to the evolution of RBF advanced skills designed specifically to provide a set of practices for people to use to work together and improve the life circumstances of all the families, children, and adults in communities. I would like to thank them for the generosity of their contributions and the warmth of their friendship:

- *Victoria Goddard-Truitt,* for her contributions as a thought partner, editor of the *RBF Primer* and the *Theory of Aligned Contributions Primer,* lead researcher developing the evidence base for practice, and codeveloper of the coaching and practice methods and developer of the High Action/High Alignment Assessment Tool.

- *Raj Chawla,* for his dedication to the mastery and extension of the skills and as the co-author of many of the results-based leadership applications and as the author of *The Ten Conversations.*

- *Steven Jones, Phyllis Rozansky, Ron Redmon, Kathleen Pogue White,* and *Mark Friedman,* all of whose work has contributed over the years to the development and application of the advanced skills.

- *Molly McGrath Tierney,* director of the Baltimore (Maryland) City Department of Social Services, and her staff, for their application of leadership skills in improving the lives of children and families.

- *Alice Shobe, Crystal Collier,* and *Olymphia Perkins,* for their leadership in applying the advanced skills to improve the well-being of children, youth, and families.

- *Connie Revell, Catherine Saucedo, Reason Reyes* and all the staff of the Smoking Cessation Leadership Center, for the successful implementation of Performance Partnerships across the country and the use of the advanced skills.

- *Donna Stark, Barbara Squires, Jennifer Gross,* and *Ashley Stewart* of the Annie E. Casey Foundation, for almost two decades of partnership, their support of the development and practice of RBF, and their use of RBF both within the Foundation and as part of the Foundation's results-based leadership programs. Many of the advanced skills were tested and refined in the crucible of these programs, as leaders worked to contribute to improve the well-being of the most vulnerable families and children.

- *Kate Shatzkin, Kathryn Shagas, Victoria Goddard-Truitt* and other members of the editing and design team who worked so hard to produce *RBF Advanced Skills, second edition.*

I also would like to acknowledge the leaders too numerous to mention by name who, by their willingness to practice RBF skills in service of improving results, have informed and made possible the development of the RBF skills and practice methods. I hope that the advanced skills are useful to them as they continue to do the hard, courageous, and meaningful work of moving from talk to action.

My deepest gratitude goes to Robert D. Pillsbury, my husband and cofounder of the Results Based Facilitation Network. This work would not have been possible without his helpful insights, unflagging support, extraordinary creativity as an iconographer, and lifelong commitment to being my closest thought and practice partner.

This book is dedicated to all the people who get up every day and with dedication, patience, and perseverance do the hard work of making a measurable difference in the lives of children, families, and communities.

Jolie Bain Pillsbury, Ph.D. (ENTJ)
President, Sherbrooke Consulting, Inc.
Cofounder, Results Based Facilitation Network
Cofounder, Results Based Leadership Consortium
December 2015

IMPORTANT ICONS

	Awareness of a skill
	Application of a skill
	Mastery of a skill
	Participant practice guide
SF ST NF NT	Myers-Briggs Type Indicator® (MBTI®)

GLOSSARY OF ACRONYMS

ACRONYM	FULL NAME OR PHRASE
3Rs	Results, Relationships, and Resources
ARE	Acknowledge, Rephrase, and Explore
B/ART	Boundaries of Authority, Role, and Task
CS	Context Statement
EQ	Effective Question
LF	Listen For
MBTI®	Myers-Briggs Type Indicator®
PBDM	Proposal-Based Decision Making
PRS	Person-Role-System
RBF	Results Based Facilitation
RBL	Results-Based Leadership
SBI	Situation, Behavior, Impact

CONTENTS

OVERVIEW

WE HAVE TO DO THE BEST WE CAN. THIS IS OUR SACRED HUMAN RESPONSIBILITY

-ALBERT EINSTEIN

Results Based Facilitation (RBF) advanced skills are for the specific purpose of putting results, the well-being of people, at the center of people's collective work. The practice of these advanced skills builds on those in *Results Based Facilitation: Book One — Foundation Skills.*

To stimulate new levels of thinking, Book Two introduces a repertoire of mental models designed to support groups in clarifying issues, addressing challenges, and building the relationships needed to move from talk to the kind of action that produces measurable, observable results in programs, organizations, and communities. These advanced skills support a group's ability to make decisions that stick, to be accountable for moving to action, and to address and use data to improve execution and accelerate progress toward program and community results.

RBF is a skill set grounded in a daily practice method that leads to mastery and efficacy. Daily practice makes the skills available when people need them most — in those moments of risk and opportunity when frustration and inaction can pivot to become action and results. This book is about the translation into actual practices that if repetitively pursued, catalyze the idea of community well-being into a reality that is lived, felt, and experienced by people.

People often know what to do (such as, listen well, address conflict constructively); their challenge is actually doing what they know with sufficient consistency and skill to make a difference in the way things are. The premise of this book is that persistent, continuously improving practice enables people to act effectively.

As a practice guide, this book gives you a rubric to assess how well you practice now, exercises and methods to develop your skills, and ways to gather information about the impact you are having when you use the skills. The intent of the focused practice and skill improvement is to give you the opportunity to achieve mastery of the advanced skills that enable groups to work together to achieve improvement in the well-being of populations.

The six RBF competencies, including the advanced competencies of Hold Mental Models and Hold Action and Results, are listed in the table below.

THE SIX RBF COMPETENCIES AND 22 SKILLS

RBF FOUNDATION SKILLS AND COMPETENCIES (BOOK ONE)
HOLD ROLES: Be aware of and make choices about roles that contribute to achieving results.
Use B/ART to define and differentiate roles as they relate to meeting results
Use B/ART to understand group dynamics and achieve meeting results
Hold neutral facilitator role
Give the work back to the group
HOLD CONVERSATIONS: Listen with openness, curiosity, and attentiveness to frame dialogues that achieve meeting results.
Demonstrate appreciative openness
Use Context Statements, Effective Questions, and Listen Fors
HOLD GROUPS: Support groups in having focused conversations that move to results.
Use flip chart to display the group's work
Sequence
Summarize
Synthesize
Check in and check out
HOLD 3R MEETINGS: Use the 3R framework to design and facilitate meetings that move groups from talk to action.
Use the 3Rs to design the meeting
Use the 3Rs in the meeting to achieve results
RBF ADVANCED SKILLS AND COMPETENCIES (BOOK TWO)
HOLD MENTAL MODELS: Use a repertoire of perspectives that contribute to achieving meeting results.
Use proposal-based decision making to move from talk to action
Use conversations to develop convergence
Name and address barriers to convergence
Make and help others make action commitments
Be and help others be accountable for action commitments
Observe and respond to group dynamics
Assess and address conflict
HOLD ACTION AND RESULTS: Make a difference in programs and community populations.
Be accountable in role for contributions to results
Use RBF skills to work collaboratively to accelerate progress toward results

When people are locked in conflict — unable to implement, unable to move from small-scale success to larger impact — or when they are tempted to walk away from failure rather than using failure as an opportunity to learn, RBF advanced skills help people move from talk to action.

RBF equips people with a perceptual framework and skill set that moves groups toward a series of consensus-based decisions in a short time. The method integrates the use of data, appreciative inquiry, problem solving, and conflict resolution in the practice of proposal-based decision making. This specific practice enables groups to overcome one of the major barriers to successful action: their inability to make decisions together that stick and lead to accountable, aligned action.

Emergent research indicates that Results Based Facilitation, as part of a larger collaborative leadership skill set, enables groups to contribute to improved results.[1] RBF accelerates the adoption of practices that frame complex issues. These practices focus people on making measurable progress against a baseline and rapidly moving to develop and implement action plans.

RBF is a competency-based approach to participating in and facilitating meetings in order to get results. The six RBF competencies used by participants and facilitators move groups from talk to action by focusing on meeting results and by developing an accountability framework for commitments to aligned action. RBF skills ensure that participants, conveners, and facilitators work together, entering a meeting with results in mind and leaving with action commitments in hand.

The advanced skills in this book are built on the foundation skills found in *Results Based Facilitation: Book One.* Book Two is most easily understood by those who have gained an understanding of the theory underlying RBF: the competencies, the developmental continuum, and the practice methods, including how to give and receive skill-focused feedback, found in Book One.

RBF COMPETENCY ASSESSMENT CONTINUUM

As with the foundation skills, each of the advanced skills is described at three levels. The levels allow the practitioner to differentiate between awareness, application, and mastery as described in the following table.

RBF SKILL LEVELS

Developing awareness begins with an initial understanding of the concepts — and a rudimentary command of the skill. You are developing awareness when you can see and *name the skill.*	**Begin by seeing**	
Applying the skill involves a deeper and broader understanding of the skill and the ability to use the skill well in various situations. You are applying the skill when you can *do it consciously.*	**Move to doing**	
Mastering the skill occurs when you have internalized it and demonstrated the ability to consistently integrate the skill in most situations. You have mastered the skill when you have made it your own, and the skill is now *a part of who you are.*	**Make it part of your being**	

The use of the advanced skills is predicated on an awareness and ability to apply the foundation skills. The following is a brief review of the foundation competencies. In addition, Appendix A includes a competency assessment for the four foundation skills of Book One. If your competency assessment identifies foundation skills that are not at the mastery level, you can continue to improve these skills while becoming aware of and applying the advanced skills.

THE FOUNDATION SKILLS

The foundation skills are divided into four competencies. These competencies have 13 associated skills that are briefly described below.

HOLD ROLES

To hold roles is the ability to be aware of and make choices about roles that contribute to achieving meeting results.

This first competency uses the concept of the boundaries of authority, role, and task (B/ART) to consider your own role and that of others in meetings. The competency includes the ability to name and understand the tasks and authority of the variety of roles that people hold in both their daily work and in meetings. From this role clarity, you can make the informed choices about what to say and do in a variety of roles that will be most productive in achieving meeting results. The skills enable practitioners to accomplish the following:

- define and differentiate roles as they contribute to meeting results;
- understand group dynamics to achieve meeting results;
- develop the capacity to hold a neutral facilitator role; and
- use methods for giving work back to the group.

HOLD CONVERSATIONS

To hold conversations is the ability to listen with openness, curiosity, and attentiveness to frame dialogues that achieve meeting results.

This competency includes the capacity to have conversations or facilitate meaningful conversations. These kinds of conversations create the connections that enable people to be on the same page at the same time and hear each other's perspectives and points of view. The skills equip practitioners to accomplish the following:

- demonstrate openness and genuine curiosity in their listening; and
- use a Context Statement, Effective Questions, and an awareness of what to Listen For in conversations.

HOLD GROUPS

To hold groups is the ability to support groups to hold focused conversations that move to results.

This competency encompasses the basic meeting skills needed to hold groups in focused conversations. These skills enable the practitioners to accomplish the following:

- chart to document the work;
- sequence speakers, topics, and work to have one conversation at a time;
- summarize ideas, proposals, and decisions to support the group's ability to make decisions;
- synthesize ideas, meaning, and group dynamics to enable the group to move from talk to action; and
- check in and check out to support the group in beginning and ending their work together focused on results.

HOLD 3R MEETINGS

To hold 3R meetings is the ability to use the 3R framework to design and facilitate conversations and meetings that move groups from talk to action.

This competency contains the skills that enable you to have meetings by design. These skills equip you to consider the 3Rs (Relationships, Resources, and Results) to:

- develop and articulate clear meeting results; and
- analyze group composition to understand how participants relate to each other and to the result, and support participants to align resources in service of the result.

THE ADVANCED SKILLS

Practicing and developing mastery of the foundation skills produces benefits, such as an increased ability to collaborate with others and accelerate progress toward meeting results, a heightened awareness of your strengths and how to deploy them to achieve meeting results, and an enhanced capacity to notice the impact of using skills and to learn from experience.

As you master the skills, you may find that you predictably create and contribute to more coherent conversations that address and resolve issues, and that move you and others to accountable aligned action. However, you may also find challenges that are beyond your skill set. You may be part of groups stuck in conflict, paralyzed by lack of clear decision making, or unable to hold themselves accountable for implementing their decisions. In these instances, you may not have the skills to address the complex challenge of people from different backgrounds working together to improve the well-being of the children, families, or adults in a community.

RBF advanced skills equip you to work collaboratively to have effective meetings where conflicts are resolved, action commitments made and kept, and strategies implemented at a scope and scale to make a measurable difference in people's lives. This book builds on the foundation skills in Book One and introduces advanced skills that enable conveners, facilitators, and participants to have productive meetings. The advanced skills move groups from talking to planning to execution at the scope and scale needed to achieve a collective impact.

The advanced skills consist of two competencies: Hold Mental Models and Hold Action and Results, which are listed in the table below.

ADVANCED SKILLS

HOLD MENTAL MODELS: *Use a repertoire of perspectives that contribute to achieving meeting results.*
Use proposal-based decision making to move from talk to action
Use conversations to develop convergence
Name and address barriers to convergence
Make and help others make action commitments
Be and help others be accountable for action commitments
Observe and respond to group dynamics
Assess and address conflict
HOLD ACTION AND RESULTS: *Make a difference in programs and community populations.*
Be accountable in role for contributions to results
Use RBF skills to work collaboratively to accelerate progress toward results

For each skill, information is provided that enables you to assess your level of skill. The example competency assessment shown in the next table indicates that at the *mastery* level, knowledge of Myers-Briggs Type Indicator® (MBTI®) is used to make and help others make action commitments.

SKILL 5.4: MAKE AND HELP OTHERS MAKE ACTION COMMITMENTS

AWARENESS	APPLICATION	MASTERY
Understands the intent and form of effective action commitments • *Do I set a context for making public action commitments?* • *Do I listen for action commitments with a disciplined focus on who, what, and when?* • *Do I support the group in documenting action commitments for future reference?*	Helps groups make commitments to action • *Do I help groups manage the change process associated with moving to action?*	Helps groups align action commitments • *Do I use MBTI awareness to support people making action commitments?* • *Can I use the high action/ high alignment framework?*
→	→	→

ADVANCED SKILLS ALIGN CONTRIBUTIONS

The combination of the foundation and advanced skills enables groups to overcome common barriers to moving forward together, such as difficulty in using information to decide what to do, how to do it, and if they are making a positive difference. The table below gives examples of how the skills create the capacity to overcome barriers and enable groups to align contributions for collective impact.

BARRIERS AND RBF COMPETENCIES AND SKILLS TO OVERCOME THEM

Barriers	RBF Competencies and Skills
Inability to make decisions because people lack data on which to base decisions	The foundation competency of Hold 3R meetings, in conjunction with the advanced competency of Hold Action and Results, ensures that groups gather baseline data prior to the meeting. This method of preparing for the meeting with a focus on the population to be served, the trend line data to be analyzed, and the available evidence-based practices specific to the issue accelerates the group's ability to move forward with targeted strategies.
Inability to use available data because of discomfort with quality or relevance of the data	The foundation skill of Use Context Statements, Effective Questions, and Listen Fors enables groups to have fluid and focused group dialogues that resolve issues of using the best available data to agree to a baseline and set a target. In combination with the advanced competency of Hold Mental Models, groups are able to use the data they have and commit to developing improved data.
Vested interests leading to unresolved conflict	The advanced skills of Identify and Address Barriers to Convergence and Assess and Address Conflict enable groups to understand the sources of conflict in the group and use a repertoire of approaches, ranging from adopting norms of behavior to interest-based negotiation, to resolve differences and move forward together.
Inability to make decisions that everyone supports and lead to effective follow-through	The advanced skill of Use Proposal-Based Decision Making to Move from Talk to Action provides an alternative to traditional approaches such as Robert's Rules of Order and expedites consensus building. Proposal-based decision making allows groups to more quickly formulate decisions that everyone can support.
Inability of participants to move to action quickly enough, which dissipates the urgency needed to take action	The foundation skills of Give the Work Back to the Group and Sequence, Summarize, Synthesize in combination with the advanced skill of Be Accountable in Role for Contributions to Results enables people to commit to practical, realistic next steps that are likely to produce measurable changes in the targeted performance measures.

PARTICIPANT PRACTICE GUIDES

Practicing the skills daily as a participant in meetings leads to mastery. Fortunately, such practice opportunities abound. Every day there are many conversations in which you participate, even though you may not be a facilitator. These are settings where you can use RBF skills to listen appreciatively, clarify meaning, explore issues, create greater understanding, and (where appropriate) move to action. For each skill, as with Book One, Participant Practice Guides provide suggestions for using the skills. Below is a brief summary of Book Two.

SUMMARY

THEORY: RBF — A COLLABORATIVE LEADERSHIP SKILL

Productive meetings are a prerequisite for collaboration that produces results in organizations and communities. The RBF advanced skills are grounded in the Theory of Aligned Contributions and equip people to convene, facilitate, or participate in meetings that make effective collaboration possible.

PRACTICE: PUTTING RESULTS IN THE CENTER

The practice of advanced RBF skills at the mastery level enables cross-sector leaders to put a common result at the center of their work and move through a cycle of collaborative action to produce measurable improvements in population well-being. That practice is illuminated by the application of the Hold Action and Results competency in a range of collaborative leadership programs in organizations and communities.

COMPETENCY #5: HOLD MENTAL MODELS

The Hold Mental Models competency is based on the premise that problems cannot be solved by the same level of thinking that created them.[2] To stimulate new levels of thinking, this competency introduces a repertoire of mental models designed to support groups in clarifying issues, addressing challenges, and building the relationships and making decisions needed to move from talk to action.

This competency includes seven skills that provide a repertoire of mental models to move people through the collaborative work cycle, which is the overarching mental model of Results Based Facilitation. These skills, used as either a participant or a facilitator, are particularly helpful when groups are stuck and cannot move from talk to action because they cannot make decisions that stick, hold accountability for getting things done, and/or resolve the conflicts or address the difficult issues that are barriers to action.

COMPETENCY #6: HOLD ACTION AND RESULTS

The Hold Action and Results competency focuses on examples of results when RBF skills and methods are employed. The examples include specific conversations and meeting designs that have proven effective in adopting a common result and ways to measure progress toward that result; committing to and being accountable for aligned actions; and developing the capacity to address differences across the boundaries of sector, gender, race, ethnicity, and world view to build the sustainable relationships necessary to make a measurable difference.

USING DATA TO IMPROVE PRACTICE

This chapter provides an opportunity to consider how to continue your path to mastery, find opportunities to use your skills in the coach role, and use data to improve practice.

Book Two is a guide to the daily practice needed to develop the advanced skills. It provides the opportunity to explore and reflect, experiment and conceptualize the application of the skills. The intention is to engage people in a process of knowledge development similar to that depicted in Frank LaBanca's experiential learning cycle shown here.[3]

LaBanca's Experiential Learning Cycle

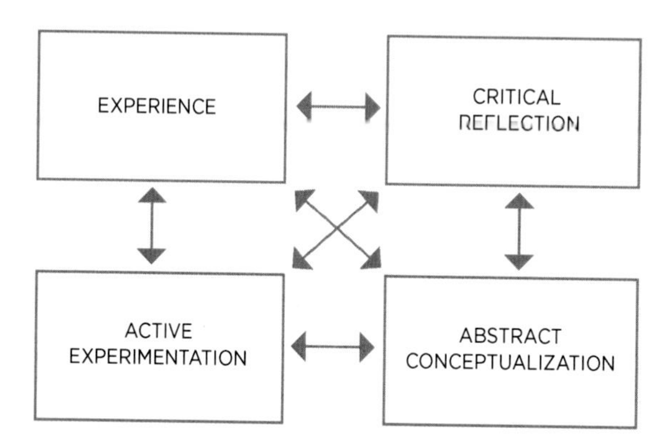

The advanced skills are built by using reading, reflection, observation, and data to inform practice. Not all these modes, though necessary, will be equally appealing to you. However, mastery requires that you work to do them all.[4]

TO LEARN, OBSERVE.
TO UNDERSTAND, READ.
TO DO, PRACTICE.
TO IMPROVE, USE DATA.
TO MASTER, TEACH.

— ANONYMOUS

In each chapter in this book, you will find detailed descriptions of the skill accompanied by specific activities to help you become aware of, apply, and master the skill. The development of each skill will be enhanced by learning through experience and observation, reading and reflection, deliberate and daily practice informed by the use of data, and ultimately, by coaching others in the use of the skills.

NOTES:

[1] Littlefield, O'Brien, and Hersey. *Participant or Spectator: Non-profit Engagement in Multi-Sector Collaboratives.* American Society for Public Administration Conference. Baltimore, MD. March 2011.

[2] Attributed to Albert Einstein.

[3] http://epltt.coe.uga.edu/index.php?title=Experiential_Learning

[4] Baker, Jensen, and Kolb. *Conversational Learning: An Approach to Knowledge Creation.* Quorum. 2002.

THEORY: RBF — A COLLABORATIVE LEADERSHIP SKILL

CONCEPTS IN THIS CHAPTER

THE THEORY OF ALIGNED CONTRIBUTIONS

USING RBF IN TWO SYSTEMS

PUTTING RESULTS IN THE CENTER

This chapter discusses the theory behind advanced Results Based Facilitation competencies and skills. By its nature, RBF requires working with others and understanding the underlying theory that governs collaborative work. RBF is a collaborative leadership skill. You'll learn how intentionally aligning individual contributions and commitments within a group improves accountability and accelerates progress toward results within both your home organizational system and a new system you may be part of creating to achieve large-scale results.

» **Collaborative:** (n) a group of people working together to align and leverage their efforts, resources, and relationships to achieve results

CONCEPTS IN THIS CHAPTER

COLLABORATIVE MEMBERS ARE SUPPORTED BY NEUTRAL, BUT SKILLFUL, FACILITATORS WHO WORK TO DEVELOP THE PARTICIPANTS' COLLABORATIVE LEADERSHIP SKILLS AND PROMOTE BOTH PUBLIC ACCOUNTABILITY FOR THE GROUP AND INDIVIDUAL ACCOUNTABILITY WITHIN THE GROUP.[1]

Results Based Facilitation (RBF) enables people to work together to make progress toward meeting results. Sometimes meetings are convened to achieve larger-scale, more complex results. In these instances, leaders might strive to ensure that all the babies in a community are born healthy, that all the young children in a state enter school ready to learn, or that all the children at risk in a community grow up in safe and nurturing families. Research shows that leaders are more effective collaborators when they use RBF skills and when they are supported by meetings designed, facilitated, and implemented using RBF skills and methods.

Using RBF to create productive meetings convened to improve population well-being is part of an emergent theory about how to achieve collective impact in organizations and in communities. That theory, the Theory of Aligned Contributions (TOAC), informs the design and execution of meetings that predictably move leaders to hold themselves accountable for implementing aligned strategies at a scope and scale to measurably improve results.

For example, using the RBF skill of making and helping others make action commitments at the awareness level involves participants making public action commitments and then documenting their progress using a template to ensure that the commitments are specific and aligned. Applying this RBF skill in a collaborative setting increases the accountability rate (e.g., the percentage of action commitments accomplished) for individuals by 17 percent and for groups by 25 percent.[2]

This chapter outlines the TOAC and provides examples of how RBF is used as a collaborative leadership skill in the design and implementation of productive meetings.

THE THEORY OF ALIGNED CONTRIBUTIONS

In the Theory of Aligned Contributions, leaders are defined as people who consciously and persistently work to contribute to a result, align those contributions to create greater collective impact, and progress toward improvement in well-being for people at the program, organizational, and community levels. According to that theory, a *leader* is, by definition, any person in any role who holds him- or herself and others accountable for making and keeping commitments to action that are aligned to accelerate progress. The following figure is a visual representation of the theory.

ILLUSTRATION OF THE THEORY OF ALIGNED CONTRIBUTIONS

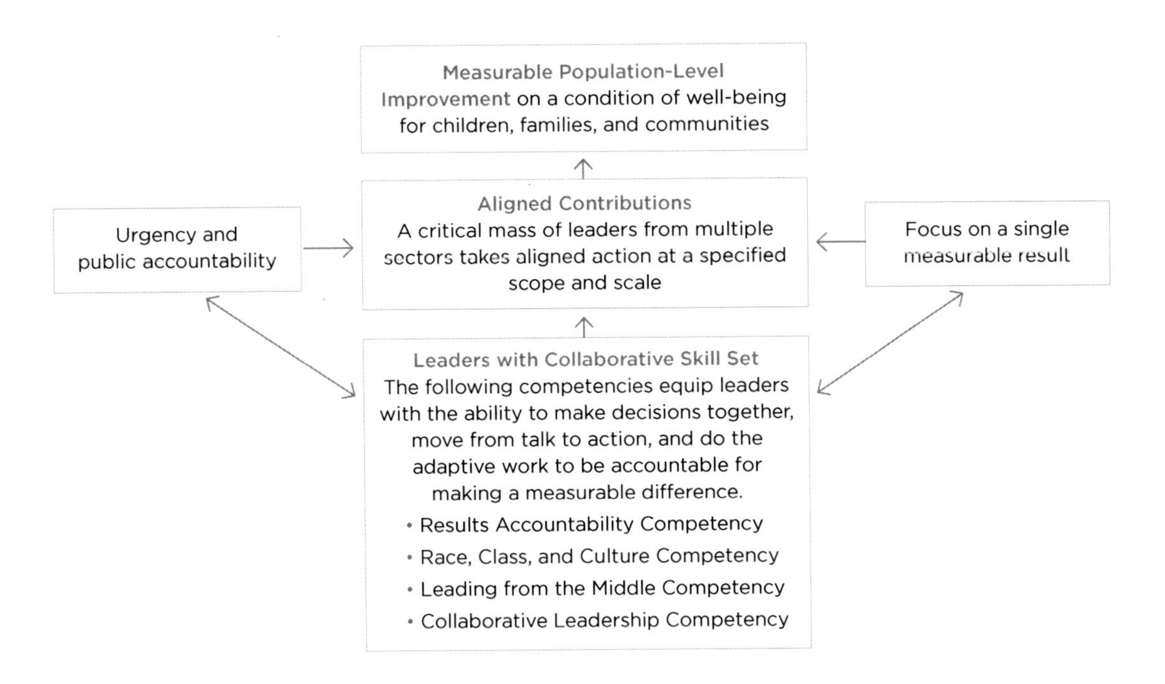

The TOAC is a collaborative leadership theory which predicts that population-level results can be achieved by leaders developing the competencies and skills to move through the collaborative work cycle together.

As leaders practice these skills and behaviors and take aligned actions, the leaders produce better results, build stronger relationships, and create a virtuous cycle. In that cycle of moving from talk to aligned action, the power of accomplishment reinforces the leadership practices that accelerate progress toward the common result. This approach is contingent on leaders practicing a set of skills together while working toward a common purpose.[3]

The theory posits that leaders who have the following four collaborative leadership competencies are more likely to create progress in improving population-level results:

- The Results Accountability competency is the ability to use a disciplined approach to making data-driven decisions. These decisions are focused on immediate action that contributes to measurable improvement in a result.
- The Race, Class, and Culture competency is the constructive dialogue that enables leaders to address race, class, and culture disparities.

- The Leading from the Middle competency is the ability to enroll those you are accountable to, those you hold accountable, and peers and colleagues to implement strategies that work.
- The Collaborative Leadership competency is the ability of leaders to make decisions and take action together in service to the result.

Mastery of the four leadership competencies is enhanced by the use of RBF skills. For example, in mastering the Race, Class, and Culture competency, the Hold Conversations competency at the mastery level enhances people's ability to listen with appreciation and curiosity to experiences different from their own. The Hold Mental Models is a complementary competency that strengthens people's ability to understand the assumptions they hold and find ways to work across the divides of race, class, and culture and implement strategies together to address disparities. The next table uses color coding to highlight how the Hold Conversations (purple) and Hold Mental Models (green) competencies enhance the ability of leaders to master the Race, Class, and Culture competency.

RACE, CLASS, AND CULTURE COMPETENCY

The ability to have constructive dialogue about race, class, and culture that enables leaders to address race, class, and culture disparities.

Skill	Awareness	Application	Mastery
Has honest conversations about race, class, and culture effects	I share my own race, class, and culture experiences and actively listen to experiences of others to deepen understanding and to clarify assumptions.	I understand the interaction of race, class, and culture, and use awareness to address race, class, and culture effects in my interactions.	I use race, class, and culture awareness to take risks and to hold own interests, and to explore interests of others to develop deeper, more trusting relationships.
Takes action to address race, class, and culture disparities	I am willing to assess the impact on disparities of my own choices and actions at the person-role-system level.	I seek out and implement best practices to address race, class, and culture disparities.	I implement best practices with partners to address race, class, and culture disparities.

Mastering the Leading from the Middle Competency is enhanced by the Hold Roles competency. The Hold Roles competency enables people to use MBTI within the Person-Role-System framework and operate within a defined B/ART. This skill supports people in working within hierarchies and across heterarchies to make aligned contributions to results. The following table highlights how the Hold Roles (blue) competency enhances the Leading from the Middle competency.

LEADING FROM THE MIDDLE COMPETENCY

The ability to enroll those you are accountable to, those you hold accountable, and peers and colleagues to implement strategies that work.

Skill	Awareness	Application	Mastery
Uses understanding of preferences to move self and others from talk to action	I understand my own MBTI and those of others and am aware of the impact of my preferences on my choices as a leader.	I use understanding of the impact of MBTI preferences to see choices or behaviors that move a group from talk to action.	I apply MBTI awareness in making choices about communication, approaches to problem solving, and conflict resolution that move to high action and high alignment.
Makes decisions and takes actions on behalf of the result	I use reflective practice and feedback to explore my own sources of authority and assumptions about what I can and can't do.	I use my own authority and enroll others to support movement from talk to action.	I contribute through choices and actions to implement strategies at the scope and scale necessary to impact the result.

The Collaborative Leadership competency is supported by the Hold Mental Models (green) and Hold Roles (blue) competencies. With its focus on proposal-based decision making, this competency depends on mastery of all the RBF skills and, in particular, the ability to apply the mental model of the collaborative work cycle in groups. Meeting designs that implement the collaborative work cycle enable leaders to enter a meeting with the results that they want to accomplish in mind and leave meetings with commitments to action in hand.

COLLABORATIVE LEADERSHIP COMPETENCY

The ability of leaders to make decisions and take action together in service of the result.			
Skill	**Awareness**	**Application**	**Mastery**
Makes proposals to develop accountability for collective decisions	I make proposals and build on the proposals of others.	I problem solve to help groups reach convergence and be accountable for implementing decisions.	I facilitate or lead proposal-based decision making and am able to resolve conflicts during the process.
Takes up leadership role in the group	I use the concepts of boundaries of authority, role, and task to address the technical and adaptive challenges.	I consciously take a leadership role in the group by facilitating joining, problem solving, decision making, and holding accountability.	I help the group move forward by taking aligned action to accelerate progress.

USING RBF IN TWO SYSTEMS

Contributing to population-level results requires using the RBF skills in two systems — your home organizational system and the larger collaborative system(s) that you join and help bring into being.

SYSTEM I: ORGANIZATIONAL SYSTEMS

Your home organizational system[4] authorizes the roles, tasks, and authority of those within the organization. RBF skills used within your primary sphere of hierarchical authority can clarify your and others' accountability for making aligned contributions to program results. Hierarchical authority and accountability include a CEO's authority in his or her own organization and accountability to the board, a supervisor's authority within his or her own unit and accountability to the manager, a publicly appointed official's authority in his or her own agency and accountability to the appointing authority, a private consultant's accountability to a client and authority over his or her own work and the work of colleagues that the consultant supervises or directs, a teacher's authority in the classroom and accountability to a principal. The skills can also be used to build collaborative heterarchical relationships across the lines of authority and functional specialties within organizations.

A defining characteristic of the organizational system is that no matter how large and diverse, a unifying authorizing body or locus of hierarchical authority defines the parameters of how people work together, what they will produce, and how accountability is held. The RBF skills provide ways to negotiate and influence the organizational system's operation to increase alignment and accountability *within* the organization to produce program results. In addition, if the individuals in the organization become part of broader collaborative efforts to contribute to population results, RBF skills are useful in supporting the alignment of organizational contributions to the population results beyond the organization's boundaries.

SYSTEM II: EMERGENT RESULTS-CENTERED SYSTEMS

In collaborative work, there is no formal authority between leaders from different systems or organizations. Instead, leaders work to build heterarchical relationships across organizational structures to address issues of authority and accountability. RBF skills are used in heterarchical roles to bring an emergent system into being to improve population well-being. In the emergent results-centered system, your B/ART and the B/ART of those you work with are an emergent property of the group's work on a population result that is beyond any one organization's scope of authority. In these results-centered emergent systems, people work across the boundaries of organizations and sectors to ignite a collaborative system that catalyzes contributions at a large enough scope and scale to measurably improve population-level results.

CATALYZE: TO BRING ABOUT; INITIATE; TO PRODUCE FUNDAMENTAL CHANGE IN; TRANSFORM

- THEFREEDICTIONARY.COM

Use of RBF skills and practices supports the creation of conditions "within which spontaneous self-organization might occur to produce emergent outcomes."[5] The Hold Action and Results competency focuses on the interactions and relationships more likely to lead to the self-organizing behaviors that improve performance.[6]

> *Emergent behavior is self-organized. Self-organization is a process in which the internal organization of a system, normally an open system, increases in complexity without being guided or managed by an outside source. This is a bottom-up process.*[7]

IT WAS A UNIQUE CATALYTIC EFFORT THAT STIMULATED MANY "SELF-ORGANIZING" EFFORTS ALL AIMED AT THE SAME OUTCOME: THE REDUCTION OF TEEN PREGNANCIES.

- JEFFREY S. LUKE

In both systems, the Hold Action and Results competency equips people to use RBF skills in the roles of convener, facilitator, or participant, and to take action and be accountable for implementing strategies that contribute to results. These skills, applied in role, build bridges across the boundaries of sector, gender, race, ethnicity, and world view to create groups with sustainable relationships among members accountable to themselves and others for measurable progress toward a common result.

Used with mastery, the Hold Action and Results competency increases the likelihood that people will have productive meetings that make progress toward measurably improved results. The intention of applying the competency is to support leaders in producing the kind of results achieved by Tillamook County, Oregon,[8] when the community came together to reduce teen pregnancy. This county-level experience later informed the development of the Oregon Option, which used a catalytic leadership model to improve population results statewide.

I ALONE CAN DO IT.
I CAN NOT DO IT ALONE.

- ANONYMOUS

PUTTING RESULTS IN THE CENTER: A COPERNICAN REVOLUTION

Heterarchical leadership is possible when a group of leaders makes the population or program result the center of their attention, thus changing their world view and sense of self. Just as the Copernican discovery that the earth revolved around the sun challenged people's understanding of their place in the universe, placing a result in the center challenges a leader to see him- or herself as part of a larger whole and commit to contributing to the result. This commitment can challenge other conscious or unconscious commitments, such as the commitment to the survival of a specific program or commitment to maximize or sustain positional power and authority.

In that sense, the Hold Action and Results competency invites the leader to develop a new identity consistent with the role, task, and authority of collaborating for the sake of a common result. It can be challenging for leaders to move from a role of hierarchical authority to a negotiated role consciously constructed with other leaders. Ultimately, at the mastery level of the Hold Action and Results competency, the leader is comfortable and confident holding both heterarchical and hierarchical roles as appropriate.

> *LAP led me to think more globally. How do we move the needle for all children in DeKalb County? It has pushed all of us in LAP to look beyond our own narrow interests.*
>
> – Allen Shaklan, Executive Director of Refugee Family Services

NOTES:

[1] O'Brien, Littlefield, and Goddard-Truitt. A matter of leadership: Connecting a grantmaker's investments in collaborative leadership development to community results. *The Foundation Review*, Vol. 5, No. 1. 2013.

[2] Results Based Leadership Collaborative. *Achieving Results with Collaboratives: Strategies for Helping Collaborative Leaders Hold Themselves and Each Other Accountable for Action.* Research Brief. The University of Maryland School of Public Policy. Fall 2011.

[3] Pillsbury. *Theory of Aligned Contributions.* Sherbrooke Consulting, Inc. 2008.

[4] In this context, organizations are considered dynamic systems as defined by Boros in *Dynamic Organizations and Organizational Dynamics, Exploring Organizational Dynamics.* Sage Publications. 2009.

[5] Stacey. *Complexity and Emergence in Organizations.* Routledge. 2001.

[6] These behaviors are consistent with a heuristic trial-and-error approach that leads to learning, discovery, and experiential problem solving.

[7] Hsu and Butterfield. *Emergent Behavior of Systems-of-Systems.* Boeing Corporation. INCOSE International Symposium. 2007.

[8] Luke. *Catalytic Leadership, Strategies for an Interconnected World.* Jossey-Bass. 1997.

PRACTICE: PUTTING RESULTS IN THE CENTER

EXAMPLES YOU'LL STUDY

THE LEADERSHIP IN ACTION PROGRAM

USING RBF SKILLS WITHIN ORGANIZATIONS: BALTIMORE CITY DEPARTMENT OF SOCIAL SERVICES

PERFORMANCE PARTNERSHIP SUMMITS

This chapter provides three examples of how advanced RBF concepts can work in programs to achieve large-scale results. The Theory of Aligned Contributions informs the design of each of these programs.

» **Practice:** the application of RBF methods to improve population results

EXAMPLES YOU'LL STUDY

The Theory of Aligned Contributions (TOAC) currently informs the design of programs that achieve results and are designed to improve community-wide results by catalyzing emergent results-centered systems. In these programs, the primary purpose is to make a measurable difference in a program- or population-level result.

In all of these programs, a facilitator or a coach/facilitator uses the RBF competencies to support the group. In the programs with a leadership development purpose, the participants learn and use RBF as part of the TOAC's Collaborative Leadership competency. When using RBF skills to improve population well-being, the program participants are developing mastery of the Hold Action and Results RBF competency that is described later in this book.

The Hold Action and Results competency includes two skills:

- Be accountable in role for contributions to results
- Use RBF skills to work collaboratively to accelerate progress toward results

To illuminate how the Hold Action and Results competency can be used, examples are provided below from the implementation of TOAC in three types of programs.

1. The first type involves leaders from multiple organizations and multiple sectors participating in the development of an emergent results-centered system. This program, the Leadership in Action Program (LAP), builds the skills of the program participants while they are working to improve community-wide population results. In LAPs leaders master the Hold Action and Results competency.

2. A second type of program takes place *within* an organization, having the dual purpose of measurably improving program results and building leadership skills.

3. In a third type of program, multi-sector leaders work together to measurably improve population-level results. In this program, RBF is used by a team that supports implementation of the program; however, the leaders are not engaged in skill building as part of the process. In this program, the Performance Partnership Summit Model,[1] the team uses the Hold Action and Results competency to create productive meetings where, in a day and half, leaders move to action and commit to reduce smoking prevalence in community or statewide populations.

The following table summarizes the implementation of TOAC in the three types of programs.

TOAC IMPLEMENTATION IN THREE TYPES OF PROGRAMS

Program design elements	Leadership in Action Program (LAP)	Results-based leadership program within organizations	Performance Partnership Summits
Primary purpose	Measurably improve *population* results	Measurably improve *program* results	Measurably improve *population* results
Complementary purpose	Build leadership skills of the cross-sector leaders and catalyze a collaborative system to sustain progress toward results	Build leadership skills of the executive and management teams of the organizations	Catalyze a collaborative system to sustain progress toward results
Who uses RBF skills	The cross-sector leaders and the implementation team	The organizational leaders and the coach/facilitators	The implementation team
Duration	18 months to three years with on-site support of implementation team. LAP leaders continue to work together without implementation team support for two to 10 years	Six months to four years	One-and-a-half days with the on-site support of an implementation team; ongoing effort with technical assistance and off-site support for six months to two years
# Participants	30 - 40	15 - 50	12 - 80

EMERGING EVIDENCE OF EFFECTIVE PRACTICE (1): THE LEADERSHIP IN ACTION PROGRAM

The strongest research on implementation of the TOAC and the practice of RBF comes from implementation of the Leadership in Action Program (LAP). LAP is recognized as a leadership development approach that supports leaders as they collaborate and take aligned actions to achieve measurable results.[2] TOAC is the underlying theory of change that informs the design of LAP. Over the past five years, LAP has contributed to and benefited from a research and quality improvement effort at the Results Based Leadership Collaborative (The Collaborative) at the School of Public Policy, University of Maryland, College Park.

The Collaborative's data analysis and research have aided the development and practice of the TOAC's four leadership competencies and methods for integrating the RBF competencies into the LAP design and execution. This interactive effort to produce and use data to improve program design and execution has led to a more pragmatic understanding of what makes a measurable difference in population-level results. Emerging evidence[3] indicates that leaders using RBF skills as part of the Collaborative Leadership competency work together more effectively and take aligned action leading to greater collective impact.[4] This research and the ongoing quality improvement effort led to the articulation of the Hold Action and Results competency and positioned RBF to become part of a set of data-informed leadership practices.

The Leadership in Action Program, sponsored by the Annie E. Casey Foundation since December 2001, is an example of a program in which multi-sector leaders develop RBF skills as part of the Collaborative Leadership competency. In LAP, leaders from different sectors come together to make a measurable improvement in a result for a specific population. For example, in Baltimore, Maryland, more than 40 leaders from the education, nonprofit, faith, early education, health, and business sectors came together to accelerate progress toward all children in Baltimore City entering school ready to learn.

The LAP leaders held themselves publicly accountable for making progress toward the result. The Baltimore City LAP, launched in 2004, contributed to increasing the number and percentage of children entering school ready to learn.

BALTIMORE CITY LAP DATA

MARYLAND AND BALTIMORE CITY 2002-2009
STUDENTS ASSESSED "FULLY READY"

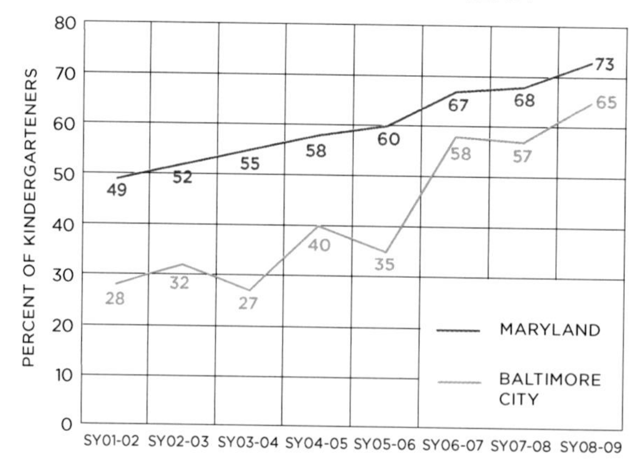

Quality improvement and research informed the design and execution of 14 LAPs implemented between 2001 and 2012. Based on the quality improvement and research findings from the implementation of this first LAP, the Indianapolis/Marion County LAP was implemented with an enhanced focus on RBF as a collaborative leadership skill. This was launched in 2008 when 40 leaders from city and state government, business, faith, corrections, health, adult education, corrections, law enforcement, judicial, and human service sectors came together to accelerate the successful reintegration of Marion County ex-offenders into the community.

The leaders learned and practiced RBF skills, as did leaders in the Elkhart County Indiana LAP launched in 2010. The development of RBF and other leadership competencies enabled the leaders to sustain their work together and make measurable progress toward the result.

MARION COUNTY LAP DATA

MARION COUNTY REARRESTS OF PRISONERS WITHIN ONE YEAR OF RELEASE DATE

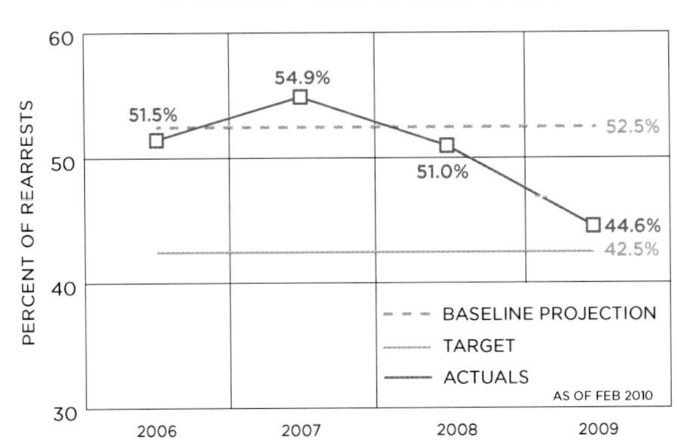

- LAP INITIATIVE LAUNCHED SEPT 2008
- NEW BASELINE PROJECTION 52.5% (AVG OF 2006, 07, 08 ACTUALS)
- NEW TARGET SET TO 42.5% (10% BELOW NEW BASELINE)
- DATA INCLUDE OUTRIGHT ARRESTS, EXCLUDE WARRANT ARRESTS

EXAMPLE DATA POINT: LAP RESULTS 2009, VALUE 44.6%
44.6% of the prisoners released from DOC in 2008 were rearrested within one year of their release date

As shown in the previous chart, the Indianapolis/Marion County LAP contributed to a measurable improvement in helping ex-offenders successfully reenter the community, as shown by changes in the recidivism rate. Using RBF tools, methods, and competencies, LAPs engage leaders in the collaborative work cycle and provide opportunities for them to commit to action and be accountable for implementing strategies at a scope and scale to make progress.

MAKING AND KEEPING ALIGNED ACTION COMMITMENTS IS A PRECURSOR TO GROUPS HOLDING THEMSELVES ACCOUNTABLE TO EACH OTHER AND RESULTS. GROUPS WHO RATE THEMSELVES AS BEING ACCOUNTABLE AS MEASURED BY COMPLETION OF COMMITMENTS ARE MOST LIKELY TO BELIEVE THAT THEY HAVE CONTRIBUTED POSITIVELY TO THE ACCELERATION OF RESULTS AND THERE HAS BEEN A REDUCTION IN THE INCIDENCE OF THE PROBLEM.[5]

The research to date highlights the effectiveness of leaders armed with the skill to make and keep commitments to aligned action.

Research further indicates that formal public accountability for contributing to results contributes to the efficacy of leaders who collaborate in sustained and aligned action. LAPs with formal accountability processes saw a 25 percent increase in the likelihood that group commitments would be completed and a 17 percent increase in the likelihood for individual commitments.

> *This demonstrates the importance of such processes for collaborative groups. High- to mid-performing LAPs internalized the use of formal accountability systems. They tracked commitments made by the group more effectively than low-performing groups.*[6]

The Hold Action and Results competency includes the skills that enable leaders to be accountable for taking aligned action to improve results. The LAP programs were designed to create a community-wide collaborative work cycle to measurably impact a population-level result in a relatively short time, e.g., 18 months on average.

The implementation of the LAPs has generated extensive data on what contributes to leaders taking aligned action. That research shows that "the TOAC model provides a means for setting in motion a series of events and actions that can result in important changes on the ground."[7] The Hold Action and Results competency provides you with the tools and methods to have productive meetings that implement the Theory of Aligned Contributions in communities.

EMERGING EVIDENCE OF EFFECTIVE PRACTICE (2): USING RBF SKILLS WITHIN ORGANIZATIONS

The Baltimore City Department of Social Services (BCDSS) senior leadership team has used RBF foundation and advanced skills as part of its efforts to improve the well-being of children in Baltimore City. Under the leadership of Director Molly McGrath Tierney, the situation improved dramatically. For example, from 2008 to 2010 the number of annual adoptions rose 59 percent, from 265 to 422, and the number of children with permanent families rose 47 percent, from 1,327 to 1,946.

The members of the BCDSS leadership team have used RBF skills to make decisions together and carry through on strategies to improve service delivery. Tierney attributes some of the department's success to using RBF skills in conjunction with the other leadership skills based on the Theory of Aligned Contributions.

The Hold Action and Results competency provides the skills to have productive meetings within organizations that help staff implement effective service delivery strategies.

> PART OF WHAT CAUSED THINGS TO SUCCEED DRAMATICALLY WAS THE USE OF ACCOUNTABILITY AND THE SKILLS MY STAFF LEARNED TO IMPLEMENT A VERY DIFFERENT BUSINESS PRACTICE IN A BIG URBAN CHILD WELFARE SYSTEM.[8]
>
> - MOLLY MCGRATH TIERNEY, DIRECTOR, BALTIMORE CITY DEPARTMENT OF SOCIAL SERVICES

EMERGING EVIDENCE OF EFFECTIVE PRACTICE (3): PERFORMANCE PARTNERSHIP SUMMITS

The Smoking Cessation Leadership Center has implemented more than 27 Performance Partnership Summits across the country. The summits are one-and-a-half day meetings implemented using RBF foundation and advanced skills. During a summit, leaders from multiple sectors create and commit to implement action plans to measurably reduce smoking prevalence in their communities. In every instance, the summits produced action plans that were subsequently implemented by the leaders who attended the summit. Data from seven states implementing summits as part of a partnership between the Center and the Substance Abuse and Mental Health Services Administration (SAMHSA) show that six months after the summit, all of the states were implementing the action plans. In six of the seven states, the leaders reported that the strategies were already producing measurable improvements for the populations served.[9]

The Hold Action and Results competency, used to implement the Performance Partnership Summits, has contributed to their consistent success.[10]

NOTES:

[1] The Performance Partnership Summit (PPS) Model uses the catalytic leadership model in which multi-sector leaders come together to improve results. The model was developed in Oregon in the 1990s. The Smoking Cessation Leadership Center at the University of California at San Francisco further refined the model, and summits are being held across the country. www.smokingcessationleadership.ucsf.edu/performancepartner.htm

[2] Meehan. *A New Leadership Mindset for Scaling Social Change.* Leadership for a New Era Series. Learning Community. 2012.

[3] Results Based Leadership Collaborative. *Achieving Results with Collaboratives: Strategies for Helping Collaborative Leaders Hold Themselves and Each Other Accountable for Action.* Research Brief. The University of Maryland School of Public Policy. Fall 2011.

[4] The concept of collective impact developed by Kania and Kramer has some features in common with the Theory of Aligned Contributions, the concept of Mutually Reinforcing Activities is similar to aligned action. John Kania and Mark Kramer. Embracing emergence: How collective impact addresses complexity. *Stanford Social Innovation Review.* 2013.

[5] Littlefield and O'Brien. *Policymaking Through Collaborative Networks: Issues of Accountability and Performance.* Poster presented at the annual conference for the Association for Public Policy Analysis and Management. Boston. 2010.

[6] Results Based Leadership Collaborative. *Achieving Results with Collaboratives: Strategies for Helping Collaborative Leaders Hold Themselves and Each Other Accountable for Action.* 2011.

[7] O'Brien, Littlefield, and Goddard-Truitt. A matter of leadership: Connecting a grantmaker's investments in collaborative leadership development to community results. *The Foundation Review.* Vol. 5, No. 1. 2013.

[8] The Annie E. Casey Foundation. *Sharpening Leadership Skills to Improve Child Outcomes in Baltimore, Maryland.* 2011.

[9] SAMHSA-SCLC State Leadership Academies for Wellness and Smoking Cessation in Behavioral Health. *Reports from 7 States.* Smoking Cessation Leadership Center. 2012.

[10] Revell and Meriwether. The Performance Partnership Model to smoking cessation: Lessons learned by the Smoking Cessation Leadership Center. *Health Promotion Practice.* Vol. 12, No. 6, Supplement 2. 2011.

HOLD MENTAL MODELS

THE PROBLEM IS NOT THAT WE HAVE MENTAL MODELS, IT IS THAT WE DON'T RECOGNIZE THAT WE HAVE MENTAL MODELS.

– SRIKUMAR RAO

DEFINITION: USE A REPERTOIRE OF PERSPECTIVES THAT CONTRIBUTE TO ACHIEVING MEETING RESULTS

CONCEPTS IN THIS CHAPTER

THE USE OF MENTAL MODELS

PROPOSAL-BASED DECISION MAKING

SKILLS FOR THIS COMPETENCY

5.1 USE PROPOSAL-BASED DECISION MAKING TO MOVE FROM TALK TO ACTION

5.2 USE CONVERSATIONS TO DEVELOP CONVERGENCE

5.3 NAME AND ADDRESS BARRIERS TO CONVERGENCE

5.4 MAKE AND HELP OTHERS MAKE ACTION COMMITMENTS

5.5 BE AND HELP OTHERS BE ACCOUNTABLE FOR ACTION COMMITMENTS

5.6 OBSERVE AND RESPOND TO GROUP DYNAMICS

5.7 ASSESS AND ADDRESS CONFLICT

The Hold Mental Models competency supports the use of new ways of thinking by individuals in groups as they make decisions and move from talk to action. There are seven skills in this competency. These skills enable groups to use proposal-based decision making to move groups from talk to action; use conversations to develop convergence, maintain momentum, and establish accountability for carrying through on action commitments; observe and respond to group dynamics; and assess and address conflict.

» **Mental models:** differing world views and assumptions that shape people's behavior

In 1805, the Jacquard loom revolutionized weaving.[1] Patterns, punched in cards, in the hands of a skilled weaver created woven pictures in cloth. This innovation increased the productivity of the skilled weaver by a factor of 24. RBF's foundation skills are like the loom; the mental models are like the cards. They weave the threads of a conversation into new and different patterns that can increase group productivity.

Hold Mental Models builds on the foundation competencies of Hold Roles, Hold Conversations, and Hold Groups. For example, the Hold Roles competency enables you to be aware of and make conscious choices about roles and understand the differences in the authority and tasks associated with a variety of roles. The mastery of that competency is the platform to better understand the mental models that influence how people hold roles in different systems.

Mastery of the Hold Conversations competency provides the disciplined ability to hold a mental model with awareness and to consciously use that mental model to intentionally listen for information relevant to that model.

The Hold Groups competency at the mastery level provides the context for using multiple mental models to observe and understand group dynamics. As you begin your practice of the Hold Mental Models competency, take the time to review the foundation competencies of Hold Roles, Hold Conversations, and Hold Groups to enhance your ability to easily recognize, name, and use a broad repertoire of mental models.

CONCEPTS IN THIS CHAPTER

THE USE OF MENTAL MODELS

The RBF theory and practice methods are grounded in a set of mental models illuminating assumptions about how groups can work together to measurably improve results in programs, neighborhoods, and communities. In this context, mental models are defined as follows:

> *A mental model is an explanation of someone's thought process about how something works in the real world. It is a representation of the surrounding world, the relationships between its various parts and a person's intuitive perception about their own acts and their consequences. Our mental models help shape our behavior and define our approach to solving problems and carrying out tasks.*[2]

Striving to understand mental models of others provides insight about emotion and motivation:

> *Mental models give you a deep understanding of people's motivations and thought processes, along with the emotional philosophical landscape in which they are operating.*[3]

An understanding of differing world views, assumptions, emotions, and perspectives enable groups to understand their own dynamics and address factors that keep them from aligned action. The Collaborative Work Cycle shown below is one of RBF's underlying mental models. It provides a context for understanding and using a repertoire of mental models to support the work of groups.

COLLABORATIVE WORK CYCLE

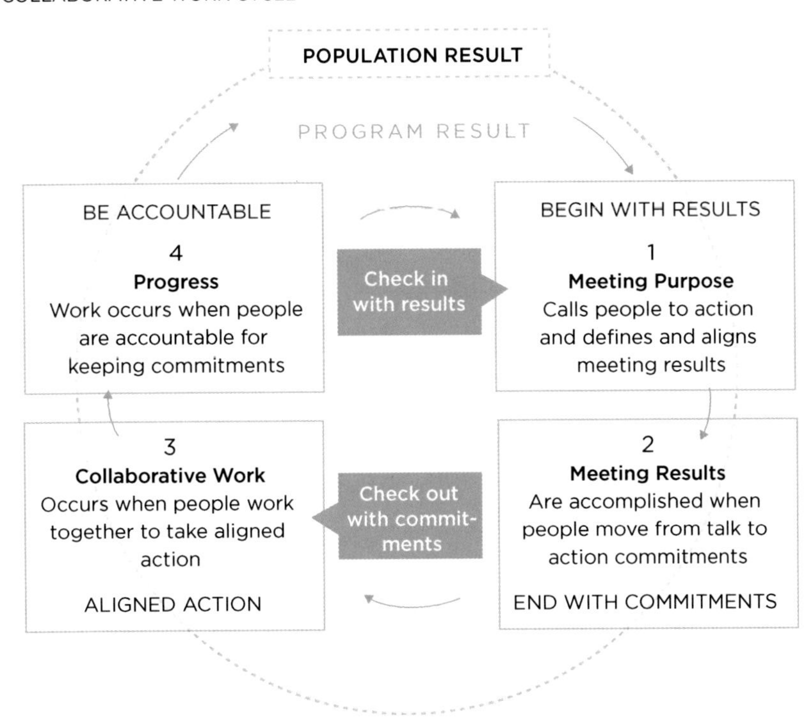

The skills in this competency equip you, in the role of either participant or facilitator, to move through the Collaborative Work Cycle and flexibly deploy a range of responses when a group gets stuck on the path from talk to action.

PROPOSAL-BASED DECISION MAKING

Proposal-based decision making (PBDM) is a technique that can be used by groups to rapidly assess consensus (or the lack thereof).

HETERARCHY IS A SYSTEM OF ORGANIZATION REPLETE WITH OVERLAP, MULTIPLICITY, MIXED ASCENDANCY, AND/OR DIVERGENT-BUT-COEXISTENT PATTERNS OF RELATION.

FOR EXAMPLE, THE POWER AND AUTHORITY OF COLLABORATIVE LEADERS IS CONSIDERED HORIZONTAL (NON-HIERARCHAL). EACH PERSON HAS EQUAL VOICE, POWER, AND AUTHORITY TO ENGAGE IN DECISION MAKING.

PBDM: A MENTAL MODEL FOR DECISION MAKING

People move through the Collaborative Work Cycle by having a series of linked conversations. The transition from one conversation to another occurs when a decision is made, even if the decision is only that people are ready to move to the next conversation.

The precursor to doing is deciding. However, groups often get stuck in talk and can't move to action because they cannot make decisions together. Therefore, an explicit mental model for collaborative decision making is the first skill in the Hold Mental Models competency.

- A PBDM decision is one everyone supports and no one opposes.
- A PBDM decision is reached when everyone in the group can say: *I can live with the decision and support it, even though it may not be exactly what I want.*

PBDM is a heterarchical model of collaborative decision making. In other words, every member of the group has the opportunity and obligation to participate in the shaping and making of a specific decision that they and everyone in the group can support. The opportunity and obligation are that the individual members of a group engage in the task of reaching convergence. A PBDM decision is one that the people affected by the decision own. They will act in accordance with the decision out of choice and acceptance, and be motivated to take action and persist in their work together to achieve a desired result based on the decision.

An effective PBDM decision creates a condition in which group members are autonomous in their actions. Those actions are informed by the group's decision, with the result that group is committed to achieving. This type of decision — heterarchical and owned by the members — contrasts with the more common hierarchical decisions that people make and experience in many families, organizations, and community groups. In a family, for example, the parents have authority to make decisions for their minor children. In an organizational system, supervisors have the authority to make decisions about their employees.

Given that most people operate in hierarchical decision-making systems, having a role in an intentional system of heterarchical decision making is often a new experience and a new way of thinking. The Hold Roles competency and the Person-Role-System framework facilitate people's ability to step into their role in a heterarchical decision-making system and, as appropriate, shift to a different role in a hierarchical system. The next table contrasts PBDM as a heterarchical approach with the more common hierarchical decision making. The differences are highlighted for purposes of making the distinction between heterarchical and hierarchical; however, people's experience is often in hybrid models of decision making. For example, supervisors may delegate decisions to a group of subordinates and expect the group to reach consensus.

COMPARISON OF HETERARCHICAL AND HIERARCHICAL DECISION MAKING

CATEGORY	PBDM (HETERARCHICAL)	HIERARCHICAL
Participation	Individuals are obligated as members of a group to be active participants in creating a solution they and the group can support.	Subordinate members of the group are expected to accept decisions of those with hierarchical authority whether the group supports the decision or not.
Inclusion of different points of view	Individuals in the group have active roles in expressing their own point of view and eliciting and understanding perspectives of other group members.	Differences in perspective and viewpoint can be ignored or discounted by the subordinates and the hierarchical authority.
Commitment to the decision	Through engagement in the PBDM process, group members create ownership and the capacity to act based on decisions.	The acceptance of the hierarchical authority to make the decision produces compliance with the decision.

Understanding of other viewpoints, participation in the definition and resolution of the issue, and ownership of the decision are the intended effects of PBDM. These effects are accomplished through a process that engages all group members in behaviors that lead to decisions owned and acted on by the group. How individuals participate in the decision making is central to the quality of the decision.

HIERARCHY IS A SYSTEM IN WHICH PEOPLE OR GROUPS ARE RANKED ONE ABOVE THE OTHER ACCORDING TO STATUS OR AUTHORITY.

> *The thing we're trying to emphasize is that it's the individuals and how they interact with one another...[that]...can influence whether or not they make a good decision...What matters is who they are, what they know and how they interact.*[4]

PBDM: A MENTAL MODEL OF INQUIRY

Many groups have had experience at different times with unstructured consensus decision-making processes and/or with Robert's Rules of Order. The author developed PBDM in the early 1990s as an alternative to both. Robert's Rules of Order is an approach based on a mental model of advocacy[5] and majority rule. When using Robert's Rules, group members debate each other and as advocates present arguments to convince others to support their ideas. The idea is expressed as a motion, and a decision is made when debate ends and a majority votes in favor of the motion.

Robert's Rules has many strengths in providing a process for group decision making. However, often those in the minority do not own the decision and, therefore, may not support it; thus emphasis on debate and the criticism of competing ideas may not lead to creative problem solving or the development of ideas that everyone can support.

In contrast to the Robert's Rules advocacy approach, PBDM uses the mental model of inquiry. In the PBDM process, people make proposals and build on each other's proposals. Instead of voting yea or nay for a motion, people show their level of support as follows:

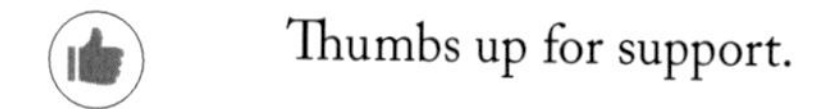

Thumbs up for support.

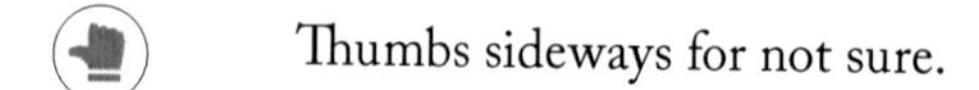

Thumbs sideways for not sure.

Thumbs down for don't support.

People with their thumbs sideways or down are engaged through inquiry to share their concerns. They are encouraged to articulate what they need to support a proposal. Everyone in the group then works to address these concerns and modifies the initial proposal or develops a new proposal that everyone can support.

Using thumbs to show their level of support for a proposal makes it easier for people to act in the new way of thinking that underpins the mental model of PBDM. The act of showing where you are and noticing where others are provides information to the individuals in the group that is immediately useful in moving toward convergence.

By using PBDM, groups can address differences, resolve conflicts, uncover what people need in order to own a decision and move to action, and make decisions that lead to action.

PBDM and consensus decision making are not appropriate for all settings or all decisions — for example, when decisions need to be made by one person exercising his or her hierarchical authority. PBDM is appropriate when the group is collaborative and either has or has been given the authority to make decisions based on the collective will of the group. Proposal-based decision making is often used to complement the use of Robert's Rules of Order. For example, during a board retreat, the group may use PBDM to develop consensus supported by a facilitator, and then pause for a formal vote using Robert's Rules with the chair of the board conducting the voting. This hybrid allows the group to have the benefit from PBDM and still operate in accordance with bylaws that specify the use of Robert's Rules of Order.

SKILLS FOR THIS COMPETENCY

SKILL 5.1: USE PROPOSAL-BASED DECISION MAKING TO MOVE FROM TALK TO ACTION

The following self-assessment presents the levels of using PBDM to move groups from talk to action.

AWARENESS	APPLICATION	MASTERY
Understands and uses proposal-based decision making • *Do I make proposals and build on proposals?* • *Do I set a context and ask an Effective Question to elicit proposals?* • *Do I use the rule of thumb to scan levels of support?* →	Synthesizes proposals and gives the work back to the group • *Do I concisely introduce the concept of PBDM?* • *Do I label proposals as options?* →	Helps groups stay in the hard work of decision making • *Do I attend to pace to support engagement?* • *Do I recognize when a group is not moving forward in decision making?* →

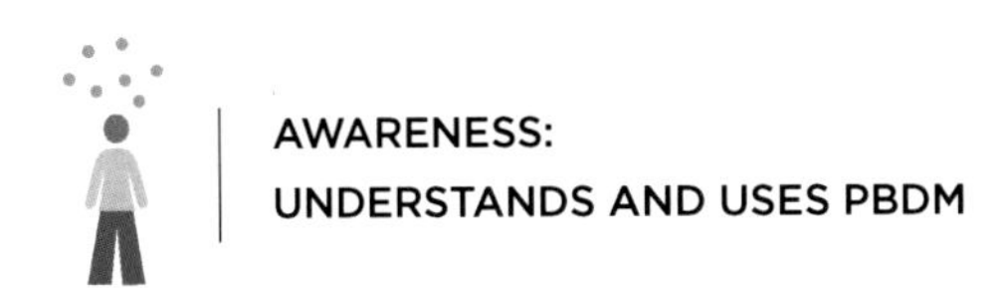

AWARENESS: UNDERSTANDS AND USES PBDM

You are aware of this skill when:

- *you make proposals and build on proposals.*
- *you set a context and ask an Effective Question to elicit proposals.*
- *you use the rule of thumb to scan levels of support.*

PBDM: The Rule of Thumb

The PBDM process is described below. It is a six-step iterative process. Suggested wording for interaction with and within the group is included.

THE SIX-STEP PBDM METHOD

STEP	POSSIBLE SCRIPT WORDING	STRATEGY
1. Make a proposal.	I propose that ... [insert a short phrase describing what you want].	Use a calm, constructive tone of voice.
2. Add to or make a new proposal.	Do you want to add to it or make a new proposal?	Consider the proposals as different options or possible decisions the group might make.
3. Show thumbs.	Do you support it? Do you not support it? Are you not sure?	Ask people to show where they are by a show of thumbs.
4. Build support.	What will bring your thumb up?	Build proposals everyone can support. Listen to their issues and encourage proposals that address the issues. Invite everyone to make proposals that everyone can support. Ask people to do the work of finding convergence.
5. All thumbs up!	Proposal adopted!	A proposal is adopted and becomes a decision when everyone's, or almost everyone's, thumb is up and the group decides there's enough support to move forward because people whose thumbs are not up are okay with the group going forward.
6. Commit to action.	Who will do what when?	The group moves to action by deciding who will do what when to implement the decision.

Using PBDM in the Participant Role

THE SITUATION: THE GROUP IS STUCK

You are a participant in a budget preparation meeting that is now in its third hour. Everyone is tired. Although all the information has been shared about budget requests and available resources, no decisions have been made. Aware of your own exhaustion and frustration, you suggest a break and invite people to come back ready to discuss what they would like to do next. Everyone accepts your suggestion with relief.

IDENTIFY ISSUES

During the break, you check in with your colleagues about issues they think need to be addressed so the group can move forward. You also share your own idea that the group needs to agree to a process for making budget decisions.

MAKE PROPOSALS

After the break, you raise the issue of developing a process for making budget decisions. You then propose that a process be developed to examine the costs and benefits of funding one program versus another. Another group member builds on that proposal by suggesting that the budget office provide the relevant data for the analysis.

FIND PROPOSALS THAT EVERYONE CAN SUPPORT

After the discussion, the group is thumbs up on doing a cost-benefit analysis using budget office data.

ADOPT PROPOSAL AND MOVE TO ACTION

Everyone agrees to complete a cost-benefit analysis using budget office data for the programs they supervise and present the analysis at the next meeting.

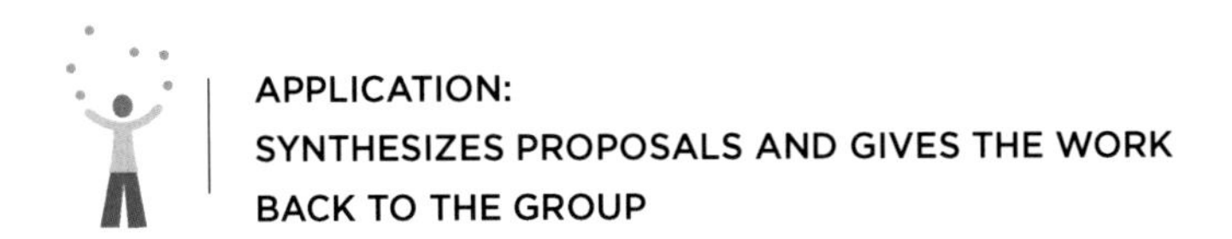

You are applying this skill when:

- *you concisely introduce the concept of PBDM.*
- *you label proposals as options.*

PBDM can be used in both facilitator and participant roles. Applying the skill in the facilitator role can be done in a straightforward and brief manner, as outlined below.

Using PBDM in The Facilitator Role

A facilitator supports PBDM as follows:

- Introducing the method
- Asking Effective Questions to clarify issues
- Listening for proposals (options to address the issues)
- Summarizing and flip charting the proposed options

- Giving the work back to the group in ways that encourage convergence around a proposed option
- Documenting the adopted proposal as a decision
- Holding neutral despite the group's frustration or confusion

1. BRIEFLY INTRODUCE PBDM AND USE IT IMMEDIATELY.

Introduce PBDM by providing a very brief description of the process, then move directly to using the rule of thumb. The group will learn more quickly by doing PBDM than by hearing it described at length. Below is a script you can use to introduce PBDM; it should take only two minutes.

- Proposal-based decision making is a process for reaching a decision everyone can support: making proposals, building on each other's proposal, or making other proposals.
- This may be new for many of you. If you try it, you may like it!
- (Note: Use humor and lightness to encourage people to play with PBDM and try it out.)
- For the issue being discussed, does anyone have a proposal? (Pause to hear proposals.)
- This is the proposal I heard: (insert proposal here).
- Are there any questions for clarification?

2. LISTEN FOR AND MODEL THE USE OF PROPOSALS.

Listen for proposals and summarize what you are hearing. Flip chart these options quickly or label your existing flip charts with option numbers or letters. To encourage building proposals rather than critiquing proposals, refer to brainstorming rules that ask groups to refrain from critiquing in the generative phase of the conversation.

- I think I heard two proposals. Let's call one Option A and the second Option B. In the process of making a proposal, building on a proposal, or making another proposal, we don't trash each other's proposals.
- Would anyone like to build on these proposals (A & B) or make another proposal.

3. BUILD A PROPOSAL EVERYONE CAN SUPPORT.

Once people understand a proposal, they are invited to show their level of support with their thumbs and scan the room to see what work needs to be done to build convergence.

- Repeat proposal to reflect the original language or any modifications.
- Ask the participants to show where they are in relation to the proposal by using their thumbs. Let them know the following:
  - Thumbs up means they support the proposal.
  - Thumbs sideways means they are not sure.
  - Thumbs down means they cannot support it.
  - If your thumb is sideways or down, you will have an opportunity to say what would "bring you up."
- Take a moment to see which thumbs are sideways or down.
- Go to each person with a thumb sideways or down.
  - What is your concern? What would bring your thumb up?
  - Would anyone like to ask questions to better understand the concern?
  - What are your suggestions to build on the proposal to address the concern?

4. MAKE A DECISION AND MOVE TO ACTION.

When everyone or almost everyone shows a thumbs up, the group decides that there is enough support to move forward. The group knows it can move forward when the people who did not give a thumbs up signal indicate that they are okay with group's decision to adopt the proposal; in other words, they can support the group's decision.

The group can use the "okay" symbol to enable people to signify that even if they are not in full agreement they support the group's decision. (Groups often discover on their own the need for a fourth symbol that allows people to indicate their comfort with the group moving forward even though their thumbs are not up.)

Carefully choose when to introduce the concept of the "okay" symbol. If introduced too early, it may shortcut the development of the group's ability to authentically use PBDM to constructively explore differences and develop convergence.

- The group has made a decision and adopted the following proposal: [insert proposal here].
- Based on this decision who will do what when to implement it?
- Chart the decision and the action commitment.

Tips may be helpful to reinforce that PBDM is a proposal-based tool and that the group owns the process.

TIPS: USING OPTION LANGUAGE TO DEVELOP PROPOSALS

- Label proposals *options* and flip chart them as you hear them.[6] The use of option language signals the group that their work is to explore possibilities and move toward convergence.
- Use multiple flip charts with one option per flip chart. Point to the flip chart with the proposed option as the group works on each proposal. Annotate the flip chart as people build on the proposal.
- People often start to synthesize or create hybrid proposals early in the process. Name and encourage this synthesis by using language like:
  - "I am hearing a synthesis of Options A and B. Is that right? That will be Option C."
- You may hear implicit proposals in complaints, questions, or statements of frustration. Name what you hear and explore whether people might have a proposal to offer. For example:
  - "You have posed a question. Do you have your own answer to that question that might be another option?"

TIPS: LABELING PROPOSALS AS OPTIONS

- Listen for differing viewpoints. Synthesize one viewpoint and call it Option A; another viewpoint as Option B.
- Invite people to build on Option A or B, or propose additional options.
- Ask the group how it would like to proceed given the options that have been proposed.
- Notice the impact on the group of your use of PBDM.
  - Did the group recognize their proposals in your synthesis of the options?
  - Did the members of the group begin to work toward convergence?
  - Was the group able to make a decision and move to action? In what ways did your use of PBDM support the group's ability to make a decision?
  - What might you do differently in the future based on this exercise?

MASTERY: HELPS GROUPS STAY IN THE HARD WORK OF DECISION MAKING

You are demonstrating mastery of this skill when:

- *you attend to pace to support engagement.*
- *you recognize when a group cannot move forward in making a decision.*

Decision making in groups is hard work. People have a natural tendency to defer to others, avoid conflict, and duck responsibility. The facilitator can notice these behaviors and respond as indicated in the table below. Similarly, the table on the next page shows ways to help the group move forward and ways to help the group shut down.

OBSERVING AND RESPONDING TO ENGAGEMENT CUES

OBSERVATION	RESPONSE
Nonverbal cues (facial expressions, hesitancy to lift thumb so others can see it) may indicate that people are uncomfortable using their thumbs to show their position relative to a proposal	Acknowledge there may be differences of opinion, that some people may need more time to process, or that people may not yet be comfortable assessing proposals.
Someone not using the thumb to show where he or she is relative to a proposal	When you see each person's thumb, acknowledge the person and encourage everyone to notice where people are. If you see someone is not using the thumb, go back and check in with him or her. Remind people that PBDM is only an effective tool when everyone participates.
Someone, despite a couple of invitations to participate, still not comfortable showing where he or she is with the thumb	Give small groups time to talk. Use paired conversations. Acknowledge that this process might feel like pressure. Invite people to discuss their concerns about participating in PBDM.
Verbal and nonverbal behavior (bored expression, perfunctory participation) may indicate that some people are giving up and not authentically engaged in the process.	Pause the discussion and emphasize the opportunity people have to influence a decision by participating. Mention that groups often go in new directions or find new solutions because one member is willing to say clearly what he or she thinks, even if that person is the only one holding that viewpoint at the time.

ENCOURAGING ENGAGEMENT

DO	WHEN
Encourage proposals.	When people voice criticisms, offer them the opportunity to express the criticism as an alternate proposal.
Have people state their concerns directly.	When people advocate a point of view instead of addressing the concerns of those not in support, list the concerns and ask them to address the concerns.
Invite inquiry.	When people restate their own viewpoint, invite them to ask exploratory questions of those with different viewpoints.
Support full participation.	When people withdraw from the process, invite them to share their viewpoint.

PARTICIPANT PRACTICE GUIDE 5.1:
USE PROPOSAL-BASED DECISION MAKING TO MOVE GROUPS FROM TALK TO ACTION

Here are ways of using PBDM as a participant in meetings, by level of risk.

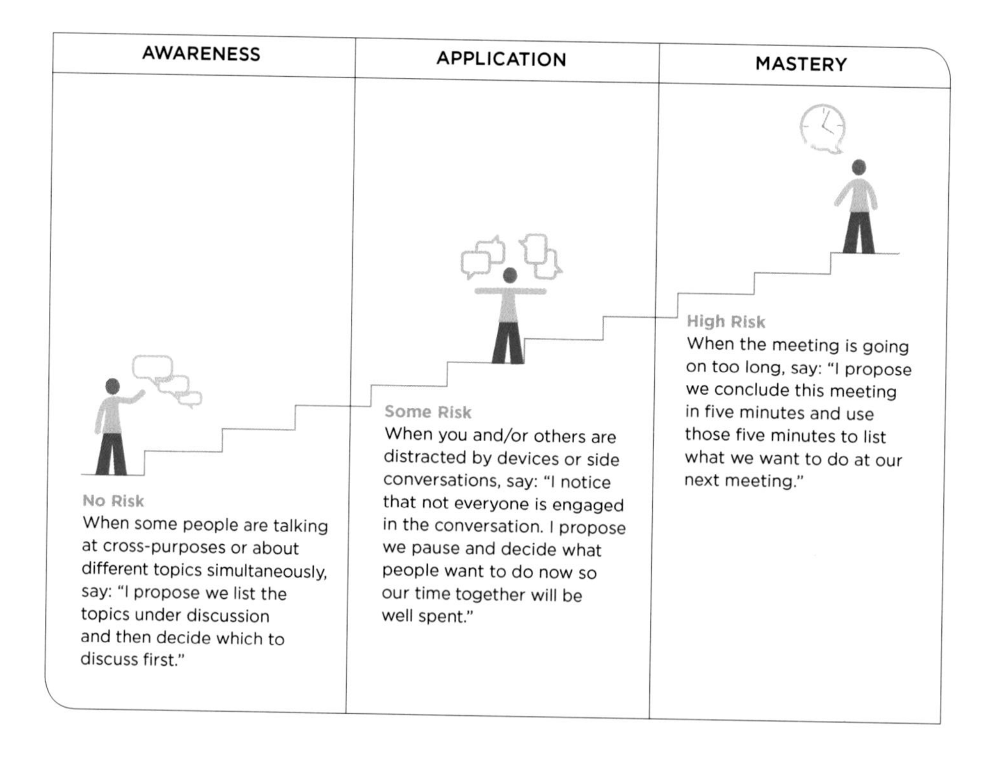

AWARENESS	APPLICATION	MASTERY
No Risk When some people are talking at cross-purposes or about different topics simultaneously, say: "I propose we list the topics under discussion and then decide which to discuss first."	**Some Risk** When you and/or others are distracted by devices or side conversations, say: "I notice that not everyone is engaged in the conversation. I propose we pause and decide what people want to do now so our time together will be well spent."	**High Risk** When the meeting is going on too long, say: "I propose we conclude this meeting in five minutes and use those five minutes to list what we want to do at our next meeting."

SKILL 5.2: USE CONVERSATIONS TO DEVELOP CONVERGENCE

Conversation as a way to develop group convergence is a powerful tool. When used properly groups can move from talk to action. The three levels of skill are outlined in the self-assessment below.

AWARENESS	APPLICATION	MASTERY
Frames conversations that move people toward convergence • *Does my synthesis of the group's work support movement toward convergence?* • *Do I set a context so the group can work with emotion-laden proposals?*	Labels where the group is in the process of convergence and supports forward movement • *Do I share observations about the group and invite others to share theirs?* • *Can I use Effective Questions to move the group forward toward convergence?*	Recognizes, labels, and synthesizes conversations to support the group's ability to make choices about what to do next • *Can I support the group in making choices about the process of decision making?* • *Do I regularly and quickly help groups choose the conversation that will move them forward?*
→	→	→

AWARENESS:
FRAMES CONVERSATIONS THAT MOVE PEOPLE TOWARD CONVERGENCE

You are aware of this skill when:

- *you synthesize the group's work to support movement toward convergence.*
- *you set a context so the group can work with emotion-laden proposals.*

Invite the Group to Work Toward Convergence

After the group has been working for a while, encourage people to be conscious of all the proposals and people's interests. Ask them to use their creativity to develop a proposal that everyone can support. This moment is also an opportunity for the work to be given back to the group. For example, ask people in pairs or small groups to develop proposals they can support. Then have the pairs or small groups make proposals to the whole group, such as the following comment:

> *The work of the group is to build convergence toward a proposal everyone can support. Can anyone see possible convergence and make a proposal? Take a few minutes with your small group and develop a proposal that will move the whole group forward.*

Notice when a temperature check or preference check is timely. As you scan the room, identify where the thumbs are sideways and down. Encourage the group to notice as well. Go to the thumbs sequentially and check if other people with thumbs sideways or down have the same or a similar issue. If there are several thumbs sideways or down, you can choose to get all the issues expressed at once rather than working them sequentially.

Use the parking lot to track issues that are important but not yet relevant or central to the option being developed. For example, people may talk about proposals for the communication of a strategy before deciding what strategy to pursue. Track those ideas on a separate flip chart, then inquire if those ideas can be addressed after the decision about strategy is made or if they need to be addressed in parallel with the strategy decision.

Be Attentive to Emotion and Mood

During the work of convergence, have and show empathy for the emotions that are evoked. Observe body language, affect and mood. Be respectful of where people are emotionally. Particularly significant are the emotions that might make people reluctant to share their viewpoint.

As a participant, practice recognizing and accepting the group's emotions. Stay aware of your own emotional state. As a facilitator, practice holding neutral in the face of your emotional responses and keep giving the work back to the group. In either role, as the group struggles toward convergence, take the opportunity to go to the balcony and use insights from what you see, hear, and feel to frame conversations that support forward movement. The next table shows ways to handle emotions and moods in the role of participant and/or facilitator.

TIPS: HANDLING EMOTION AND MOOD

WHEN YOU OR OTHERS FEEL...	DO THIS...	DON'T DO THIS...
Vulnerable in expressing an opinion that is in conflict with views of the majority	Acknowledge the elephant in the room that may be affecting your own or other's participation, e.g., power struggles, the impact of race, class, or culture.	Don't react with either anger or withdrawal to the issues.
Unconfident in expressing a viewpoint or wary of being coerced	Suggest a paired or table conversation for people to process their thoughts and feelings.	Don't become defensive and avoid the issue.
Anxious because more time is needed for some group members than others to process the issues	Acknowledge that you or some members of the group need more time. Propose or invite others to propose allotting additional time to process and/or to defer decisions to a later time.	Don't abdicate ownership of the issue in deference to the expertise or conviction of some group members.
Frustrated at how long the process is taking	Invite the wisdom of the group by asking people to go to the balcony and say what they observe or by asking them to reflect on past success in reaching convergence. Query if group has suggestions for how to move forward.	Don't accept or project blame for the fact that the group is not moving forward.
Disengaged from the conversation and signaling an intent to make the decision in another forum, e.g., using their hierarchical authority	Name, or invite others to name, assumptions about the group's B/ART regarding the issue being discussed or the decision being made. Address differences of opinion about the B/ART with the group.	Don't allow disagreements about B/ART to be unspoken.

Awareness of MBTI Preferences

Emotional intelligence,[7] is the capacity to identify, assess, and express emotions in yourself and others. An approach to developing that capacity is to use awareness of MBTI preferences to guide your practice.

The functional pairs — Intuitive Feelers (NF), Sensing Feelers (SF), Sensing Thinkers (ST), and Intuitive Thinkers (NT) — provide insights regarding how individuals manage emotions. Developmental areas for each of the four functional pairs include the following:

NF Reflecting on the sources of and emotional responses to information; developing an internal framework for dealing with conflict and discontent.

SF Establishing a mental framework to analyze the big picture and cause-effect relationships; developing conflict management strategies, including competitive styles.

ST Working to identify feelings and emotional responses as useful information; developing a system for examining information from diverse sources.

NT Learning to identify emotional responses and how they affect behavior; developing the ability to label emotions to enhance empathetic understanding.

APPLICATION:
LABELS WHERE THE GROUP IS IN THE PROCESS OF CONVERGENCE AND SUPPORTS FORWARD MOVEMENT

You are applying this skill when:

- *you share observations about the group and invite others to share theirs.*
- *you use Effective Questions to move the group forward toward convergence.*

Be Attentive to the Pace and Progress

Judge the pace and support progress by observing the group's work on PBDM in terms of degree of specificity and potential to move to actionable proposals. The figure depicts this progression.

PROGRESSION OF CONVERSATIONS

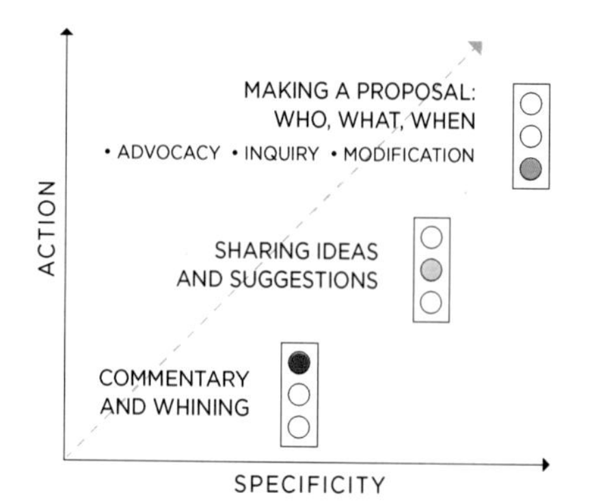

Do not go to proposals or use thumbs too soon or too late. Encourage people to turn their table tents to the vertical position to signal when they are ready to move on. Invite people to notice the time spent on developing consensus. The group may choose to set a time or do time checks to limit the amount of time spent on reaching consensus.

When a group is stuck, take the opportunity to support progress up the line to higher specificity and action. First observe where the group is, respond with Effective Questions and Context Statements, and then see if the group can move to the next stage. For example, the Context Statements and Effective Questions in the following table can support movement from one stage to the next.

CS AND EQs FOR MOVING TO ACTION

CS	EQs	MOVEMENT
I hear you are unhappy with the situation ...	Do you have an idea of what might make the situation better?	From complaining to sharing ideas
These are the ideas that have been shared ...	Does anyone have a specific proposal that builds on one or more of these ideas?	From sharing ideas to a specific proposal
The following proposal has been adopted ...	Who will do what when to implement the proposal?	From proposal to action

People may need to reflect and spend time in the sharing ideas and suggestions stage before they make a specific proposal. This time is an opportunity for the individual or group to think twice and speak once, thereby offering more coherent proposals. For example, if the first gentle prompt doesn't work and the participant continues complaining for two or more minutes, the facilitator or participant can try again:

These are the concerns I have heard: __________. Are you ready to address those concerns? Or do you have an idea of what might help you address these concerns?

If the person is unable to address his or her concerns, the facilitator or participant can invite the group into the work of developing convergence:

Is there anyone who has an idea or proposal that might address these concerns or help the group move forward?

If no one in the group can help move the group forward, e.g., if the group is stuck in red or at yellow, label the situation and invite or make hypotheses:

I notice that the group is struggling to move forward and address concerns. Does anyone have an idea about what is preventing us from moving forward?

Based on the hypothesis, the group may pause and have conversations that directly address the barriers to convergence.

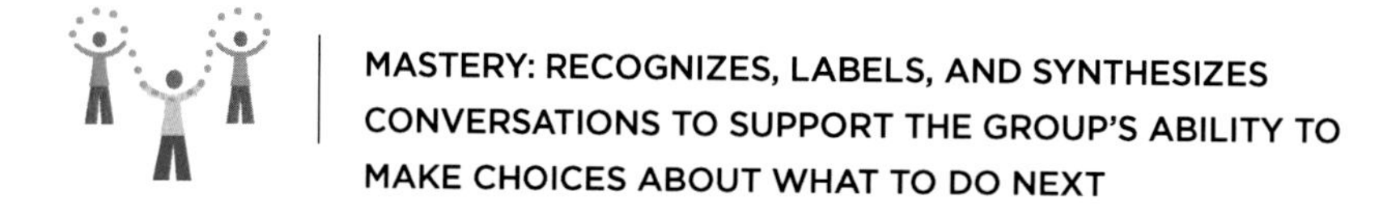

MASTERY: RECOGNIZES, LABELS, AND SYNTHESIZES CONVERSATIONS TO SUPPORT THE GROUP'S ABILITY TO MAKE CHOICES ABOUT WHAT TO DO NEXT

You are demonstrating mastery of this skill when:

- *you support the group in making choices about the process of decision making.*
- *you regularly and quickly help groups choose the conversation that will move them forward.*

Flexibility is important when you apply PBDM. Sometimes the PBDM structure will feel too confining and groups need to have free-flowing conversations. Give groups opportunities to pause, caucus, dialogue, take breaks, breathe, and laugh along the way, as needed.

Most groups working on challenging issues get stuck at some point in the process. When a group is stuck and can't find a path to convergence, a facilitator or participant might ask the group members what they want to do and/or acknowledge the underlying issues that might make it difficult for the group to deal with challenges when there is uncertainty about what to do.

Be aware of the conversation or multiple conversations being conducted simultaneously. Keep in mind the types of conversations that move groups from talk to action, name what conversations the group members are in, invite them to choose one conversation to discuss further, and focus clearly on that conversation to bring it to closure. Here is an example:

> *I am hearing two conversations right now: __________ and __________. Some people might be exploring the issues, and others might be beginning to develop some options to address the issues. Which conversation would you like to have right now?*

When a group is struggling to reach convergence, people may benefit from examining the process and making decisions about how to proceed. As a participant or facilitator, use your awareness of the different decision-making processes to support the group in making informed choices about the process. In effect, you are providing the opportunity to adopt, by consensus, supplemental decision rules of the types described in the following table.

TYPES OF DECISION-MAKING RULES

TYPE	CIRCUMSTANCE WHERE TYPE IS APPROPRIATE	IMPLEMENTATION EXAMPLES
Delegation	The group identifies issues and who needs to do what to address the issues and then bring the proposal back to the group.	Groups often work to reach consensus on mission statements that require editing. The group can name a poetry team (a group of two or three people delegated to wordsmith for the group) to synthesize, edit, and bring back the proposed wording to the group.
Caucus	The group invites those who are most interested and have diverse opinions to caucus and bring back options to the larger group.	There may be subgroups who can more efficiently work with their allies to formulate options. Those people can caucus while the rest of the group takes a break.
Lobbying	The group declares a pause during which people get up, move around, and lobby others in the group to build support and convergence.	When different groups support different proposals, declare a five-minute lobbying break. Encourage people to move around and talk with someone with a different opinion to see if convergence can be developed.
Super Majority	The group adopts a decision rule by consensus that allows it to invoke supermajority voting when the group agrees by consensus that consensus cannot be reached.	Groups often work hard to adopt this decision rule, and then, paradoxically, never or rarely use it.
Deferral	The group defers a decision or decides not to decide.	When the people in the group scan thumbs and notice there is a long way to go to achieve consensus, they can decide not to try to reach consensus at that time and return to the proposal at a later date.
Overcoming Obstacles	The group names what needs to be done so that consensus can be reached.	In the process of working toward convergence, a group can explicitly identify what is preventing movement. The group then decides who needs to do what to overcome the obstacle. For example, before making a decision, some may need more or different data while others may need authorization or endorsement from their home organization or affiliation. In each instance, the group finds ways to address those needs.

PARTICIPANT PRACTICE GUIDE 5.2: USE CONVERSATIONS TO DEVELOP CONVERGENCE

As a meeting participant, you may be able to help the group develop convergence, using the elements in this Participant Practice Guide.

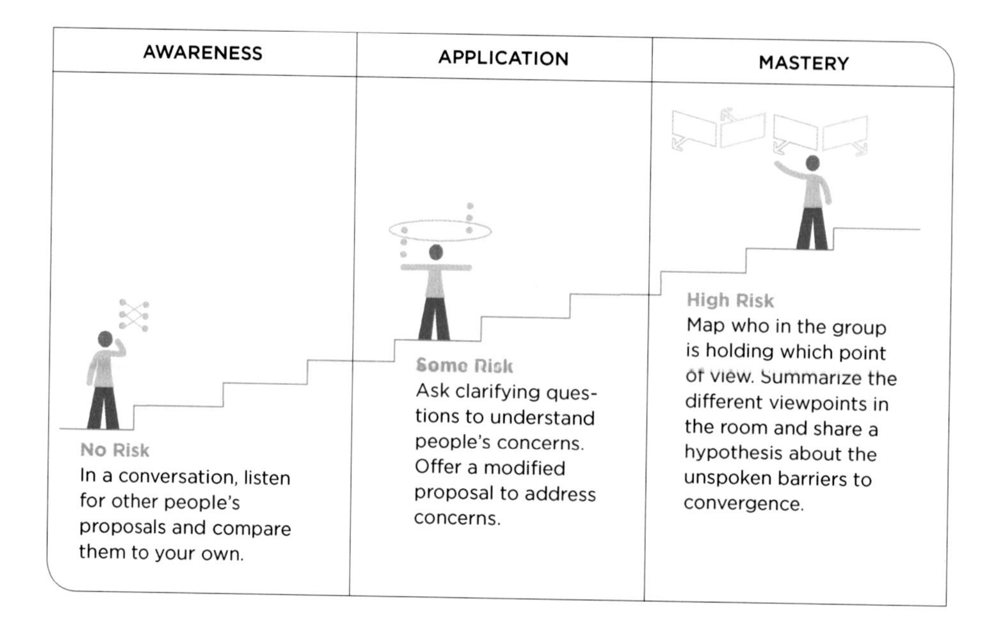

AWARENESS	APPLICATION	MASTERY
No Risk In a conversation, listen for other people's proposals and compare them to your own.	**Some Risk** Ask clarifying questions to understand people's concerns. Offer a modified proposal to address concerns.	**High Risk** Map who in the group is holding which point of view. Summarize the different viewpoints in the room and share a hypothesis about the unspoken barriers to convergence.

SKILL 5.3: NAME AND ADDRESS BARRIERS TO CONVERGENCE

Naming and being able to help the group address barriers to reaching agreement is an important skill for the facilitator. The table below lists the three levels for this skill.

AWARENESS	APPLICATION	MASTERY
Names divergent mental models • *Do I label my own mental models and listen for the mental models expressed by group members?* • *Can I use the ladder of inference or the 5Fs (Feelings, Frames, Filters, Facts, Findings) to listen for other people's mental models?*	Uses mental models to develop solutions and make decisions • *Do I apply the underlying concepts of interest-based negotiation to help the group develop solutions?* • *Do I use the MBTI communication preferences Z model to sequence discussions and move groups toward decisions?*	Uses a repertoire of mental models to address barriers • *Do I readily identify and shift to another mental model to address barriers?* • *Can I use mental models that do not represent my own world view or values?*

As groups address complex issues and experience challenging dynamics, sometimes people hit a barrier that prevents them from moving to convergence. The ability to understand the mental models that might be causing the barrier and to introduce a new way of thinking or a new approach can help groups move forward. In either the participant or facilitator role, you can catalyze a new way of thinking by being able to name the barrier to forward movement and offer an alternate mental model for the group to consider.

A new mental model can inform a Context Statement, frame an Effective Questions, and direct your Listen For; inform how the participant or the facilitator labels what is occurring in the group; and provide an example just in time of how a group might want to frame a conversation.

Using mental models is a two-step process. The first is to develop the ability to name your own and others' implicit and explicit mental models. The second is to be familiar with a wide range of mental models useful in helping groups move from talk to action. The next section provides approaches to help you name your own and others' mental models. It also introduces a range of mental models to add to your repertoire.

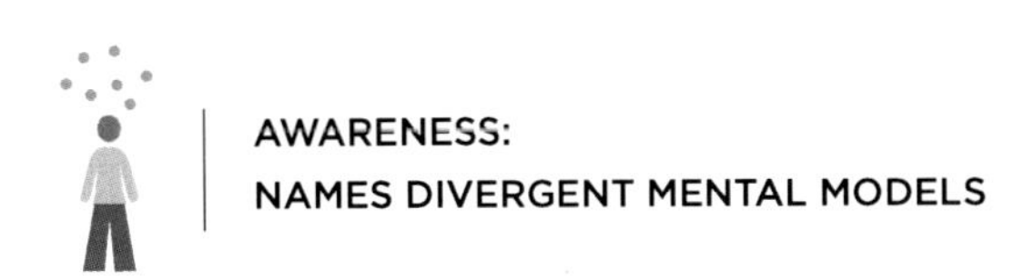

You are aware of this skill when:

- *you label your own mental models and listen for the mental models expressed by group members.*
- *you use the ladder of inference or the 5Fs (Feelings, Frames, Filters, Facts, Findings) to listen for other people's mental models.*

Labeling Your Own and Others' Mental Models

The implicit and explicit mental models of the group members inform the group's conversation. An important step in developing the skill of using mental models is to become aware of your own mental models and be able to name them.

PRACTICE: NAMING YOUR OWN MENTAL MODELS

When listening, information is not only received, it is also processed and reactions occur — liking or not liking what is being said, agreeing or disagreeing with the speaker. Notice your reactions in conversations, and practice asking yourself the following questions:

- What are my assumptions? Are they similar to or different from those of others?
- What preconceived ideas are being brought to the discussion, by me and by others?
- What mental model is the source of my assumptions or preconceived notions?
- What is the name I would give the mental model that informs my viewpoint?

Using the Ladder of Inference to Listen For Mental Models

You can explore and name mental models using the Argyris-originated and Senge-popularized ladder of inference.[8] The ladder of inference illuminates the interactive connection among actions, beliefs, conclusions, assumptions, affixed meaning, selected data, and real data and experiences.

The ladder of inference can be used as a visual, a handout, a way to flip chart, a frame for synthesizing a conversation, or a guide to setting context and asking Effective Questions.

The illustration below shows the interrelationship of mental models and how people take in information, make decisions, and behave or act. The exercise on the following page lists a series of steps for using the ladder of inference in group situations.

LADDER OF INFERENCE

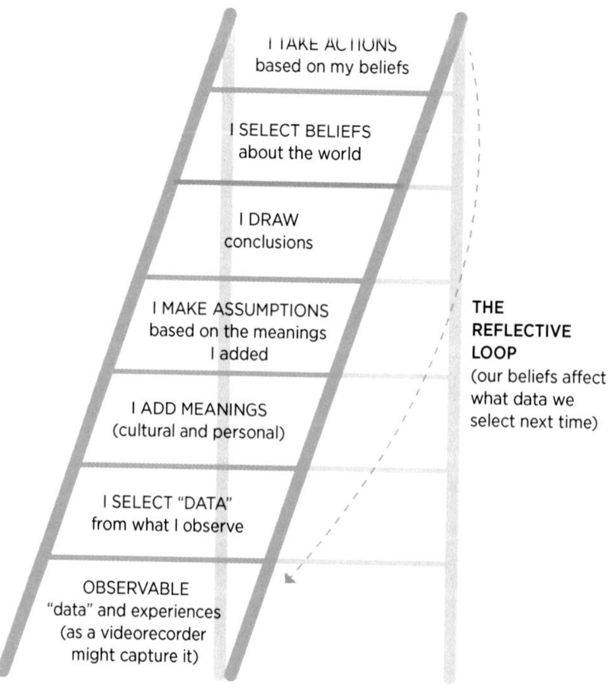

PRACTICE: USING THE LADDER OF INFERENCE

1. Draw a copy of the ladder of inference.
2. As you listen to a conversation, map what you are hearing from others to the steps in the ladder.
3. Notice what is missing in the conversation. For example, people might be sharing different sets of facts without being explicit about the mental models that make those facts relevant and not others.
4. Elicit information for all steps of the ladder. Explore what the conversation is about for different group members and how members are making connections among data, meaning, assumptions, beliefs, and proposed actions.

Mental Models Through the Person-Role-System Lens

The Person-Role-System framework, which illuminates how a person's unique characteristics influence how they hold a role and how the authorizing systems shape roles, is a useful lens for seeing and naming mental models. In the Hold 3R Meetings competency, you use the Person-Role-System framework to do a composition analysis of the group. The analysis specifies who the people are, what roles they play in the meeting and in their organizations, their relationships to each other and to the meeting result, and what interests and resources they bring to the meetings.

The information from the composition analysis can inform hypotheses about the mental models that influence people's participation in the conversation. As in all RBF work, hypotheses are used to explore what might be occurring and gather information to test those hypotheses. The practitioner uses inquiry and observation to explore the hypotheses, using them constructively and intentionally to generate multiple hypotheses about the same circumstances, systematically gather information to test hypotheses, and foster the ability to let go of hypotheses in the face of experience.

In the Person-Role-System framework, the way people describe their identity at the person level (e.g., their gender, race, sexual orientation, cultural, socioeconomic, religious, geographic, age, political, professional, national identity) can illuminate potential mental models that influence their person-in-role-in-system behavior. Considering how a woman supervisor exercises her authority in a predominantly male profession is an example of person-in-role-in-system analysis.

Knowing how a person declares his or her identity in a particular context can illuminate the mental model he or she might be applying in a particular conversation. Feminist, conservative or liberal, religious believer or atheist, member of a generation (X, Millennial, Boomer, Greatest), urban or rural, white or blue collar, member of a minority racial or ethnic group — all are examples of labels for mental models that might be linked to identity. The tips on the following page list some things to notice as participants self-identify.

Often, the conversation and the group membership will shape which mental model takes precedence — what is in the foreground versus what is in the background. For example, in a group of older people, a younger person might signal her mental model of age identity as follows: *As a member of Generation X . . .* That same person in another conversation and/or with another group might bring race and gender identity to the foreground by saying: *As an African-American woman . . .*

Below are some phrases to listen for as participants self-identify.

TIPS: USING PERSON-ROLE-SYSTEM TO LISTEN FOR MENTAL MODELS

In conversations, listen for people using the phrase "As a... "

For Person
Notice what is shared after that phrase and if there is a predictable pattern that reveals an identity linked to a mental model. For example, someone with a feminist identity might have a conscious or unconscious mental model that would bring issues of gender equality and the relative power and status of men versus women to the foreground.

Conversely, when you hear people express an interest or take a position in a conversation, see if there is a connection between how they describe their identity and a mental model that informs their perspective.

For Person-in-Role
Notice what role the person is speaking from. For example, in a discussion about flex time, is a person wearing the hat of management concerned with coverage and workflow or wearing the hat of an employee who needs flexibility and is concerned with meeting personal needs.

For Role-in-System
Notice what is implied about the authority and tasks of similar roles in different systems. For example, a supervisor in a public system with both civil service and union protections for employees exercises authority differently than a supervisor in the private for-profit sector guided solely by the organization's personnel practices.

The 5Fs: Feelings, Frames, Filters, Facts, Findings

A common barrier to convergence is the intense emotion evoked when mental models connected to identity are challenged. The individuals and the group may not be aware of the source of the intense emotion and may react with either fight or flight.

The 5F model is an approach that uses emotion as a pointer to understand mental models. The 5Fs is a mnemonic for an approach that illuminates the connections between emotional reactions (feelings) and the mental models that are the context for the emotional reactions.

Awareness of the emotional reaction (Feelings) can be used to generate a hypothesis about identity. This hypothesis, in turn, can inform the naming of an explicit or implicit mental model (Frames). The named mental model frames the conversation, in effect, determining what is relevant (Filters) to the conversation (Facts). In psychological terms, framing effects "generally refer[s] to the relationship between context and information as it determines meaning ... a template or data structure that organizes pieces of information." [9]

The feelings are connected to a frame that defines the filter, which acts as a set of criteria for selecting the facts that lead to a person's findings, e.g., the conclusions that lead to actions. The 5Fs and some EQs are listed below.

THE 5Fs AND THEIR EQs

5Fs	DEFINITION	EQs
Feelings	The emotional reaction, stance, or orientation to a conversation or topic	What are the feelings evoked by the topic: • How do you feel about...? What aspect of identity evokes the emotional response • Who are you in the conversation? • With whom do you empathize? • In whom do you see an aspect of yourself? • Are there aspects of your identity that position you in the conversation? What is the emotional orientation toward the topic or conversation: • *What makes this important to you?*
Frames	The mental model that is coherent with the source of feelings and reinforces the underlying identity associated with the feelings	What is the mental model that underlies your emotional response and may be connected to your identity: • Based on how you feel and who you are in this conversation, what is your perspective? • How do your viewpoint, philosophy, or values inform you? • What story are you telling yourself about this? What is your narrative?
Filters	The elements of the mental model that act as criteria for selecting facts	What are your criteria for selecting the relevant facts? • Based on your narrative, what do you think is important? • What facts do you consider irrelevant? • What information carries weight with you? What do you tend to discount? • Are there any facts that would change your mind?
Facts	The facts that meet the criteria of the filter and reinforce the frame	What is your supporting evidence: • What categories of information are important? • What information do you need to make a decision? Take action? • What are your preferred sources of information?
Findings	The interpretation of the facts that inform conclusions that lead to actions	What are your conclusions: • What leads you to that specific conclusion? • What actions are being proposed? (What might you do? What are you doing?) • What do you think will happen or what might be the consequences of the proposed action? (What do you hope will happen? What are the consequences?)

TIPS: USING THE 5Fs MNEMONIC

As you listen for the feelings, frames, filters, facts, and findings, explore and test whether they represent a mental model with a preexisting name, or can be given a name to bring the mental model to the foreground for conscious exploration by the group. Being aware of some of the commonly held mental models associated with different types of conversations can give you a broader repertoire to use as you practice naming mental models.

For example, the relationship between identity and emotion may make it useful to develop a repertoire of mental models that often inform conversations about race. For example:

- Anti-racism (structural racism frame)
- Civil rights advocacy and anti-discrimination (legal rights frame)
- Community building (relationship-building frame)

In a conversation about race, listen for feelings and identity and then formulate a hypothesis about the person's frame. Notice how people holding different frames use those as a filter for relevant facts that inform their proposals (findings) about solutions and actions.

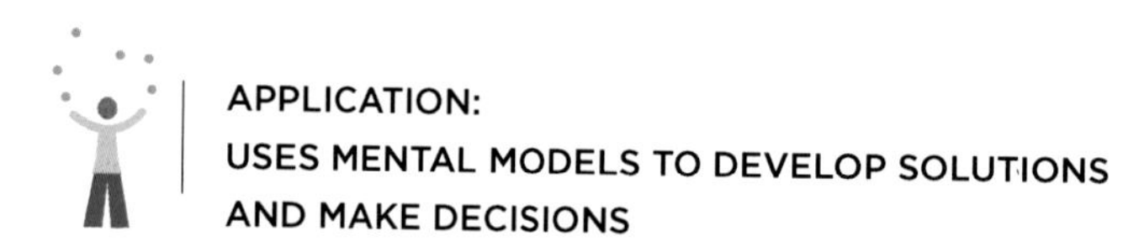

APPLICATION: USES MENTAL MODELS TO DEVELOP SOLUTIONS AND MAKE DECISIONS

You are applying this skill when:

- *you apply the underlying concepts of interest-based negotiation to help the group develop solutions.*
- *you use the Z model to move groups toward decisions.*

Groups often get stuck in moving toward convergence because they approach the problem with a zero-sum rather than a win-win approach. The zero-sum approach is based on the assumption that for every gain there is a loss. This approach is, in and of itself, a barrier to finding generative, collaborative solutions. Interest-based or win-win negotiation addresses the barrier of a zero-sum perspective.

Interest-Based Negotiation

Fisher and Ury's[10] approach to Interest-Based Negotiation (IBN) is a well-developed and effective approach to moving groups forward when people are stuck in positions and not open to listening to each other and finding common ground. Whether as a participant or facilitator, the ability to use EQs to evoke the process of IBN helps people move through difficult conversations and develop solutions together. Definitions of key terms and related EQs are provided below.

Party: A person or subset of people in the meeting who have interests.

- Who is the party/are the parties who hold interests?

Position: The initial demand, or what people think they should ask for or get.

- What is the benefit of your position to you?
- What do you hope to gain (or prevent) by holding your position?

Interests: What people are pursuing and want to have as a result of a negotiation.

- What is your interest?
- What do you need to be satisfied?

Underlying Interests: The fundamental needs that can be brought to the surface through exploration; what people really care about.

- What do you care about?
- What is most important to you?
- What do you need?

Options: What people do to meet interests and maximize mutual gain. Encourage people to be creative in achieving this goal.

- Is there an option that meets multiple interests?
- Can you imagine an option that creates benefits for more than one party?
- Can you imagine an option that addresses, at least in part, everyone's needs?

Best Alternative to a Negotiated Agreement (BATNA): An articulation of how interests might be met if a negotiated agreement cannot be reached. For example, a person negotiating with a current employer for salary and conditions of employment creates a BATNA by simultaneously seeing what other employers can offer. Exploring a BATNA can help people see possibilities for a win-win agreement and not feel that reaching agreement through IBN is the only option to meet their interests and needs.

- What are other ways to meet your interests and underlying interests?
- What can you do now to develop alternatives to meeting your needs that do not depend on reaching agreement with the parties to this negotiation?

THE SIX STEPS OF IBN

IBN is introduced through a six-step process that supports a group in developing options and making decisions based on those options.

1. Help the group see the difference between position and interest, and interest and underlying interest, through inquiry.
2. For each position, encourage people to explore why the position is important to them or what purpose it serves.
3. As people clarify their interests and underlying interests, name those interests and underlying interests.
4. Invite people to be aware of the range of interests and underlying interests and identify opportunities to meet those interests in a variety of ways. Include in this exploration a discussion of how a BATNA might meet people's interests.
5. Build on the discussion of how interests and underlying interests might be met to develop multiple options for mutual gain.
6. Use proposal-based decision making to reach agreement on options the group can support.

Holding the IBN mental model, whether you are a participant or facilitator, provides a range of responses to what you observe in groups, as shown in the table below.

USING IBN

YOU OBSERVE ...	YOU RESPOND ...
People stating positions	Invite the people to speak to their interests and underlying interests. Synthesize the interests and underlying interests and invite people to brainstorm options that address multiple interests.
People speaking from a win-lose or zero-sum game mentality	Invite people to consider that options may exist for mutual gain and lead to win-win solutions.

The Z Problem-Solving Model

Another barrier to decision making is that people have different approaches to problem solving and may get stuck because they do not bring the strengths of their MBTI preferences to the work. The Z Problem-Solving Model shown in the figure is a four-step process that connects MBTI insights, preferences, and awareness to the process of PBDM.

This model was discovered through research that examined the effectiveness of group problem solving. The most successful groups followed the sequence of Sensing, iNtuition, Thinking, and Feeling.[11]

Each step in the sequence benefits from using an EQ specific to that step[12] as shown in the following exercise. Groups using the Z-Model have the opportunity to draw on the strengths of all members, to challenge members to use their abilities by engaging in a way that is not their preference, and to come up with an understanding of the issue and the possible solutions that reflect the perspectives of many group members.

THE Z PROBLEM-SOLVING MODEL

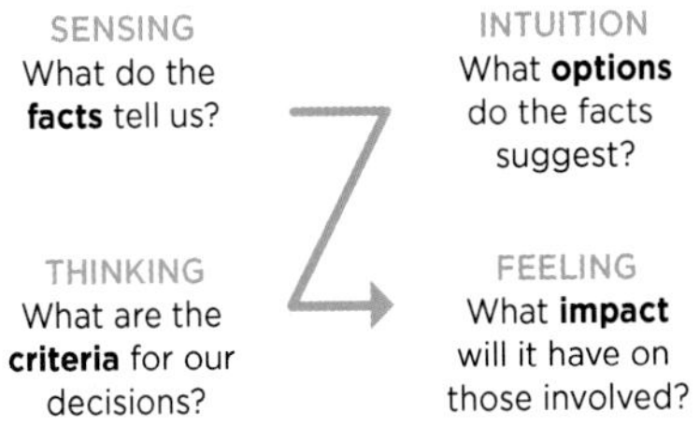

PRACTICE: USING THE Z-MODEL WITH MBTI PREFERENCES

Use the following EQs to elicit information at each of the four steps of the Z-Model.

1. **The Facts (Sensing)**
   - What are the relevant facts?
   - What specific data are available about the situation?
   - What does experience tell us?
   - What are the realistic constraints?
   - What incremental steps have already been taken?
   - What facts describe where we are?
   - What should we keep that works?

2. **The Options (iNtuition)**
   - What are all the possibilities?
   - What is the big picture view of where we want to be?
   - What are the alternatives?
   - What might address many factors at once?
   - What might happen in the future?
   - What trends or patterns can inform different approaches to the problem?
   - What could we do?

3. The Criteria (Thinking)

- What needs to be considered in assessing the options?
- What are the criteria that will determine the best decisions?
- What are the best options, with their pros and cons?
- Is there a model that we can apply to better understand the options?
- What are the fundamental assumptions underlying the options?
- What are the logical consequences of implementing each option?
- How does each option contribute to the desired result?
- How will we objectively assess progress and success?

4. The Effect on People (Feeling)

- With whom do we need to collaborate and in what ways?
- How will people feel about the implementation of the selected option?
- How will our stakeholders react?
- Which solutions will promote maximum acceptance and ownership?
- Is the option consistent with our values?
- Who will the option's implementation affect?
- How will we communicate with others about the selected option?
- Are there other parties to the solution who should be included?

The Z-Model supports PBDM in many ways. For example, when small groups at tables are generating proposals, invite them to use the Z-Model to develop their proposals. Remind a group struggling among multiple options to refer to the Z-Model. Invite explicit consideration of MBTI and encourage the group to first use S to gather data and ensure that people understand the concerns of those with their thumbs sideways or down. Then use N to explore possibilities and use the information gathered to creatively address specific interests. Highlighting criteria (T) first to sort choices and then exploring the impact on people (F) incorporates the strengths of all preferences into the decision-making process.

MASTERY:
USES A REPERTOIRE OF MENTAL MODELS TO ADDRESS BARRIERS

You are demonstrating mastery of this skill when:

- *you readily identify and shift to another mental model to address barriers.*
- *you use mental models representing world views and values that are not your own.*

Another barrier to convergence is some people's inability to see the world from another person's viewpoint or to be aware of how mental models shape participation in conversations to reach convergence. This barrier is overcome when you can, as a participant or facilitator, not only name a wide range of mental models — but also consciously use another model and see the impact of using a different model on your own and others' ability to work together toward convergence.

The advanced practice of consciously adopting a mental model that is not your own and using it in a conversation or a facilitation requires work. The steps and EQs below will help you identify mental models in conversations and practice consciously holding a model not your own.

TIPS: USING A REPERTOIRE OF MENTAL MODELS

When in a conversation:

1. Consider the focus of the conversation and name to yourself a number of mental models that might be at play.
2. Choose a mental model that is not one you would naturally use in a conversation.
3. Practice holding the frame of your chosen mental model as you participate in or facilitate the conversation.
4. After the conversation, reflect on the experience of holding the alternate frame:
   - What was foreground and what was background?
   - What was relevant? What was irrelevant?
   - What feelings were evoked?
   - What seemed possible or desirable? What seemed impossible or undesirable?
   - How was the experience similar to or different from the experience you have when participating in the conversation with your more typical mental model as the frame?

Repertoire of Mental Models About Race, Class, and Culture

In many problem-solving conversations about results, people often consider how to address disparities. Disparities in this context are disparate outcomes associated with factors such as gender, race, class, or culture. A disparity might be revealed by data indicating that the high school graduation rate for Asian boys from low-income families is higher than that of Hispanic boys of similar economic status. However, people's negative experiences in trying to address disparities become a barrier to the work. That barrier can be overcome by listening for the mental models that people bring to these conversations and by being aware of how the models frame their participation.

A repertoire of mental models enables you to listen to conversations and generate hypotheses about the different models people use. For example, several years ago while listening to a conversation about early childhood education, I noticed that the group members had very different perspectives. As people explored how to improve the number and percent of children of all races, genders, and cultural and economic backgrounds who succeed in school, I generated hypotheses about people's perspectives about race, class, and culture and used those hypotheses to name to myself the five mental models listed below.

1. **We are all one race, the human race.** Yes, there are racial differences, but those are outweighed by our common humanity. We are all the same under the skin and the work is to discover our common humanity.

2. **Race matters most.** Those with darker or darkest skin color experience oppression and disparities because institutionalized power and privilege protect people with lighter skin (i.e., white privilege). White privilege operates through many mechanisms (structural, cultural, etc.). The work is to combat white privilege by anti-racism awareness and action.

3. **Enslaved ancestors matters most.** The legacy of slavery is the most important factor to be addressed. African Americans who are descendants of slaves experience a unique and toxic mix of structural, cultural, and economic inequity. The work is to use multiple mechanisms to redress historical inequity and address current barriers to equity.

4. **Race (as defined by ethnicity or group identity) is only one factor and not always the most significant in understanding disparities.** Many factors are important to understanding disparities: language, economic status, class identity, culture, race, gender, religion, and geography, to name a few. The work is to address multiple factors in the context of how each factor or a combination of factors creates disparities.

5. **Oppression is experienced by many people in many different circumstances.** Hatred and oppression are based on a multitude of factors: religion, ethnic identity, skin color, economic class, language, gender, sexual preference. The tendency to generate in-group boundaries with special privileges and relationships based on identity occurs whenever groups form. The work is to create more conscious awareness and choice regarding the consequences of the dynamic of identity formation and the processes of inclusion and exclusion.

PRACTICE: EXPERIMENTING WITH MENTAL MODELS ABOUT RACE, CLASS, AND CULTURE

1. Consider your own assumptions about what matters for children entering kindergarten ready to learn.
2. Give a name to that set of assumptions or mental model.
3. What do you consider to be important strategies to implement at the Person-Role-System level to ensure that all children enter school ready to learn?
4. Review the five mental models.
5. Choose one that is different from your own.
6. Consciously hold the chosen mental model and think again about the challenge of all children entering school ready to learn.
   - What strategies are important within this mental model?
   - Are they similar to or different from those you generated with the first mental model?

A Repertoire of Complementary Mental Models to Frame Problem-Solving Conversations

As groups discuss problems and solutions, individuals bring with them mental models (often unconscious) that limit their ability to see possibilities for solutions. Sometimes the mental model that is limiting the possibilities has a corollary, one that complements the mental model and puts it into a broader perspective that encourages groups to move toward convergence. Naming a common mental model and its corollary or complementary model to frame the conversation can help a group move forward. A repertoire of complementary mental models is listed in the following table.

COMMON AND COMPLEMENTARY MENTAL MODELS

COMMON MENTAL MODEL	COMPLEMENTARY MENTAL MODEL	INTRODUCING THE COMPLEMENTARY MENTAL MODEL — CONTEXT STATEMENT AND EFFECTIVE QUESTIONS
either/or	both/and	**Context Statement:** People are looking at either/or options. • Are there any helpful both/and solutions?
will happen	if/then	**Context Statement:** People often have implicit assumptions about what will happen. • Ask people to articulate their ideas about causality by expressing what they think in this way: If X happens, then Y will follow.
focus on the part not the whole	part/whole	**Context Statement:** Several people might be proposing solutions to part of the problem. • When you look at all the proposed solutions, what do they add up to? What is the larger whole of which these solutions are a part? • What is possible when people can see both the whole and the parts?
favored ideal compared to unfavored real	ideal compared to ideal and real compared to real	**Context Statement:** When you are evaluating the proposed alternatives, you are describing the best-case scenario for your favored alternative and comparing it to the worst-case scenario for your least favored option. Take a moment to consider all the options. • What is the best-case scenario for each (the ideal)? What is the worst-case scenario (more realistic) for each? • Compare the ideal to the ideal and the real to real for each scenario. • What does that comparison reveal?
assumed equilibrium	consider disequilibrium	**Context Statement:** People might assume that their own past experiences are relevant to the current situation or that the current situation will continue unchanged into the future. • What are your assumptions about how the current situation is similar to past circucmstances? • What are your assumptions about what might change in the future?

As you use complementary mental models in conversations, notice other complementary models that are being used or could be used.

- What is the impact of introducing complementary mental models into conversations?
- What are some complementary models that you have noticed in conversations?
- How would you name the complementary mental models?
- What CS and EQ can be used to introduce complementary mental models into a conversation?
- What are some opportunities to use a complementary mental model in a conversation to move it forward?

PARTICIPANT PRACTICE GUIDE 5.3: NAME AND ADDRESS BARRIERS TO CONVERGENCE

A participant in a meeting can practice using mental models through these steps.

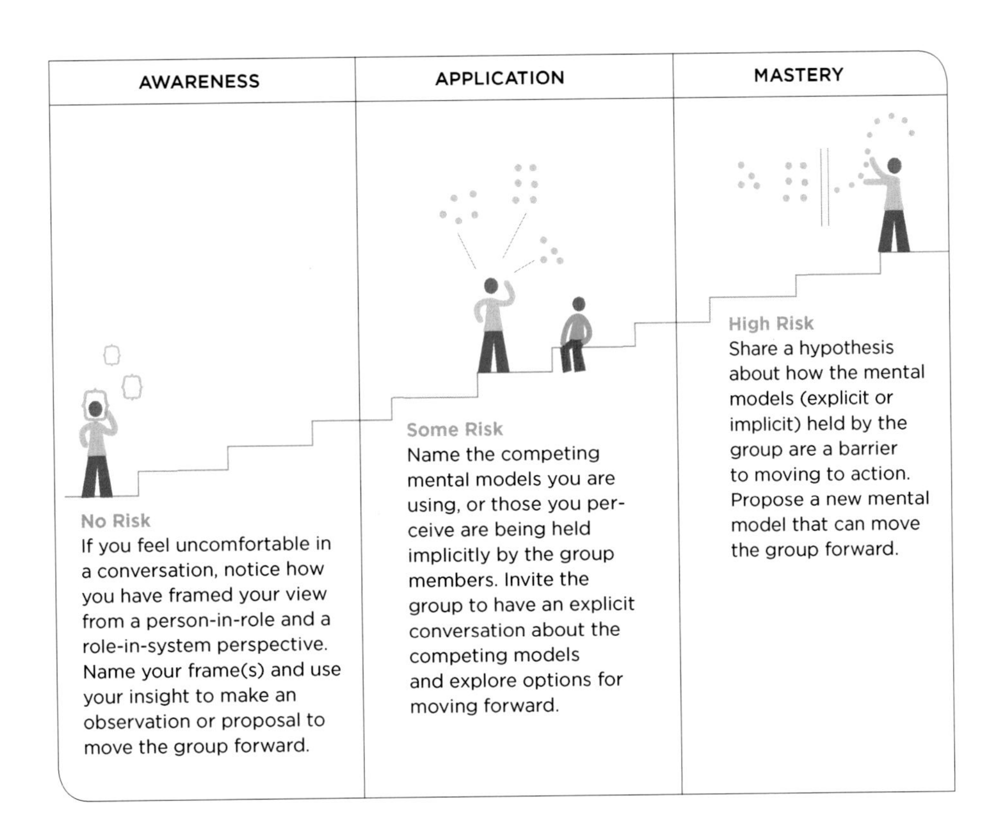

SKILL 5.4: MAKE AND HELP OTHERS MAKE ACTION COMMITMENTS

Once a group has reached convergence on a proposal and adopted it, the group's work becomes translating decisions into effective action. The following table shows the skill self-assessment that can help groups in this step.

AWARENESS	APPLICATION	MASTERY
Understands the intent and form of effective action commitments • *Do I set a context for making public action commitments?* • *Do I Listen For action commitments with a disciplined focus on who, what, and when?* • *Do I support the group in documenting action commitments for future reference?*	Helps groups commit to action • *Do I help groups manage the change process associated with moving to action?*	Helps groups align action commitments • *Do I use MBTI awareness to support people making action commitments?* • *Can I use the High Action/ High Alignment framework?*
→	→	→

Experience and emerging research suggest that what contributes to effective action is a public commitment to action that is specific: who will do what when, with whom, and with what impact or contribution.

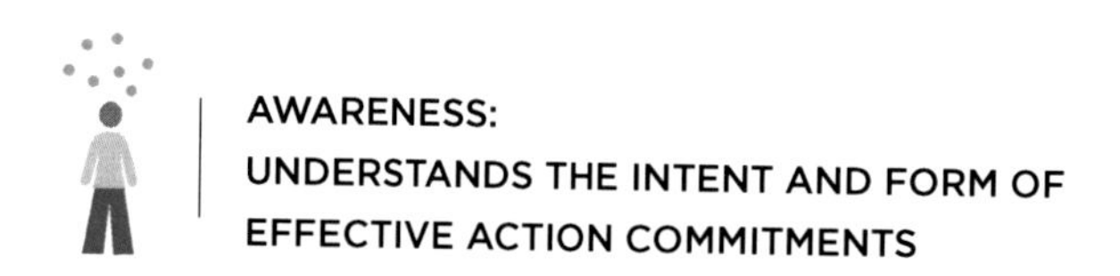

You are aware of this skill when:

- *you set a context for making public action commitments.*
- *you Listen For action commitments with a disciplined focus on who, what, and when.*
- *you support the group in documenting action commitments for future reference.*

The Action Commitment Conversation

When participating in or facilitating an action commitment conversation, use the following CS, EQ and LF:

CS: Based on the decision just made (or proposal adopted)...

EQ: Who needs to do what when to accomplish the intended purpose of the decision (or adopted proposal)?

LF: Who will do what when, and with what impact?

When charting a conversation, structure your flip chart so that every what has a who and a when. This information is needed for individuals and groups to hold accountability for action. In addition, listening for the intended impact of action supports groups in making stronger connections between their effort (what they are doing) and their desired results.

Documenting Action Commitments

The documentation is the mechanism of accountability that helps people keep commitments that they make in meetings.

Documenting action commitments can be done in several ways. For example, people can use personal journals to note their action commitments and share those action commitments out loud at the end of a meeting. At the next meeting, people refer to the commitments in their journals and share the progress made with others.

In another documentation method, a facilitator charts the action commitments and brings that chart to the next appropriate meeting to be updated. The chart could also be transcribed and the commitments distributed electronically after the meeting, then updated at the next meeting. Or, people could be provided with carbonized action commitment forms to document their commitments — taking one copy as a reminder to themselves and leaving another copy to be transcribed for a public record of all action commitments.

These three methods of documentation have a common thread: all action commitments represent public, shared accountability, with a mechanism for reporting on progress that helps groups hold transparent and constructive conversations.

The three templates for documenting action commitments are shown on the following page.

ACTION COMMITMENT TEMPLATES

TEMPLATE #1: FOCUS ON CONTRIBUTION TO THE RESULT

NAME	ACTION	WITH WHOM	WHEN	CONTRIBUTION TO THE RESULT	PROGRESS

TEMPLATE #2: FOCUS ON EXECUTION

NAME	WHAT WILL YOU DO?	HOW WILL YOU DO IT?	WHAT ARE THE STEPS TO GETTING IT DONE?	WITH WHOM WILL YOU DO IT?	WHEN?	PROGRESS

TEMPLATE #3: FOCUS ON MEASUREMENT

WHAT	HOW	WHO	WHEN	IMPACT	MEASURE	PROGRESS

PRACTICE: CHALLENGES AND OPPORTUNITIES OF DOCUMENTING ACTION COMMITMENTS

Practice using one or more of these formats to document your own and others' action commitments, then use the documentation at a later date.

- What is the impact of documenting action commitments mentally, emotionally, and/or relationally?
- What did you learn from using the documentation at a later time for accountability?
- What form of action commitment documentation might you integrate into your roles of participant and facilitator?

You are applying this skill when:

- *you help groups manage the change process associated with moving to action.*

Groups and individuals often get stuck when moving from a decision to execution of the decision. One barrier to making action commitments is that action commitments often require people to implement changes at the Person-Role-System level. Change is challenging. Approaches that support groups in making and in keeping commitments to actions that require and cause change help groups move. Following are two ways to support groups to manage the change associated with moving to action.

In both instances, the models provide a CS and EQs that engage people in the dialogues that support forward movement to action. In using the models, as participant or as a facilitator, you can assess the stage of change you or the group are in and then, depending on that assessment, use the EQs to create forward momentum.

Managing Transitions Approach to Change

The Bridges' transition model[13] helps groups to deal with the changes at the Person-Role-System level needed to maintain a commitment to action. The model identifies three stages people go through as they face making changes. Use this approach to help people explore the implications of change and decide how to manage the change associated with endings, being in a neutral zone between the old and new, and with new beginnings. The following table illustrates some of the EQs for each of the three stages of change.

USING EQs TO MANAGE CHANGE AND MOVE TO ACTION

STAGE	CHARACTERISTICS OF THE STAGE	EQs
Endings	People experience loss and grief, sometimes unacknowledged. People see no value or benefit to the new.	• What am I, or what are others, losing in this change? • How can people grieve and/or mark the endings?
Neutral zone	The time when people sort out their emotions and experiences about old and new. People experience discomfort and emotional stress.	• What might I do on a temporary basis while I am sorting out the old and new? • What are my opportunities for creativity in this time of change?
New beginning	As the change is implemented, people experience a combination of old and new behaviors. People often are caught by surprise at how slow the change is and are disappointed that things aren't working.	• What are your expectations? • How does your ambivalence about the change manifest itself? • What are the forces causing you and others to hold on to old behaviors?

Keep in mind that progression through the stages is not linear, sequential, or predictable. Hold the model as a hypothesis, not an expectation — in other words, without assumptions about how long a person might be in any particular stage. The key to managing the change is to recognize what stage you and others are in and explore the questions appropriate to that stage.

The Prochaska and DiClemente Stages of Change Model

The Prochaska and DiClemente Stages of Change Model[14] creates awareness about where people are and what their choices are as they move from talking about action to taking action. This model illuminates six stages involved in adult behavior change.

The following table summarizes the Prochaska and DiClemente Stages of Change Model describing characteristics of each stage and techniques helpful in moving people from one stage to another. Included are examples of the Context Statement, EQ, and LF appropriate to each stage.

SUMMARY OF THE PROCHASKA AND DICLEMENTE STAGES OF CHANGE MODEL

STEPS TO ACTION COMMITMENT	CHARACTERISTICS	CONTEXT STATEMENT, EQ, AND LF
1. Pre-contemplation	Not currently considering commitment to action; blissful unawareness	**CS:** You may not have considered what action you can take to implement this decision. Take a moment to explore the possibilities. **EQ:** What are the benefits to you if this decision is successfully implemented? What can you do to support the decision? **LF:** What they might do
2. Contemplation	Ambivalent about committing to action; sitting on the fence	**CS:** You may not be ready to make a commitment to action. Take a moment to consider your decision to make a commitment. **EQ:** What are the pros and cons of the actions you might take? **LF:** Barriers and contributing factors to action
3. Preparation	Considering moving to action; testing the waters	**CS:** It is helpful to find solutions to some of the barriers to taking action. **EQs:** Considering some of the barriers you face, who can support you in moving to action? What are some of the ways you have succeeded in the past in addressing these barriers? **LF:** Small initial steps
4. Action	Taking action; making it happen	**CS:** Carrying through on an action commitment can be challenging. **EQ:** How can you remind yourself of your commitment? What has worked for you in the past in keeping commitments to action? **LF:** Short-term losses and support needed
5. Maintenance	Sustaining action until result is achieved; maintaining momentum	**CS:** Achieving a result may be challenging. **EQ:** In what ways can you reward or recognize your progress? What can you do if you falter in achieving the result? **LF:** Coping mechanisms to reinforce success and recover from relapse
6. Relapse	Failing to act or not sustaining action until achievement of result; fall from grace	**CS:** It is very common to not complete commitments to action. **EQ:** What factors contributed to you not completing your commitment? Has your experience affected your motivation to keep your commitment? What has worked for you in the past in getting back on track with a commitment? **LF:** Motivation, barriers, and ideas for recovery strategies

MASTERY:
HELPS GROUPS ALIGN ACTION COMMITMENTS

You are demonstrating mastery of this skill when:

- *you use MBTI awareness to support people in making action commitments.*
- *you use the High Action/High Alignment framework.*

At the mastery level, groups are not only making action commitments, they are also aligning those action commitments. Alignment occurs when this awareness informs the commitments people make and how they can support each other in keeping those commitments. For example, MBTI awareness highlights what people have to offer and what support they need during times of change.

MBTI Preferences: Aligning Action to Strengths

People's MBTI illuminates their strengths, their typical challenges, and what supports them in overcoming those challenges. The next table presents these for the four functional pairs.

MBTI AND ALIGNING ACTION TO STRENGTHS

MBTI	STRENGTH	CHALLENGE	SUPPORT NEEDED
SF	Supports others, is reliable and dependable in keeping commitments and celebrating progress	Worries about everyone; can get stuck in negative feelings, especially if the SF has not received support for losses	Assurance that others' needs are addressed; feedback and information about the process of change; opportunities to support others
NF	Enthusiastically supports a new plan and has a vision of the future; energizes everyone	Often underestimates how long or how much effort something will take Takes on too much and becomes overwhelmed; becomes unable to meet competing demands	Opportunities to explore possibilities; time to talk a lot about the change; ways to focus efforts on keeping people informed and involved; taking action consistent with values
ST	Sets goals; honors schedules and makes specific commitments	Tends to do it alone: is unwilling to say no Cautious; needs specifics before making commitments	Opportunities to process the change and gather specific information that will allow people to implement change well; needs information about why the change is beneficial and how it will work
NT	Sees change as an opportunity; designs systems and makes logical plans; keeps everyone on track	Becomes critical or dictatorial and impatient with pace of change, especially with acknowledging loss; does not pay sufficient attention to the details of change	Opportunities to provide analyses and solutions and the ability to move forward into action

MBTI Preferences: Aligning Strengths to Tasks

Using the MBTI functional pairs (SF, NF, ST, NT) lens provides an alternative to the more typical practice of committing to tasks based on the role people have in a system and the expectations or projections that people have about that role. When, for example, the top authority of an organization is expected to provide the vision and the system design to inform action (a strength of NTs) but the top authority is an SF, under appropriate circumstances, the authority might use this strength to support people's needs and rely on others in the group to align their action commitments and produce the vision and systems design. The next table illustrates how the strengths of people's preferences can be aligned with tasks typical of groups moving to action.

ALIGNING STRENGTHS WITH TASKS FOR THE FOUR MBTI FUNCTIONAL PAIRS

PAIR	STRENGTHS
SF	Figures out how to meet people's needs and provides practical support for execution
NF	Researches and brings back to the group innovative ways to accomplish the results
ST	Ensures that execution steps are realistically planned with enough time allotted to do things well
NT	Designs systems and creates logical approaches to track implementation

High Action/High Alignment

When people make action commitments, certain conversations can move them to being in high alignment and high action. These conversations build relationships of trust, shared accountability, and purpose among people who are committing to action in service of a common result. The following five conversations based on the concept of high alignment/high action contribute to forward movement.

1. **Context Statement:** Alignment occurs when people work together to achieve a common result that they cannot accomplish alone.
   - Is there a result you are committed to achieving that you cannot achieve alone?

2. **Context Statement:** High action requires people to examine what they do, how much they do it, and whether what they do contributes to the result.
   - Are your actions timely and sufficient to make a difference?

3. **Context Statement:** Achieving alignment with peers is hard when you are not the boss or the expert and cannot tell people what to do. It takes time, energy, and risk to change how you work in relationship with others to achieve high alignment.
   - What are you willing to do differently in how you work with others to align your actions?

HIGH ACTION/HIGH ALIGNMENT GRID

High action/Low alignment	High action/High alignment
Low action/Low alignment	Low action/High alignment

4. **Context Statement:** Achieving high alignment/high action requires knowing where you are and knowing where others are in the strength of their action commitments. The High Action/High Alignment Grid can help you visualize the degree to which you and others are aligned.
   - What quadrant are you in now?
   - Where do you perceive others to be?
   - What is revealed about what you and others need to do to stay in aligned action?

5. **Context Statement:** Commit to aligned action and specify what you will do, how you will do it, when you will do it, and with whom you will do it.
   - What can you do and with whom to align your action for greater impact?

PRACTICE: MOVING TO HIGH ALIGNMENT/HIGH ACTION

Select a project or task you are working on that involves you and several others.

1. Assess the degree to which you and others are in high alignment.
2. Map yourself and others onto the High Alignment/High Action Grid.
3. Do a composition analysis with B/ART information about each person's relationship to the task.
4. Practice setting a context and asking an EQ to move people to aligned action.

PARTICIPANT PRACTICE GUIDE 5.4:
MAKE AND HELP OTHERS MAKE ACTION COMMITMENTS

You can make and help others make action commitments as a meeting participant. Depending on what is an acceptable level of risk, you can choose any of the actions below.

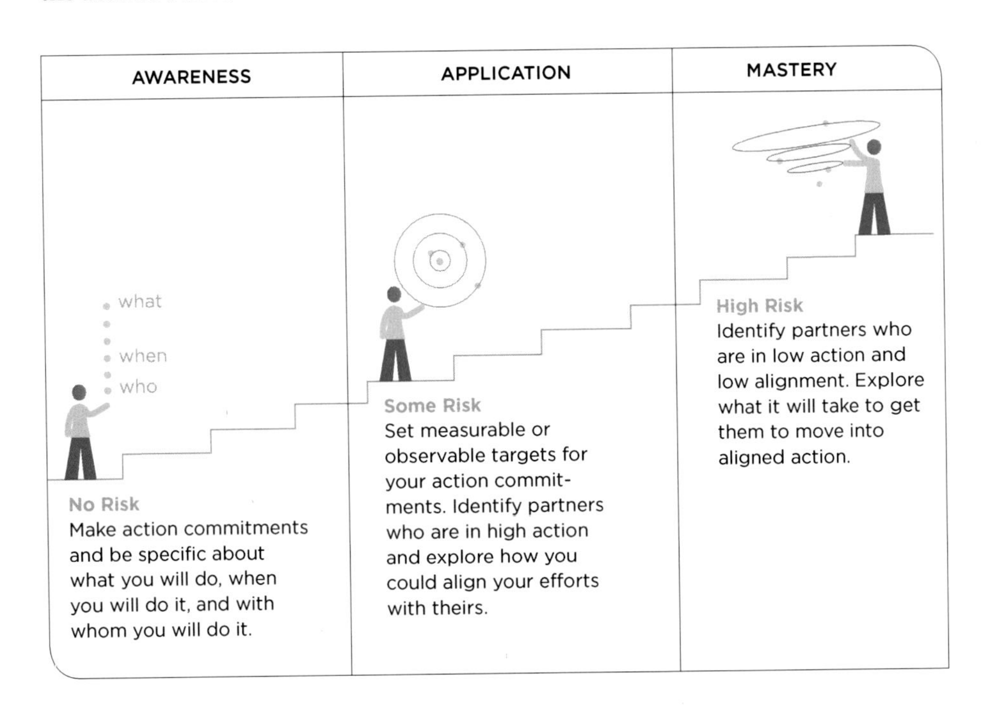

SKILL 5.5: BE AND HELP OTHERS BE ACCOUNTABLE FOR ACTION COMMITMENTS

A critical characteristic of RBF is the accountability for action commitments. The following table shows the self-assessment continuum for this skill.

AWARENESS	APPLICATION	MASTERY
Understands and uses the Accountability Pathway • *Do I introduce the Accountability Pathway as a method for people to keep commitments to action?* • *Am I comfortable and do I help others become comfortable holding genuine accountability conversations?*	Helps groups hold accountability for action commitments • *Do I use EQs that make it easy for me and others to assess progress along the Accountability Pathway, move to owning action commitments, and make them happen?*	Strengthens the group's capacity to be accountable for action • *Do I label the emotional reactions of myself and others and use EQs to support the group in making and keeping commitments to action?* • *Do I use MBTI awareness to support groups in holding accountability for action?*
→	→	→

The Importance of Accountability Conversations

Meeting results are a step along the way to neighborhood and community results only if the meeting participants commit to action, are accountable for keeping commitments to action, and learn from the consequences of their actions. Participating in and facilitating accountability conversations is an essential part of this process.

Accountability conversations occur in many different settings: parishioners form circles of support and accountability; 12-step addiction programs include group meetings for accountability; for-profit companies have accountability conversations as part of their performance management systems; nonprofit organizations have accountability conversations addressing people's contributions to the mission.

However, the framework for these conversations and the assumptions about motivation and emotion may differ from those underpinning the RBF approach to accountability. Often, these conversations do not occur in a way that leads to better informed action over time. Contributing to this problem is that most people's experience with accountability conversations is negative.

Many people's first association with the word accountability is their experience as children when they brought home a bad report card, or their association may be with the reward and punishment systems in organizations or families. However, it is possible to normalize the accountability conversation and approach it as an opportunity for learning, awareness, and choice.

The research on accountability-for-action commitments has identified three interrelated activities that increase accountability, as measured by the quality of action commitments and execution of commitments.[15] Those activities are: (1) making written commitments; (2) making commitments public; and (3) engaging in meaningful dialogue about the progress made in keeping commitments. When people hold candid accountability conversations about what they have or have not done, they can focus on their own behaviors and use the information from the dialogue to make decisions about how to proceed. These conversations contribute to people's ability to make and keep commitments and to work effectively together.

After people commit to action, these accountability conversations can take place at a later date — after people have had time to take action. In a first conversation, people report what they did, i.e., how or if they kept their commitment to action. In the second conversation, people examine the consequences of whether and how they kept their commitment to action and how what they learned from the experience will inform their future commitments to actions.

The Accountability Pathway

The mental model for these two conversations is the Accountability Pathway. For example, when people fail to keep a commitment, they often blame others. In this context, blaming others is an early step on the Accountability Pathway.

People can be at different places on the pathway at different times and in relationship to different aspects of their lives and careers. For example, in one area of a person's life or career, he or she may be highly accountable, owning his or her commitments and finding solutions to make those commitments happen while simultaneously, in another area of his or her life or career, be at the step of making "I can't excuses."

The Accountability Pathway is an adaptation of an approach developed by Bell Atlantic in the mid-1990s for creating organizational culture change. Bell Atlantic presented the concept as a ladder of accountability with the first rung of the ladder indicating a lack of awareness of a commitment and the top rung of the ladder representing accomplishing a commitment. Bell Atlantic's accountability ladder was used by people in the company trained to act as agents of change to frame conversations with their peers about taking action and implementing needed changes in the company's operations. The original accountability ladder image, with the symbolism of climbing up and falling down, conveyed an impression that was more critical than appreciative and developmental.

The Accountability Pathway graphic with the friendly icons, shown below, was created to enable people to have accountability conversations as a normal part of everyday discourse.

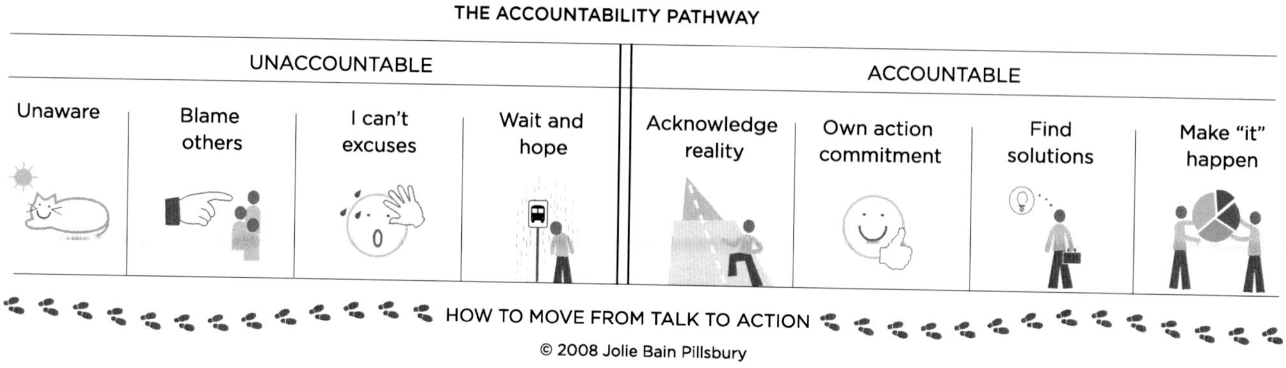

THE ACCOUNTABILITY PATHWAY

UNACCOUNTABLE				ACCOUNTABLE			
Unaware	Blame others	I can't excuses	Wait and hope	Acknowledge reality	Own action commitment	Find solutions	Make "it" happen

HOW TO MOVE FROM TALK TO ACTION

This developmental image conveys opportunities for awareness, choice, and growth over time. As a group conversation or as an individual reflection, the Accountability Pathway provides a way for people to assess, with minimal frustration and unproductive self-criticism, where they are in keeping commitments to action and to consider what it would take to move to the next step.

The progression along the continuum moves from left to right. The beginning of the conversation often entails making an individual aware that he or she committed to action and is accountable for that commitment. The facilitator uses CS, EQs and LFs to support movement from "unawareness," to "blaming others," to "I can't excuses," to "wait and hope."

The step "from wait and hope" to "acknowledging reality" is the dividing line between unaccountability and accountability. Unaccountability is associated with a victim mentality; accountability for commitment to action is associated with an efficacy mentality. When people acknowledge reality, they step over the line into the side of the continuum that moves from talk to action.

Accountability for action exists at each of the four steps to the right of "wait and hope." For example, people are accountable at each of these stages if, upon reflection, they decide that the commitment to action is either not feasible or is undesirable, and they let people know that they are either rescinding or changing the commitment. Accountability also is held when people try to take the action and discover that the action does not produce the desired effect, and they adapt the action and inform others of what has been learned and what they are doing with that learning. Finally, people are accountable when they acknowledge the barriers to taking action, persist in the commitment, find a way to overcome the barriers, and share the experience with the group.

Accountability exists when people consciously choose to keep an action commitment and communicate their progress and choices to others. Accountability is an interaction between an individual and a group. It is both the public declaration of the commitment and the public reflection on the progress of the commitment to action that creates a context for groups to continuously move from talk to action leading to results.

The evidence that accountability conversations have succeeded is when participants hold themselves accountable for action commitments and have insights about what works and what does not.

PRACTICE: ACCOUNTABILITY IN MULTIPLE ROLES

Reflect on the commitments you hold yourself accountable for in several roles — in a family role, a work role, a community role. Use the Accountability Pathway to assess where you are relative to keeping your commitments to action in your different roles. Notice any differences in how you hold accountability in different roles.

- What insights do you have about what helps you hold accountability?
- What are some lessons you can take from one role in your life to other roles that support you in making action commitments you can keep?
- Do competing commitments affect your ability to keep action commitments?
- What conversations might you have to enhance your ability to keep action commitments in all your roles?

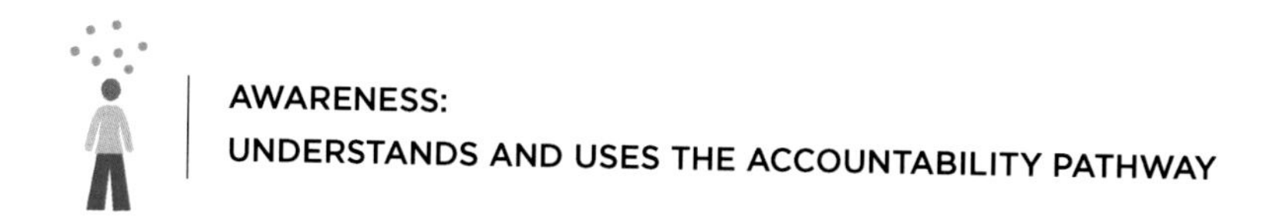

You are aware of this skill when:

- *you can introduce the Accountability Pathway as a method for people to keep commitments to action.*
- *you are comfortable and help others become comfortable holding genuine accountability conversations.*

The Accountability Pathway informs the facilitation of accountability-for-action conversations. There are seven steps in the Accountability Pathway conversation.

1. Ask people to review their progress toward meeting their commitments to action made at a previous meeting.
2. Use a CS and EQs to prompt people to share their progress on their commitments and their insights about what it takes to move to successful action.
3. In the progress report on action commitments, listen for where an individual is on the pathway.
4. Based on the individual's self-assessment of where they are, frame EQs. The EQs are designed to enable the person to see the next step on the pathway and move toward action-commitment accountability.
5. Hold neutral and, through affect and nonverbals, make it okay for people to be anywhere along the pathway.
6. Use an awareness of the range of emotions that can be evoked in the conversation to create an atmosphere of open inquiry and support.
7. Facilitate people sharing where they are, what they are learning, and how they might move forward.

SAMPLE DIALOGUE: USING THE ACCOUNTABILITY PATHWAY

FACILITATOR: *Everyone has had an opportunity to discuss with a colleague his or her progress on the action commitments made at the last meeting. What did you discover?*

PARTICIPANT: *I completely forgot what I said I would do.* (unawareness)

I thought I was going to get a reminder in the notes, but I didn't see the email. (blaming others)

You know, I am so busy that without someone reminding me, I can't fit this sort of thing into my schedule. ("I can't excuses")

FACILITATOR: *Is this action commitment something you are still interested in doing?* (appreciative inquiry to see if the commitment still exists)

PARTICIPANT: *Yes, it is a good idea, and if I could do it, it would make a difference.* (affirming commitment)

FACILITATOR: *What might help you?* (appreciative inquiry to see what stage the person is after affirming the commitment)

PARTICIPANT: *Well, maybe this time I'll remember.* (wait and hope)

FACILITATOR: *Is this coming week going to be as busy as last week?* (EQ to move the participant from wait and hope to acknowledging reality)

PARTICIPANT: *No, it actually will be even busier.* (acknowledging reality)

FACILITATOR: *Is it important to accomplish the commitment now?* (EQ regarding ownership of commitment)

PARTICIPANT: *Yes, I have to accomplish the commitment this week; next week will be too late.* (owning it)

FACILITATOR: *Is there something that you might do that could help you accomplish the commitment even in a busy week? Anything that has helped you under other circumstances?* (EQ to move to finding solutions)

PARTICIPANT: *Hmm...Well, I can write it down on my calendar for tomorrow morning and tell my supervisor that I have to get this done first thing in the morning — before I forget!* (finding solutions)

FACILITATOR: *Is there anything else you can do now to make it more likely that you can do it?* (EQ to move to making it happen)

PARTICIPANT: *Yes, I'll put it on my calendar right now. Also, during the break I'll call my supervisor and get her support for me spending some time on this, which will help my whole unit. I know my supervisor is interested in this, too.* (making it happen)

PRACTICE: FACILITATING THE ACCOUNTABILITY PATHWAY CONVERSATION

Choose a place and time you can practice facilitating an Accountability Pathway conversation with one other person, a small group, or a large group.

1. Do a composition analysis of the group and of yourself in relation to the group.
2. Create a 3R agenda that provides a context for the Accountability Pathway conversation. Position the meeting result from that conversation so that it is a step along the way to moving to action.
3. Facilitate the conversation and observe the impact of your facilitation of the conversation on the group.
   - In what ways did your facilitation of the accountability conversation move the group toward accountability for action?
   - What did you learn from this experience that you can take into your daily practice of being part of or facilitating conversations?

APPLICATION:
HELPS GROUPS HOLD ACCOUNTABILITY FOR ACTION COMMITMENTS

You are applying this skill when:

- *you use EQs that make it easy for you and others to assess progress along the Accountability Pathway, move to own action commitments, and keep commitments to action.*

The facilitator supports the accountability conversation by holding to the integrity of the process. The integrity involves creating conversations in which every person has the opportunity to be accountable for making commitments to action, to review the progress on the commitments to action, to learn from his or her experience in keeping the commitments to action, and to understand the consequences of action.

TIPS: HOLDING ACCOUNTABILITY CONVERSATIONS

- Hold the integrity of the conversation by setting the context for the work so that each person publicly reports on his or her progress. These reports include people saying they did not make a commitment, that they made a commitment and didn't act on it, that they made a commitment and acted on it with an unknown effect, or that they acted on the commitment with a desired, undesired, or unanticipated effect.
- In small groups at tables, chart each person's name and progress. Making this a public display on a flip chart brings the progress to light.
- Have conversations about what people have learned from keeping or not keeping their commitments.
- Use the Accountability Pathway framework to facilitate a dialogue. The dialogue creates the opportunity for the individuals to move along the pathway and for the group as a whole to gain the capacity for supporting the movement from talk to action.
- The flip chart format (see below) can be used in large or small groups to provide information for the dialogue.
- The structure of the dialogue catalyzes accountability and ownership of action that supports aligned, accountable action at every level.
- Individuals hold themselves accountable; smaller work groups hold accountability for implementing their strategies; and the whole group shares accountability for all the strategies aligning and contributing to measurable progress toward a common result.
- The dialogue is ignited with the following CS and the EQs.

Use Context Statement and EQs

CS: You now have an opportunity to understand the progress made and discover what it will take to move forward together.

- What progress have you made on your commitments to action?
- What do you and others need to do now to keep moving forward together?
- What are your insights regarding keeping commitments to action?
- How can you use your insights to strengthen your ability to keep your commitments?

FLIP CHART FORMAT

NAME	PROGRESS	INSIGHTS

MASTERY:
STRENGTHENS THE GROUP'S CAPACITY TO BE ACCOUNTABLE FOR ACTION

You are demonstrating mastery of this skill when:

- *you label your own and others' emotional reactions and use EQs to support making and keeping commitments to action.*
- *you use MBTI awareness to support groups in holding accountability for action.*

People experience both comfortable and uncomfortable emotions during an accountability conversation — often occurring at the same time in the group and sometimes in the same person. For example, people may manifest anxiety/confidence, frustration/satisfaction, shame/pride, cynicism/celebration, hopelessness/hopefulness, indifference/enthusiasm, resentment/appreciation, and anger/curiosity.

The facilitator's role is to support people in accepting these emotions and moving toward working together to make informed choices about future commitments and actions. (The Accountability Pathway conversation is designed to normalize the range of emotions and support an orientation toward accountability that helps people hold accountability for action commitments.)

Orientation Toward Accountability

Holding accountability is developmental. Holding accountability in different roles requires practice and experience. Through reflection and experimentation people can discover what works for them in holding accountability and can make more conscious and informed choices about when and how to make commitments.

Variation in holding accountability is normal. At any given moment, people are at different stages along the pathway at work, in the family, or in the community. People may be at different places along the pathway over the course of completing an action commitment. This variability is a common experience and provides opportunities to discover more about what it takes to be accountable.

Discussing accountability can be uncomfortable. Exploring the sources of discomfort produces useful insights for moving forward and opportunities for reciprocal support. The capacity to tolerate the discomfort contributes to the individual's and the group's ability to make and keep commitments.

Direct and candid conversations about accountability are productive. The accountability conversation immerses people in their own and others' frustrations, with the risk that people become unproductively critical of themselves and others or are too indirect or polite to speak directly. The simultaneous risk of having people in a conversation being either aggressively judgmental or too indirect or cautious is detrimental to the work; but the Accountability Pathway supports the individual's and group's ability to be clear in their commitments, to directly address whether the commitments have been kept, and to accept the consequences.

PRACTICE: WHAT IS YOUR ORIENTATION TOWARD ACCOUNTABILITY

- How does your orientation toward accountability compare to the foregoing conversation?
- What would it take for you to hold the orientation toward accountability, outlined above?

Accountability Conversations: Hold with Lightness

Used deftly, the Accountability Pathway brings light and lightness to difficult conversations about the choices we make by creating an atmosphere where people can find the humor in their common experience. That lightness helps people find a way to normalize the conversation and join together to find creative solutions to the challenges of making and keeping commitments.

PRACTICE: MAKING THE HUMAN BAR CHART: CATALYZING LEARNING ABOUT HOLDING ACCOUNTABILITY

1. Display the pathway on the wall with a banner or a series of flip charts, with room for people to stand below each step of the pathway.
2. Use the pathway to review progress on commitments to action. Did you make it? Where did you get stuck along the way? What helped you move along?
3. Encourage acceptance of where people are on the pathway.
4. Have people note where they are on the pathway and then walk to that place at the wall poster, forming a human bar chart.
5. Have people look around and notice the distribution of people along the pathway.
6. Form small discussion groups of the people at the same place on the pathway.
7. In each small group, address these questions:
   - What got you to this step of the pathway?
   - What will help you move to the next step?
8. Have people hold a dialogue to discover the experience of others at different steps along the pathway and learn more about being accountable for action.

The figure below shows examples of the EQs people can use to support each other in accountability conversations.

EQs FOR ACCOUNTABILITY CONVERSATIONS

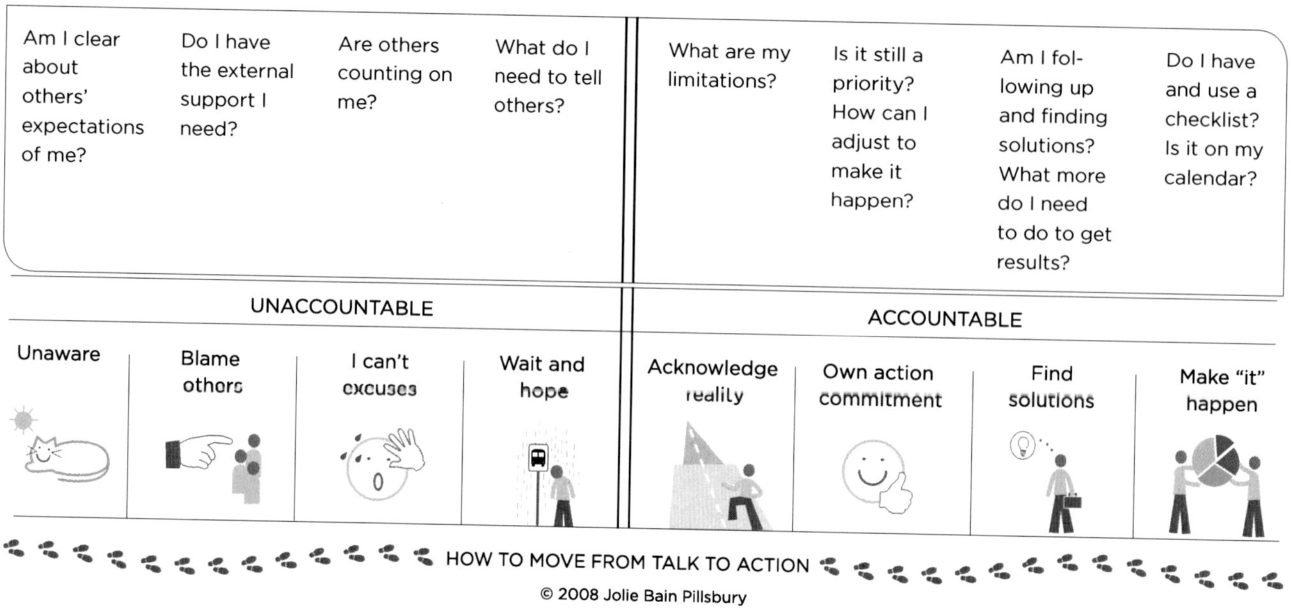

UNACCOUNTABLE				ACCOUNTABLE			
Am I clear about others' expectations of me?	Do I have the external support I need?	Are others counting on me?	What do I need to tell others?	What are my limitations?	Is it still a priority? How can I adjust to make it happen?	Am I following up and finding solutions? What more do I need to do to get results?	Do I have and use a checklist? Is it on my calendar?
Unaware	Blame others	I can't excuses	Wait and hope	Acknowledge reality	Own action commitment	Find solutions	Make "it" happen

HOW TO MOVE FROM TALK TO ACTION

MBTI Insights: Owning Accountability

Public accountability — the willingness to share your progress and own where you are on the Accountability Pathway — is a necessary but insufficient condition for achieving results. Achieving aligned action that moves toward results also requires the ability to give and receive candid and direct feedback about what people are doing (or not doing) that affects progress. This directness and candor are often countercultural to many family, organizational, and community systems, but achieving aligned action requires overcoming the natural hesitation to take risks and experience the discomfort associated with holding shared accountability.

People manage the risks of holding accountability for action in different ways. The next table lists what those participants with Judging and Perceiving preferences need in order to be accountable. The exercise that follows illuminates how MBTI preferences can support people holding these uncomfortable yet necessary conversations.[16]

J-P NEEDS IN ORDER TO BE ACCOUNTABLE

JUDGING	PERCEIVING
People with a preference for Judging need: • Not to be viewed as rigid or obsessive • Not to have the discussion open too long • A plan of action that will be followed • A back-up plan in case an alternative is needed • Evidence that the process of getting to the decision was sound • A list of checkpoints to monitor progress • Designated people with pieces of the project that each can own • Respect for their attachment to time and deadlines • Everyone to honor a deadline once it is agreed on	People with a preference for Perceiving need: • The joy of knowing the project will be complete and productive • Room to experiment with ideas associatively during discussions • Permission to take a circuitous route rather than a direct line to results • Space so as not to feel judged while collecting information • Not to have his or her style viewed as a character flaw • The possibility of achieving flow during the process • Belief that the plans are open to change with new information • Knowledge that decisions may not be final • Ample time to pause and gather information about alternate pathways to outcome • Not to feel rushed to decide without all the information • Flexibility and spontaneity — padded deadlines and understanding of their strength

PRACTICE: MBTI INSIGHTS FOR ACCOUNTABILITY

Use the information on J and P preferences in the previous table to build the group accountability for action:

1. Have everyone in the group review the information.
2. Form two affinity groups — one of all the Js and the other all the Ps.
3. Have both groups explore how they can support each other and work well with those in the other group with a different preference.
4. Have both groups share their insights with the other group.
5. Decide how the group as a whole will use these insights to improve individual and collective action accountability.

PARTICIPANT PRACTICE GUIDE 5.5: BE AND HELP OTHERS BE ACCOUNTABLE FOR ACTION COMMITMENTS

As a meeting participant, you can hold yourself accountable with no risk. As shown in this guide, you can help others be accountable with increasing risk.

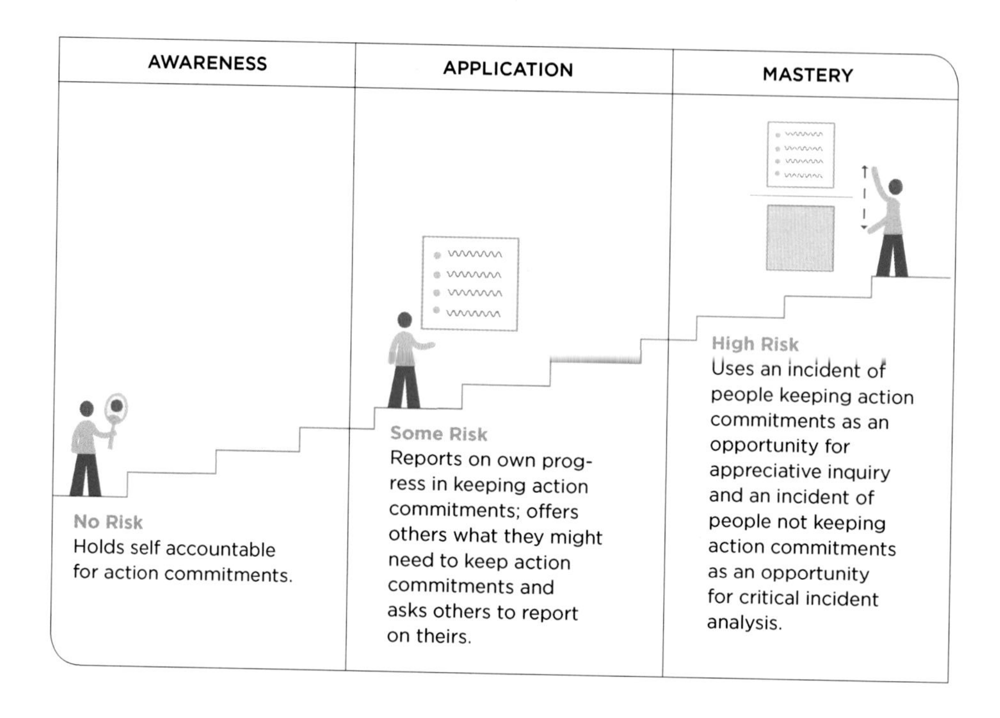

SKILL 5.6: OBSERVE AND RESPOND TO GROUP DYNAMICS

During meetings, the facilitator needs to be aware of and respond to the behavior of individuals and the group as a whole. The following table shows the self-assessment continuum for this skill.

AWARENESS	APPLICATION	MASTERY
Maps who is saying what and what role he or she plays in the group • *Do I notice and remember who is saying what when? Their affect? Their body language?* • *Do I see, label, and generate hypotheses about patterns in the group?* • *Do I consistently use the five-step process to create engagement?*	Observes, understands, and responds to patterns of behavior in groups • *Do I respond to group behaviors in ways that give the work back to the group?* • *Do I observe pace and know when to slow down and when to speed up?*	Helps groups move through difficult conversations • *Do I make in-the-moment observations about the group that enable it to move forward?* • *Do I invite group members to make observations about facts and feelings, generate hypotheses, and respond to what they observe in group?*
→	→	→

Results Based Facilitation is based on the premise that the facilitator supports the group in doing its own work. Results-based meetings are dynamic events. For the results based facilitator to use the skills appropriately and support the group in pursuing meeting results, the facilitator must constantly observe and respond to group dynamics.

For example, the choice of CS, EQs, and LFs is informed by the content of the conversations, the emotion and mood, the relationship dynamics, the presence of any underlying or overt conflict(s), and the physical condition or energy level of the group members. The facilitator uses his or her eyes, ears, feelings, and reactions to gather information about what is occurring. Through a conscious process of observing the group, generating hypotheses about the meaning of what is being observed, and using the hypotheses, the facilitator chooses how to respond. This skill provides approaches and methods to sharpen observation, expand the range of hypotheses generated, and use the hypotheses as a bridge to an informed response.

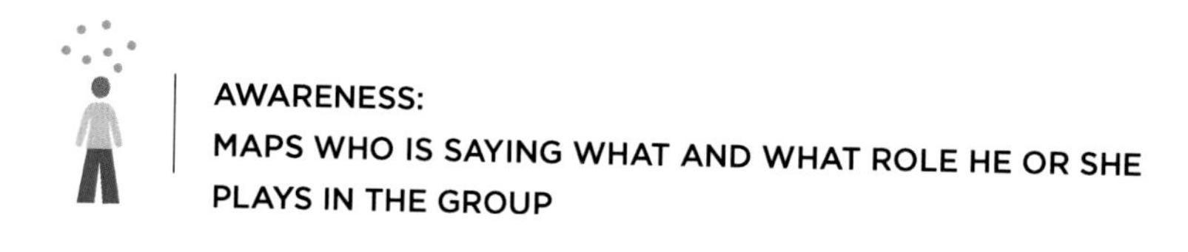

You are aware of this skill when:

- *you notice and remember who is saying what when, including the person's affect and body language.*
- *you see, label, and generate hypotheses about patterns in the group.*
- *you consistently use the five-step process to create engagement.*

Mapping

Mapping is a basic observational technique to make note of what people are doing, saying, and expressing through their body language. Mapping is the practice of drawing a picture that helps you see, remember, and make meaning of what is happening in a group.

Initially, you practice mapping by writing notes of who is saying or expressing what in a conversation. The notes make an explicit correlation between the who and the what of conversations. This information is used to hypothesize about what is happening in a group or with an individual. From these hypotheses, you can respond to what you see in the group.

Conversations are held by individuals with different points of view, different emotions, different levels of engagement, and different levels of awareness. Mapping allows you to track, remember, and see patterns in who said what when.

Mapping can also capture pace, when and how conversations proceed or get stuck, and if there are any patterns related to certain topics or transitional moments (e.g., when decisions are about to be made). Mapping can capture those triggers — either what is being said or who is speaking — that produce silence, discomfort, and/or flight from the topic. Flight can be either verbal (changing the subject) or physical (people leaving the room).

Mapping focuses your conscious attention on sustaining a precise and extensive approach to observation. Over time the practice enables you to recall longer conversations and reflect more deeply about what you are observing in a group.

PRACTICE: MAPPING

Consider your level of awareness and the focus of your attention in conversations.

- What do you notice now?
- Of what you notice, what do you retain?
- How do you use what you notice to inform your choices about how to participate in a conversation?
- In what ways could mapping strengthen your ability to take informed action?

TIPS: USING MAPPING TO MAKE CONNECTIONS AND SEE PATTERNS

Start your map with a diagram or sketch of who is sitting where.

Where people sit can reveal patterns about affiliation, perceived authority, and relatedness in the group. For example, the supervisor may always take a seat at the "head of the table," friends may sit close to each other, people from the same unit may always cluster, and/or people in conflict may choose to sit across or distant from each other.

Annotate your map with information about the people from your composition analysis.

Notations about role, expertise, what resources people bring to the conversation, MBTI, race, class, culture, age, and gender can all be useful in generating hypotheses about what you are hearing and seeing in the group.

As the conversation unfolds, make notes about what each person says and in what sequence.

Sequence can be shown with numbers, letters, or arrows showing the order of who said what when. Sequence can illuminate patterns about affiliation, interest, potential conflict, or work avoidance.

As you notice them, use color or symbols to identify the themes or patterns that will emerge during the conversation.

Several threads may emerge simultaneously. For example, one person might bring up the same topic repetitively — you can put a check by the original comment every time you hear it again. You may notice a subgroup is holding a similar mood or emotion — a smiling, frowning, or puzzled-looking emoticon can link them. Circle in different colors the subgroups that seem to share an interest or viewpoint.

Make notes of the unspoken as well as the spoken.

Make notes about body language and nonverbal cues that may reveal the unspoken issues or the issues that are hard for people to address. A person sitting back in his chair and crossing his arms might indicate that he is pulling back from a conversation. An exchange of glances between two people in response to an issue might indicate that they are silently communicating something about the topic that they are not sharing with the group.

Map as many conversations of all types as you can.

With practice, your notation system will evolve. Your capacity to observe and remember group behavior will grow, and your ability to notice patterns will be enhanced. Practicing this skill when you are a participant and can unobtrusively make your map builds your capacity to map conversations without the aid of notations when you are a facilitator. However, even when you are facilitating, you will find it useful to prepare in advance a map of who is sitting where with notes from the composition analysis. That will enable you, in the moment, to notice patterns and see connections between people's Person-Role-System characteristics and B/ART during the conversation.

Mapping can be used for straightforward purposes, such as noticing who has spoken and who has not and using that information to sequence speakers so that everyone has an opportunity to be heard. Mapping is also a useful tool for generating hypotheses about what is happening in a group and using those hypotheses to choose how to respond to the observed dynamics. In this approach, as in all RBF, it is important to generate multiple hypotheses and hold them lightly. The following is an example of how one observation about who speaks when can generate multiple hypotheses.

The Mapped Observation

Whenever Ms. Smith speaks, Ms. Jones will almost always want to speak next. The multiple hypotheses:

- If Ms. Jones speaks in contradiction to Ms. Smith, the pattern may reveal competition or conflict.

- If Ms. Jones speaks in support of Ms. Smith, the pattern may reveal a special relationship (they are friends), an alliance (they have common interests), or an authority relationship (if Ms. Smith is Ms. Jones's supervisor, Ms. Jones may be looking for approval or showing deference).

- If Ms. Jones repeats what Ms. Smith has said, as if Ms. Smith had not spoken, the pattern may reveal an unconscious or conscious bias indicating that Ms. Jones is discounting Ms. Smith's participation. If Ms. Smith and Ms. Jones are of different races, cultures, age, or levels of professional credentials, the discounting may be related to biases in areas that are likely to create disparities in the power dynamic unconnected to formal authority.

The range of responses:

As a facilitator or participant, your role is to hold the hypotheses lightly and gather additional information. If or when the observed pattern affects the group's ability to move forward, you use one or two of the likely hypotheses to inform how to respond. Below are two possible hypothesis/response pairs:

- Based on the hypothesis that Ms. Jones is discounting Ms. Smith, the facilitator's response is to intentionally sequence speakers to enable Ms. Smith to speak before Ms. Jones. This sequencing can bring Ms. Smith's voice and viewpoint more fully to the conversation.

- Based on the hypothesis that Ms. Jones is deferring to Ms. Smith's authority, the facilitator's response is to use a small group conversation and pair Ms. Jones and Ms. Smith with other participants. In the paired conversation, a conversation that does not involve Ms. Smith, Ms. Jones can contribute more fully from her own authority. To further support Ms. Jones, the facilitator invites Ms. Jones's pair to report before Ms. Smith's pair.

The Five-Step Process to Observe and Respond

When you observe circular discussions, a group that does not seem to know what conversation it wants to have, or only a few people talking and the rest checking out, you can take the opportunity to implement the five-step process that supports engagement. This process (shown below) is based on the principle that people do better, whether Es or Is, when they think before they speak and are generally more comfortable in conversations with one other person or a small group. The five-step process of engagement ignites thinking before speaking, sharing in pairs or small groups, creating ownership, through the higher participation levels made possible when smaller group processes are created within the larger group processes. The expected benefit from implementing the five-step process is higher energy, more active listening, more ideas shared out loud, more interest, and commitment to the work.

THE FIVE-STEP PROCESS

1. Set the context and ask EQs based on what you observe in group.
2. Provide private think time for individuals:
   - At the beginning of the conversation, this process is more formal. Say: *Take a minute to think, and jot down your thoughts.*
   - During a conversation, the process is more informal. Say: *Take a moment to think.*
3. Arrange for paired sharing, i.e., have two people share their ideas with each other.
   - Use this pairing to get people comfortable talking.
   - Use this pairing when you think a topic is complex and people need to clarify their thinking.
4. If there are four or more pairs, form small groups and have them share ideas with each other. This practice is helpful under the following circumstances:
   - There isn't time to process the conversations of all the pairs.
   - The group has to resolve issues before it can process a topic in a large group.
5. Return to the larger group and have the small groups share their ideas with the large group.

APPLICATION: OBSERVES, UNDERSTANDS, AND RESPONDS TO PATTERNS OF BEHAVIOR IN GROUPS

You are applying this skill when:

- *you respond to group behaviors in ways that give the work back to the group.*
- *you observe pace and know when to slow down and when to speed up.*

Groups influence how an individual communicates, makes decisions, and engages in the group's work. The patterns of group behavior can either contribute to movement toward action or retard forward momentum.

From observation, patterns can emerge that illuminate who is holding authority; the effect of race, gender, or culture on the content and process of conversations; and how the group might be avoiding the work required to move toward action. This skill supports you as a facilitator or participant to respond in a way that the group can own and be accountable for its behavior pattern.

The following tips address how to respond to common group behaviors that can be a barrier to accomplishing results.

TIPS: RESPONDING TO GROUP DYNAMICS

WHEN YOU OBSERVE...	DO...	DON'T...
One person dominating	Ask for ideas and comments from those not heard: *Now we know one point of view, are there others?*	Don't say: *Excuse me; you're taking up everyone's time.*
One or two silent members	Say: *I'd like to get opinions from those who haven't talked yet (or for a while).* Or switch to pairs-discussion format.	Don't say to the quiet ones: *You haven't said anything today. Do you have anything to add?*
Two people locked in battle	Focus on the rest of the group; ask who else has an opinion: *We've heard the X viewpoint and the Y point of view. Is there a third way to look at this?*	Don't try to resolve their conflict.
Low participation by most of the group	Switch to small group or pairs discussion for a short time.	Don't assume silence means consent.
Goofing around by many	Take a quick break. Do a 1-minute stretch or breathing exercise.	Don't say: *Okay, let's stay focused.*
Whispering or sidebar conversations	Switch to small groups so everyone can have conversations or take a quick break.	Don't ignore it and hope it goes away.
Some members of the group reacting with frustration to the behavior of other members or the behavior of the group as a whole	Bring the issue to the attention of the group with an observation or an EQ. This may lead to the group choosing group norms for listening, decision making, relationships, and communication.	Don't try to resolve the issue.
The group has adopted norms and some group members are not following the norms	Share your observation about how the group is or is not following its norms. Ask what, if anything, people would like to do in response.	Don't enforce the group norms.
Participants making statements disguised as questions	Respond by bringing to their awareness that their questions may actually be statements conveying their viewpoints, or invite them to share their answers to their own questions.	Don't answer the questions or facilitate the group in answering the questions that in effect have already been answered by the person posing the question.
People using the same word to mean different things	Respond by asking people to be specific, e.g., *What would that look like?* or *Give me an example.*	Don't assume that people notice the discrepancy or understand each other.

Notice Feelings

To develop this skill, practice observing and labeling the range of emotions the group may be experiencing. Inform your observations by consciously practicing giving names to a broad and nuanced range of emotions. Reviewing a classification scheme of the range of emotions helps you to recognize and name the emotions that you observe in the group. Plutchik's Wheel of Emotions[17] (shown below) is one way to classify and name emotions.

The figure shows three graphic representations of aspects of Plutchik's wheel. In the two dimensional circumplex model, more intense emotions are indicated by darker colors. The table at the top of the next page identifies emotional triggers and responses and the table at the bottom of the next page expands the range of emotions associated with the primary emotions of joy, sadness, and surprise.

THREE WAYS OF LOOKING AT PLUTCHIK'S WHEEL OF EMOTIONS

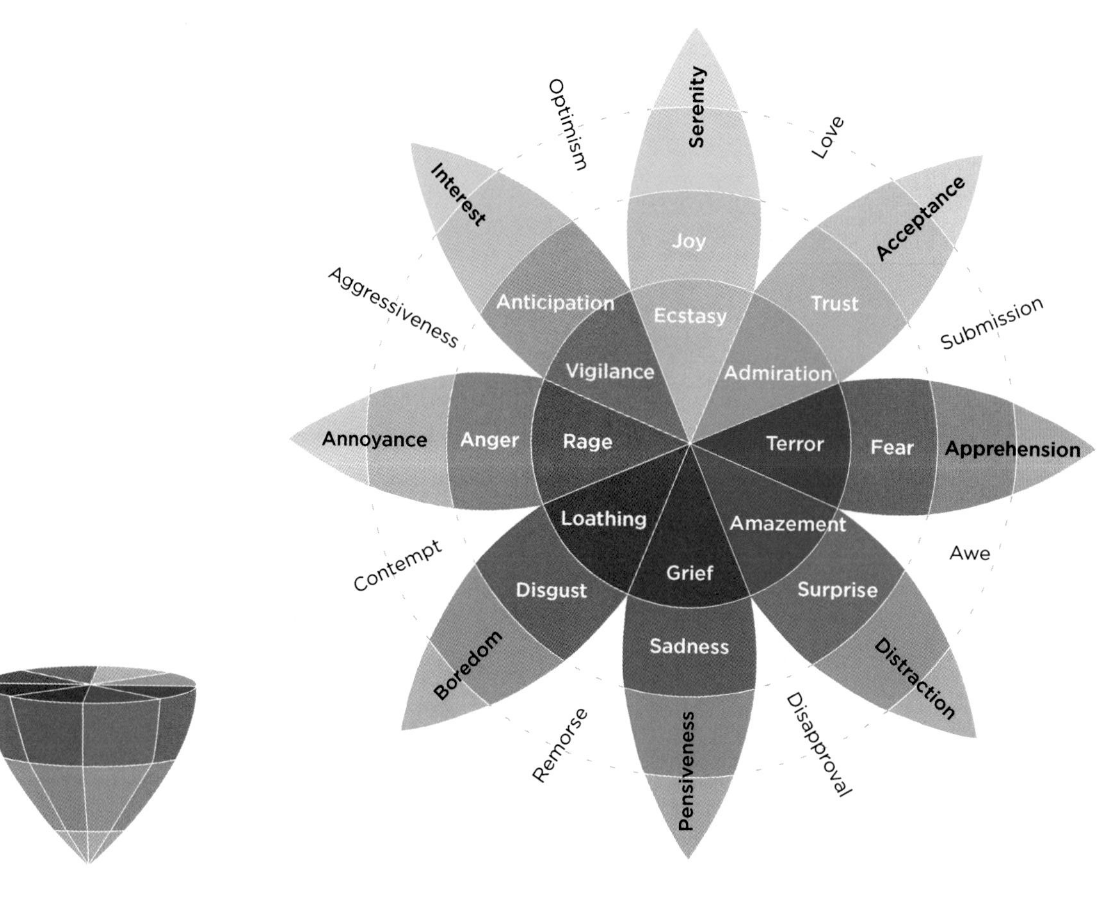

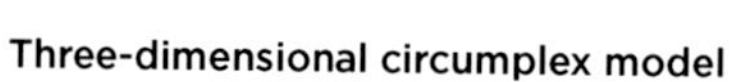

Three-dimensional circumplex model

Two-dimensional circumplex model

STIMULUS EVENT	COGNITION	FEELING STATE	OVERT BEHAVIOR	EFFECT
threat	"danger"	fear	escape	safety
obstacle	"enemy"	anger	attack	destroy obstacle
gain of valued object	"possess"	joy	retain or repeat	gain resources
loss of valued object	"abandonment"	sadness	cry	reattach to lost object
member of one's group	"friend"	acceptance	groom	mutual support
unpalatable object	"poison"	disgust	vomit	eject poison
new territory	"examine"	expectation	map	knowledge of territory
unexpected event	"what is it?"	surprise	stop	gain time to orient

JOY	Cheerfulness	Amusement, Bliss, Cheerfulness, Delight, Elation, Enjoyment, Ecstasy, Euphoria, Gaiety, Glee, Gladness, Happiness, Jolliness, Jubilation, Satisfaction
	Contentment	Pleasure
	Enthrallment	Rapture
	Optimism	Eagerness, Hope
	Pride	Triumph
	Relief	Relief
	Zest	Enthusiasm, Excitement, Exhilaration, Thrill, Zeal
SADNESS	Disappointment	Dismay, Displeasure
	Neglect	Alienation Defeat, Dejection, Embarrassment
	Sadness	Depression, Despair, Gloom, Grief, Hopelessness, Misery, Melancholy, Sorrow, Woe, Unhappiness
	Shame	Guilt, Regret, Remorse
	Suffering	Agony, Anguish, Hurt
	Sympathy	Pity
SURPRISE	Surprise	Amazement, Astonishment
		Created by: W. Gerrod Parrott, 2001

PRACTICE: RECOGNIZING AND ACKNOWLEDGING EMOTIONS

Groups always have an emotional experience as well as an analytic, relational, or physical experience. In RBF, acknowledging emotions supports the group to use the emotional dimensions of their experience to move from talk to action. This approach is informed by an understanding that people consciously or unconsciously are making decisions based on their emotional responses and that emotion is one of the motivating forces for action.

The following exercise and reflective practice are designed to strengthen your ability to recognize and acknowledge emotion.

1. Bring a classification scheme of emotions (one of those on the previous pages or another you find useful) to your next meeting.
2. While at the meeting, map your own emotions and your observations about the emotions of other group members and the group as a whole.
3. Practice using nuanced descriptors of the emotions
4. Observe if emotions are acknowledged and the effect of acknowledgment on group behavior.
    - What did you notice about your own emotions and the emotions of others and the group?
    - What emotions, if any, were acknowledged, and by whom?
    - What was the effect on the group's behavior of acknowledging or not acknowledging emotions?
5. Generate hypotheses about how and when to acknowledge emotions in groups to support progress toward results.

MASTERY: HELPS GROUPS MOVE THROUGH DIFFICULT CONVERSATIONS

You are demonstrating mastery of this skill when:

- *you make in-the-moment observations about the group that enables them to move forward.*
- *you invite group members to make observations about facts and feelings, generate hypotheses, and respond to what they observe in the group.*

Examples of Types of Conversations

When you observe that people are in a conversation that is not progressing because they are not conscious of the type of conversation or they are not using approaches appropriate to the conversation, then you respond by using a CS to name the conversation and ask an EQ to frame it. The next table lists some examples of types of conversations, each with a framing CS and an EQ in a way that you and the group can listen for a conversation result. Being conscious of the types of conversations enables groups to move through the series of conversations that lead ultimately to commitments to action. In practice, mastery of the skill is supported when you as a participant or facilitator go to the balcony, observe the conversation and group dynamics, and frame the conversation so people can consciously address difficult issues.

TYPES OF CONVERSATION, RESULTS, AND EFFECTIVE QUESTIONS

TYPES OF CONVERSATION	RESULT OF CONVERSATION	CS AND EQ
Building relationships	People know and trust each other	**CS:** People have mentioned that there may be trust issues in the group. **EQ:** What are those issues and how could you address them?
Having dialogues	Engaged exchange	**CS:** Some people are sharing their perspectives on the issue, creating an opportunity for everyone to weigh in. **EQ:** What is your perspective on the issue, and what would you like to discuss about the issue?
Brainstorming	Creative idea generation	**CS:** Some people have begun to generate ideas. **EQ:** Using brainstorming rules (all ideas are welcome), what are the two or three ideas that you want to share?
Exploring issues	Understanding assumptions and facts	**CS:** There are a number of issues being discussed. **EQ:** What are these issues, and what are the facts people are offering or the assumptions people are making about those issues?
Developing solutions	Options	**CS:** People are building a solution. **EQ:** What options can you envision that can be part of the solution?
Making decisions	Clear choices	**CS:** Some people seem ready to make a decision and move forward. **EQ:** What choices are you ready to make?
Negotiating commitments	Action and follow-up occur	**CS:** People are beginning to say what they will do next and thinking about what they need to be successful. **EQ:** What do you plan to do, and what can you offer others or do you need from others to be confident that you can keep your action commitment?

Types of Group Behavior

Making an observation about what you see in the group usually is enough to bring that behavior to the group's awareness and enable people to decide about how to deal with that behavior. Following are some examples of group behaviors that you might name and ask the group whether the behavior is okay or if they would like to address it.

- Circular conversations, i.e., conversations that repeatedly return to the same point
- People talking across each other, i.e., not hearing each other or addressing each other's issues
- Multiple conversations at once
- Conversations that ignore the elephant in the room because it makes people uncomfortable
- All talking and no listening
- Not doing the work of the people in the room
- Unfocused conversation: People talking yet unaware of what they are trying to accomplish in the conversation
- Deferring to authority/holding back

If a behavior has been brought to the group's attention and the group neither acknowledges the behavior nor chooses to deal with it, use a B/ART analysis to generate hypotheses about the persistence of the behavior, and from those hypotheses generate a response. The following practice illustrates how using a B/ART analysis can help the group address behavior that is a barrier to moving to action.

PRACTICE: USING B/ART ANALYSIS TO SUPPORT A GROUP IN ADDRESSING ITS OWN BEHAVIOR

THE MEETING PURPOSE
In a large nonprofit, a special board planning session is scheduled to set strategic goals and targets for the organization for the next five years. The session is in direct response to the rapid growth and success of the organization over the past two years.

THE PARTICIPANTS
The board chair convened the meeting. Participants include all but one of the eight board members. The chair and the board members all serve as senior executives of for-profit and nonprofit organizations in the same sector and the same community. The organization's executive director (ED) is attending with a voice but not a vote during the session.

MEETING DESIGN AND RESULTS
The meeting design calls for all participants to work as peers to determine the strategic goals and priorities. According to governance protocols, the ED will translate the strategic goals into operational objectives and implementation plans. The meeting results will be the strategic goals with a timeline of milestones for implementation. The board chair and the ED have hired and worked with an outside consultant who is facilitating the meeting.

Practice continued on next page

COMPOSITION ANALYSIS: B/ART AND PERSON-ROLE-SYSTEM INFORMATION

PARTICIPANTS	B/ART IN HOME ORGANIZATION	B/ART ON BOARD
Mr. Board Chair Retired executive of an association representing consumers in the sector	Retired director of a large association that is influential in the sector	Sets the agenda; chairs the board and the executive committee meetings; and holds accountability for ED's performance. Has a collaborative approach and where possible seeks consensus prior to final votes to make decisions.
Ms. Board Member A Nationally recognized subject matter expert in the field	President of a large for-profit competing in the same marketplace as the organization	As a member of the program committee, provides advice to the ED and senior staff regarding program strategies.
Mr. Board Member B Recently promoted subject matter expert in the field	Vice president of a large nonprofit service delivery organization that benefits from the work of the nonprofit	Vice chair of the board to succeed to chair in two years; member of the executive committee
Ms. Board Member C Expert in philanthropy and inexperienced in making grants to the sector served by the organization	Program officer of a local foundation that makes grants to the organization	As a member of the program committee, provides advice to the ED and senior staff regarding program strategies
Dr. Board Member D Senior academic expert in the subject matter	Chair of a university department that collaborates with the nonprofit in an area of common practice	Attending board for the first time; has not yet served on any of the board committees but will be a member of the program committee
Mr. Board Member E Legal expertise in the financial areas of the field	Senior partner of a large law firm with clients in the sector	Member of the executive committee and treasurer; fiduciary responsibility for financial integrity of the organization
Ms. Board Member F Subject matter expert, long-term leader in the sector and mentor of the ED	Executive director of a small nonprofit serving similar clientele in the same sector	Member of the executive committee and secretary; reviews and approves board minutes
Ms. Board Member G Subject matter expert, recently recruited from another geographic area to be CEO	CEO of medium nonprofit providing both complementary and competitive services in the same sector	Member of the program committee; provides advice to the ED and senior staff regarding program strategies.
Ms. Executive Director In role for the past five years, successful at bringing in federal grants and donations from national foundations	Has operational authority including hire and fire of all staff and budget implementation without prior board approval. Accountable to the Board Chair for meeting strategic goals and targets. Accountable to the Board Chair and the executive committee for fiduciary and policy issues.	Works with the chair and executive committee to prepare for board meetings. Authorized by the chair to work with the consultant/facilitator to design the board retreat. Active participant in the discussions about strategic goals and targets, but is not a voting member for decisions.

Practice continued on next page

The Presenting Opportunity

During the meeting, Ms. Board Member A and Ms. Board Member G, who are sitting next to each other, have engaged in sidebar conversations throughout the meeting. The group is now in a conversation about market expansion. Ms. Board Member A, when not in a sidebar conversation, weighs in after every comment made by other board members. She does not allow the facilitator to sequence her participation in the conversation, i.e., she does not wait her turn to speak.

Observed Reactions to Board Member A's Behavior

Ms. Board Member A's behavior is disrupting the discussion and the ED looks anxious.

Mr. Board Member B and Dr. Board Member D seem accustomed to being interrupted by Ms. Board Member A; however, they are beginning to disengage.

Ms. Board Members C and F look frustrated and make increasingly pointed remarks to Ms. Board Member A, including joking references to her habit of talking over others and interrupting.

Mr. Board Member E finds the behavior of Ms. Board Member A amusing; however, he checks his phone more frequently.

Mr. Board Chair notices the behavior but does not react. He had informed the facilitator prior to the meeting that Ms. Board Member A interrupts and talks over others in board meetings.

Generate at least two hypotheses for each of the following B/ART questions

- What are your hypotheses about the interaction between Ms. Board Members A and G?
- What are your hypotheses about who has a stake in the conversation, and what is that stake?
- What are your hypotheses about how Mr. Board Chair and Mr. Board Member E hold their authority and react to Ms. Board Member A?
- For each of your hypotheses, what might be a facilitator's response?

Practice continued on next page

OBSERVED BEHAVIOR	HYPOTHESES	FACILITATOR'S RESPONSE
Interaction between Ms. Board Members A & Ms. G		
Interaction of all members of the group		
Mr. Board Chair's behavior or response to Ms. Board Member A		
Mr. Board Member E's behavior or response to Ms. Board Member A		

PRACTICE: GENERATING B/ART HYPOTHESES TO INFORM RESPONSES

Compare your hypotheses and thoughts about possible facilitator responses to the examples in the following table and answer these reflective practice questions:

- What do your hypotheses illuminate about your own experience with B/ART?
- What frame (mental model) informed your hypotheses?
- How easy or hard was this exercise for you?
- As you participate or facilitate in groups, what might you practice observing to illuminate B/ART?

EXAMPLES OF HYPOTHESES AND FACILITATOR RESPONSES

OBSERVED BEHAVIOR	HYPOTHESES: FRAME SECTOR COMPETITION	FACILITATOR'S RESPONSE
Interaction between Ms. Board Members A and G	#1 A & G are forming an alliance to compete for the organization's business	Facilitator calls a break. She checks in with chair and ED to ask the chair to start the next session with a statement that reauthorizes the facilitator to hold the sequence of the conversation and request that people put on their "board member hat" in the conversation.
	#2 A & G resent the organization's success and fear its growing dominance	Facilitator creates a paired conversation where A & G can talk together. • What are your concerns? • Is there anything you are thinking or feeling about the growth and success of the organization that you have not yet voiced?
Interaction of all members of the group	#1 ED has a high stake in the conversation	Facilitator uses nonverbals and eye contact to let ED know that her reaction is being noticed. Facilitator observes that not everyone is equally engaged in the conversation and poses the following question: • What is at stake for you as a board member or for you in your day job in this conversation?
	#2 C & F have an interest in the conversation as potential beneficiaries of the organization's success	Facilitator asks the following question: • Does anyone have a personal or organizational interest in the outcome of this conversation?
Mr. Board Chair's behavior or response to Ms. Board Member A	#1 Chair is ignoring A's behavior because he is confident that C and E have an interest in the conversation and will move it forward despite A's distracting behavior	Facilitator observes that the group may be ready to move to a decision. • Does anyone have a proposal?
	#2 Chair is not confident of A respecting his formal authority because A perceives that the chair's retirement has reduced his informal influence in the sector	Facilitator observes that the sequence is not being held. • Is this process of the dialogue (without sequence) working for everyone in the group?
Mr. Board Member E's behavior or response to Board Member A	#1 E is the only member of the board without subject matter expertise and thus defers to A	Facilitator observes that there may be dimensions to the issue other than programmatic, e.g., financial, risk, public relations, communications. • Reflect on what factors, in addition to programmatic issues, are important to consider in making this decision. What can you add from your perspective?
	#2 E is confident that the chair will use his authority soon to address A's behavior	Facilitator observes that not everyone is engaged in the discussion and reminds the group that this is their retreat. • What do you each want to discuss at this time?

PARTICIPANT PRACTICE GUIDE 5.6:
OBSERVE AND RESPOND TO GROUP DYNAMICS

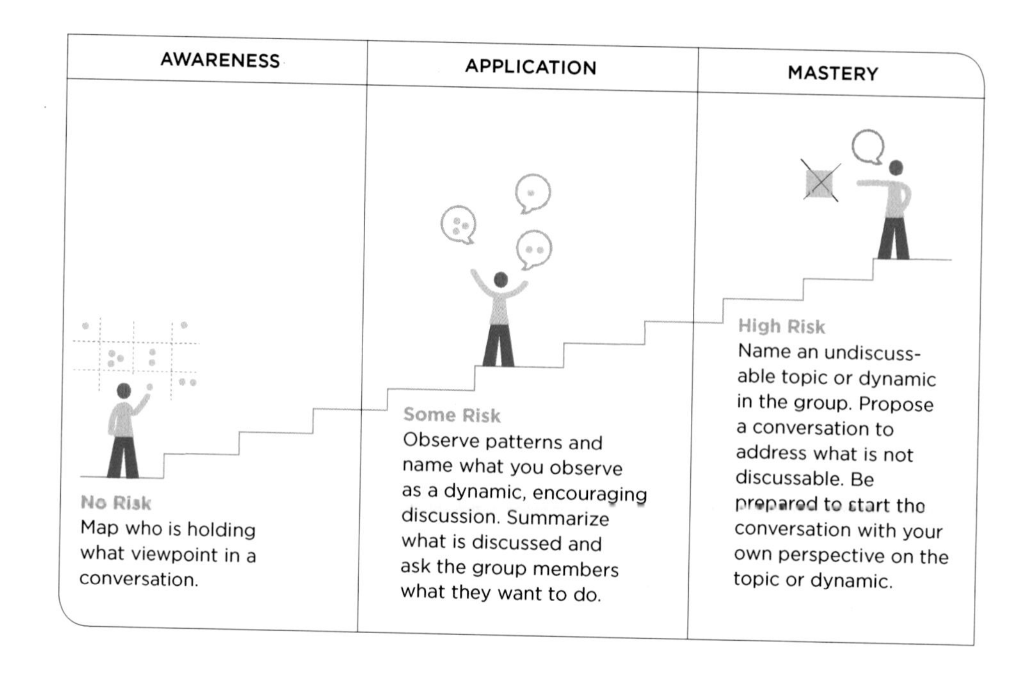

AWARENESS	APPLICATION	MASTERY
No Risk Map who is holding what viewpoint in a conversation.	**Some Risk** Observe patterns and name what you observe as a dynamic, encouraging discussion. Summarize what is discussed and ask the group members what they want to do.	**High Risk** Name an undiscussable topic or dynamic in the group. Propose a conversation to address what is not discussable. Be prepared to start the conversation with your own perspective on the topic or dynamic.

SKILL 5.7: ASSESS AND ADDRESS CONFLICT

Groups moving toward action commitments often have conflicts. The facilitator needs to notice, assess, and respond to conflict as described in the next table.

AWARENESS	APPLICATION	MASTERY
Understands own and others' orientation toward conflict • *Do I understand my own and others' orientation toward conflict?* • *Do I accept that conflict is a fact of life that can be addressed and resolved?*	Introduces and applies the Circle of Conflict • *Can I apply the Circle of Conflict to identify sources of conflict?* • *Can I frame conversations that engage people in addressing the sources of conflict?*	Supports groups in addressing conflict and moving to action • *Do I use insights from MBTI awareness to design conversations to address conflict?* • *Do I integrate the application of the Circle of Conflict into PBDM?*
→	→	→

As a participant or facilitator, the first step in mastering this skill is to understand your own orientation to conflict at the person level. From this awareness, you can adopt at the person-in-role level an orientation toward conflict that supports your capacity to address conflict and move to action.

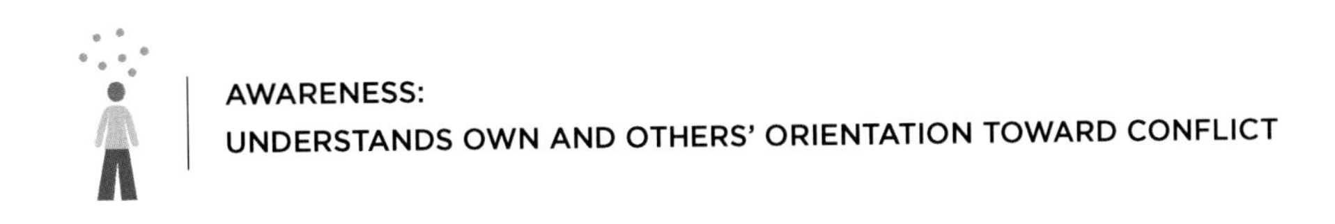

You are aware of this skill when:

- *you understand your own and others' orientation toward conflict.*
- *you accept that conflict is a fact of life that can be addressed and resolved.*

Orientation Toward Conflict

Each of us has an orientation toward conflict. That orientation is grounded in our family history, culture, and experience. For purposes of developing this skill, conflict is defined as that range of differences, disagreements, and dissonant viewpoints that can occur among participants in meetings or conversations. To determine your orientation toward conflict, consider whether you tend to move toward conflict or away from it. Once you have considered your orientation — drawn toward or moving away from conflict — reflect on what role you prefer in relation to that conflict. The next table presents examples of the roles people take in relation to conflict. Note if these examples describe you or if you take roles not listed.

ROLES PEOPLE TAKE IN RELATION TO CONFLICT

ROLES YOU PLAY WHEN YOUR TENDENCY IS TO MOVE TOWARD CONFLICT	ROLES YOU PLAY WHEN YOUR TENDENCY IS TO MOVE AWAY FROM CONFLICT
Participant in the conflict; you tend to get involved.	Observer from a safe distance; you are ready to move farther away if necessary.
Potential participant, observing closely and waiting to see if the conflict involves you. You get involved if necessary.	Guardian, observing from a distance. You are ready to call in others to help if necessary.
Protector or mediator, standing by, ready to move closer if mediation is needed or you can protect someone.	Someone moving far enough away from the conflict so as not to see, hear, or be affected by conflict.
Other role?	Other role?

FACTORS INFLUENCING APPROACH TO CONFLICT IN PERSON-ROLE-SYSTEM

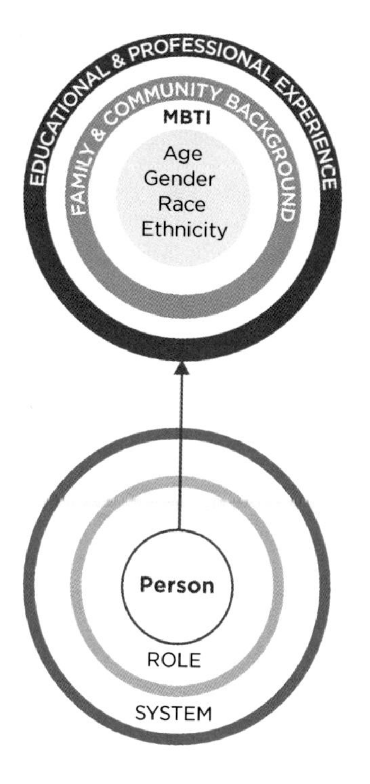

Orientation toward conflict comes from many sources and experiences, including MBTI preferences, your family's approach to conflict, your community or culture's approach to conflict, or your profession's approach to conflict. The figure illustrates some of the factors that influence a person's orientation toward conflict.

In MBTI, the preferences around decision making, the T-F dichotomy, illuminate what role the person might take in conflict and how others might perceive that person.[18] The conflict pairs provide insights about orientation toward conflict as is shown in the next table.

ROLES PEOPLE TAKE IN RELATION TO CONFLICT

CONFLICT PAIRS	ROLE	PERCEPTION
TJ	Engaged participant in the conflict, pushing to closure	Detached or angry adversary
TP	Analyst of conflict, exploring alternatives at length	Catalyst of or contributor to conflict
FJ	Alleviator of the discomfort of conflict, looking for quick resolution	Seeker of communication and harmony
FP	Mediator of conflict, seeking to include all views and feelings	Someone who includes others' values and concerns

PRACTICE: ORIENTATION TOWARD CONFLICT

- Where did your orientation toward conflict come from? Family experiences? Cultural context? Community experiences? Professional experiences?
- How do these experiences inform your assumptions about conflict?
- What is your conflict pair? Does the description for your conflict pair resonate with you?
- What other factors influence your orientation toward conflict? Gender? Age?
- If you had to summarize your orientation toward conflict, what would you say?
- Given your orientation, what are your assumptions about conflict?

Conflict Resolution Assumptions

Independent of your orientation and assumptions toward conflict, you are invited as part of this skill to develop a specific orientation toward conflict that supports your ability to use RBF skills as a participant or facilitator. This skill is built on a set of assumptions that enables you to play a role as either a participant or facilitator in resolving conflict.

The following assumptions support playing a constructive role in conflict resolution.

- Conflict is a fact of life and is here to stay.
- People can learn new skills that make conflict management and/or resolution possible.
- By applying conflict management skills, people can maximize the potential for positive outcomes.
- Therefore, destructive consequences of conflict are not inevitable.

Heifetz and Linsky's work on adaptive leadership introduces a number of concepts that are useful in holding the conflict resolution assumptions,[19] such as orchestrating conflict, regulating the temperature, and giving the work back to the group. Ultimately, when you are holding these assumptions, you are, in Heifetz's terms, holding steady in the heat of action to keep the members focused on the work.

TIPS: HOLDING CONFLICT RESOLUTION ASSUMPTIONS IN THE FACILITATOR ROLE

WHEN YOU OBSERVE...	DO...	DON'T...
People are reluctant to "own" their point of view for fear of creating conflict	Make an observation to the group that normalizes conflict. Comment that differences are common and that exploring differences can produce stronger solutions and relationships. Invite people to reflect on whether there are any differences of opinion or perspective the group would like to explore.	Don't challenge people to bring their issue to the table.
Groups have referenced conflicts but not addressed them directly	List the conflicts that have been named, and invite people to explore the benefits and risks of addressing those conflicts.	Don't ignore the conflicts that have been named.
The group is increasingly adversarial in its discussion of a topic. Some members seem about to explode while others are shutting down in reaction to the emotional intensity.	Acknowledge the intensity of the interactions. Invite the group to take a break (to stretch and breathe and imagine the benefits of resolving the conflict) so that when they return they can regulate the temperature enough to stay in the tough work of resolving conflict.	Either ignore the heated temperature in the room or shut down the conversation because it seems too dangerous.

APPLICATION:
INTRODUCES AND APPLIES THE CIRCLE OF CONFLICT

You are applying this skill when:

- *you use the Circle of Conflict to identify sources of conflict.*
- *you frame conversations that engage people in addressing the sources of conflict.*[20]

Circle of Conflict Adaptation

The Circle of Conflict is a mental model developed by Christopher W. Moore for use by mediators to examine and uncover the root causes of conflict. The model identifies five categories of conflict: values, relationships, data, interests, and structural conflicts. This mental model has been adapted in two ways: first, to add a sixth category (language conflicts), and second, to shift the orientation from use in the role of mediator to use in the roles of participant and/or facilitator.

When a group experiences difficulty addressing and resolving disagreements and differences, one or more sources of conflict may have contributed to the difficulty. The six sources of conflict in the Circle of Conflict Adaptation are shown in the figure on the next page.

> SEPARATING THE PEOPLE FROM THE PROBLEM MEANS SEPARATING RELATIONSHIP ISSUES FROM SUBSTANTIVE ISSUES, AND DEALING WITH THEM INDEPENDENTLY.
>
> – ROGER FISHER & WILLIAM URY

Relationship conflicts are barriers to building mutual trust and willingness to work together. A relationship conflict is a struggle, disagreement, or difference of opinion that takes place between two people in a relationship. Relationship conflicts are evident from nonverbal behavior, such as tense silences and awkward pauses or seating patterns that show antagonism among and between group members. In relationship conflicts, people may be distant or uncomfortable with each other, aggressive, or passive aggressive. People may also, by their tone of voice and their language, project hostility and express negative opinions of each other.

> WE ARE TWO PEOPLE SEPARATED BY A COMMON LANGUAGE.
>
> – ATTRIBUTED TO WINSTON CHURCHILL

Language conflicts are differences that prevent clear communication and joint problem solving. A language conflict is a disagreement about the definition of words or the use of words. Language conflicts include using the same words to mean different things or using words or phrases that only some members of the group understand due to differences in professional background, experience, or culture. In language conflicts, people become irritated with each other and argumentative about definitions that may in reality be about differences

CIRCLE OF CONFLICT ADAPTATION

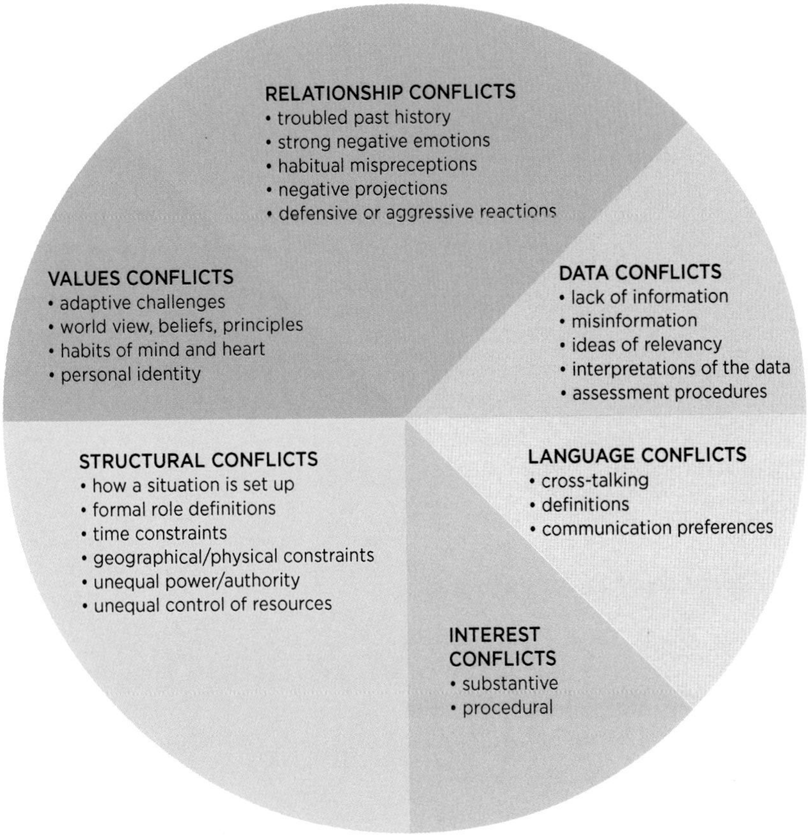

RELATIONSHIP CONFLICTS
- troubled past history
- strong negative emotions
- habitual mispreceptions
- negative projections
- defensive or aggressive reactions

VALUES CONFLICTS
- adaptive challenges
- world view, beliefs, principles
- habits of mind and heart
- personal identity

DATA CONFLICTS
- lack of information
- misinformation
- ideas of relevancy
- interpretations of the data
- assessment procedures

STRUCTURAL CONFLICTS
- how a situation is set up
- formal role definitions
- time constraints
- geographical/physical constraints
- unequal power/authority
- unequal control of resources

LANGUAGE CONFLICTS
- cross-talking
- definitions
- communication preferences

INTEREST CONFLICTS
- substantive
- procedural

in world views. The words people use are consistent with the mental structures that determine their understanding of the world, and the frames have become embedded in their thinking as well as their language.[21]

Data conflicts make it difficult to agree on the nature of the problem or the solution. A data conflict is a disagreement about information or the use of information. Data conflicts often reflect a lack of information; misinformation; persistence of myths based on inaccurate, false, or disputed information; competing perspectives on what data is relevant or how to interpret available data; a distrust of the motives of the data collectors; fear of the consequences of using the data; or discomfort with using or analyzing data. In data conflicts, people often question or discount the data others provide, get stuck, and can't make decisions.

> PEOPLE ARE ENTITLED TO THEIR OWN OPINIONS, BUT THEY ARE NOT ENTITLED TO THEIR OWN FACTS.
>
> — DANIEL PATRICK MOYNIHAN

> BRINGING ALL THE OPTIONS TO THE TABLE OPTIMIZES MUTUAL GAIN.
>
> — ANONYMOUS

Interest conflicts[22] arise from competition that prevents people from finding mutually beneficial solutions. An interest conflict is a disagreement about who will get what in a negotiation. Interest conflicts occur when there is win-lose competition over scarce resources and one or more parties believe that, to satisfy their needs, those of an opponent must be sacrificed. In interest conflicts, people get locked into positions and take adversarial approaches to each other or give up on what they want and need to preserve relationships. Interest conflicts can be about substantive issues (money, physical resources, time, etc.); about procedural issues (the way the dispute is to be resolved); or psychological issues such as perceptions of trust, fairness, or desire for participation and respect.

> CONFLICTS ACCUMULATE ALONG THE FAULT LINES THAT LIE HIDDEN WITHIN THEIR STRUCTURES.
>
> — KENNETH CLOKE AND JOAN GOLDSMITH

Structural conflicts are disputes that prevent moving to action due to external constraints. Structural conflicts reflect broader patterns of human relationships within a community, organization, or group. External forces often shape these patterns, including how formal and informal resources and authority are distributed, how political power is distributed, or what unchallenged assumptions exist. For example, meeting times, meeting places, and expectations of meeting behavior might create structural conflicts. Some members of a nonprofit board might be unable to meet during regular business hours because they can't miss work or can't afford child care. Other members might prefer to attend during business hours because their employer supports their participation as a board member. Structural conflicts often have differential impact reflecting race, class, gender, or cultural disparities. In the instance above, those who cannot attend a board meeting during business hours might have fewer economic and financial resources than those who can, revealing a class disparity.

Structural conflict manifests itself in a variety of ways, including how the situation is set up (who sits where, who speaks first, how people speak); role definitions (conscious/unconscious, formal/informal); time constraints (too little/too much); geographical/physical constraints (too far/too close); unequal power or authority in decision making or in framing the issues; unequal control of resources, (e.g., money, use of facilities, access to media, access to people with influence); or unequal accountability for making and keeping commitments.

During structural conflicts, people often behave in a way that reflects patterns and forces external to the group. Some people may appear to have a disproportionate ability to stop or start conversations, some people may look to others for permission to speak, disagreements may exist about the fairness and equity of the status quo, anger and feelings of helplessness may emerge in response to feelings of powerlessness, fear of retaliation, or anxiety about the loss of resources and relationships if the existing situation is challenged or changed.

Values conflicts are disagreements that inhibit people from coming together to work on a common result. Values conflicts are caused by perceived or actual incompatibility of belief systems. Values are beliefs that give meaning to people's lives. Values explain what is good or bad, right or wrong, just or unjust. Values disputes arise when people attempt to force one set of values on others or lay claim to exclusive value systems that do not allow for divergent beliefs. Here are three common foci of values conflict in groups.

> OUT BEYOND IDEAS OF RIGHT DOING AND WRONG DOING THERE IS A FIELD. I'LL MEET YOU THERE.
>
> — RUMI

1. *Group norms:* These are the values that inform how a group works together and how they behave together. "People listen to each other respectfully" is an example of a group norm. Explicitly adopted norms can address how groups will behave, how they relate to each other, what they value, or what values they share. When groups hold explicitly adopted norms with consistency and integrity, the norms themselves can support groups in resolving values conflicts and moving forward together. However, if there are unconscious norms held by some of the group but not all, or explicit norms that are not held consistently and with integrity, then the norms themselves can reveal values conflicts and become a source of conflict.

2. *Practice principles:* These are the values that inform fields of practice or professions. When held in common by a group, practice principles can be used to resolve differences. For example, if there are differences about how to proceed with a policy or a procedure, the practice principles that the group has agreed to can be used as criteria to make decisions about policy and procedures.

3. *Belief systems:* These are the values that people use to give meaning to their lives and explain what is good or bad, right or wrong, just or unjust. Values are often connected to people's own sense of identity. "Women should stay at home and raise their children" is an example of a belief system. During values conflicts about belief systems, people experience strong emotions and memories; fear or pain may be evoked. The emotions may lead to fight-or-flight impulses, conflict avoidance, verbal aggression, or passive-aggressive behavior. During values conflicts, if the specific belief systems that are barriers to agreement are identified, then groups can either reach agreement on how to work together in the face of differing belief systems, or they change

the group's purpose or its composition if the belief systems are so incompatible as to prevent the group from working together.

Applying the Circle of Conflict Adaptation in Different Roles

The role and authority in conflict resolution are different for each of the following three roles.

Mediator:[23] A third party to the conflict, having the role of assisting the parties to develop a resolution. The mediator plays an active role in gathering the data and shaping the alternatives. He or she often shuttles between the parties and meets with them individually and collectively. The authority to accept or reject the resolution rests with the parties.

Neutral Facilitator: The role of the neutral facilitator is to give the work of conflict resolution to the participants during a meeting. The facilitator may offer mental models (such as the Circle of Conflict Adaptation) to be used by the participants and to support the process of conflict resolution using the RBF skills and competencies. The authority to develop the alternatives and reach resolution rests with the participants.

PRACTICE: HOLDING NEUTRAL FACILITATOR ROLE IN USING THE CIRCLE OF CONFLICT ADAPTATION

- How familiar are you with the role of the neutral facilitator in conflict resolution?
- What might you do to become more familiar with the role?

Participant: A participant in a meeting may be a party to a specific conflict. In the meeting, the participants work together using the skills to resolve the conflict. Alternatively, a participant may be in a meeting where a conflict exists among other participants but does not directly involve himself or herself. In that instance, the participant is not a bystander to the conflict resolution but can use the skill in the participant role to support the parties to the conflict to use mental models to resolve the conflict. The authority to develop the alternatives and resolve the conflict rests with either all the participants or, if authorized by the group, with a subset of participants who are parties to the conflict.

Applying the Circle of Conflict Adaptation is a three-step process. The three steps are first to generate hypotheses about the sources of conflict, second to frame conversations to address the sources of conflict, and third to make decisions about how to resolve conflict. These three steps described below can be used to guide conversations toward conflict resolution in either the participant or facilitator role.

STEP 1: GENERATE HYPOTHESES ABOUT THE SOURCES OF CONFLICT

EQs for each of the sources of conflict appear below. Answering these questions in the affirmative identifies and labels the sources of conflict you are seeing or experiencing in a group.

EQs FOR PARTICIPANT AND FACILITATOR FOR EACH TYPE OF CONFLICT

CONFLICT	EQ AS A PARTICIPANT	EQ AS A FACILITATOR
Relationship	Do you habitually avoid or confront certain people because of a troubling incident in your mutual history?	Are people in the group triggering negative responses in each other that seem to be related to their history?
Language	Do you find that you and others are using the same words to mean different things or being challenged by others' communication styles?	Are people having trouble using a common language or understanding each other?
Data	Do you or others bring conflicting data to the task of defining problems and developing solutions?	Are people unable to move forward because they cannot agree on the utility, validity, or reliability of a common data set?
Interest	Do you find yourself taking competitive positions in relationship to others in the group?	Are people at cross purposes or engaging in win/lose negotiations?
Structural	Do you notice that certain conversations or solutions are not possible because of external constraints that you and others in the meeting do not influence or control?	Are people limiting their options or modifying their behavior in the group because of forces they perceive to be beyond their influence or control?
Values	Do your fundamental assumptions and world views vary so widely from those held by others in the group that there is a gap in acceptance of each other?	Are people holding tight to their own world views and strongly rejecting the world views of others, as if accepting the alternate views would challenge their identity or their definition of what is right or wrong?

STEP 2: FRAME CONVERSATIONS TO ADDRESS SPECIFIC SOURCES OF CONFLICT

Once you have generated hypotheses about the sources of conflict in Step 1, use the EQs in the table below to frame conversations that address the specific sources of conflict.

METHODS AND EQs TO ADDRESS TYPES OF CONFLICT

RELATIONSHIP CONFLICT

Provide opportunities for people to rebuild relationships by experiencing each other in a new way.

- What would it take to put the difficulties created by your past or current relationship behind you and move forward together? Redress? Reconciliation? Forgiveness? Getting to know each other in a new way? Rebuilding trust?
- What is happening in the group that is straining relationships? Supporting relationships?
- What are the trust issues that exist in the meeting? Where/when did they originate?

LANGUAGE CONFLICT

Provide opportunities to adopt norms of communication, focus on underlying meanings rather than the words themselves, adopt a common language with common definitions, commit to not using acronyms or insider jargon, be respectful of the differences in people's preferences for taking in information, provide respectful feedback on the impact of communication, and understand what words are used as code for issues that the group might not be addressing directly.

- What would it take to improve the group's ability to understand each other better?
- How would better communication benefit the group?
- What are the words that, if we used them the same way, would help us move forward?

DATA CONFLICT

Provide opportunities for data sharing and problem solving about what data to use in the work; use the criteria of data, proxy, and communication power to identify the best available data; and brainstorm the data that the group would like to have and make commitments to develop it.

- What is the available data from all sources?
- What can we do to agree on how to use the data?
- Where might the data be a concern?
- What are the consequences of using the data we have?
- How can we use the best available data with confidence, knowing its limitations?
- How will the group get correct (accurate) information into the meeting?

INTEREST CONFLICT

Provide opportunities for mutually beneficial solutions using Fisher and Ury's approach to interest-based or win/win negotiation.

- What are the interests that underlie positions people are taking?
- What do people need?

- Do people share underlying interests in common?
- Are there tensions between people that need to be resolved in addition to addressing the substantive issues? (These tensions are a pointer to address the relationship conflicts separate from the interests.)
- What does each person have to contribute, and what does each person need to get from the solution?
- How might the group first explore common interests and then address differences in interest?
- What are the criteria for choosing the options that will best meet people's interests?
- What will maximize the gains for all parties?

STRUCTURAL CONFLICT

Provide opportunities for people to explore the source of the structural conflicts and illuminate the B/ART of the group in relation to those who control or influence the source of the conflict.

- What are the conditions, relationships, or power structures that are influencing the group's ability to move to action?
- Do some people in the group influence the budget or resources of other people in the group?
- Is it easier for some people to make the time and place of the meeting than others?
- Are there ways that race, class, culture, gender, professional background, or status in the community or in organizations are contributing to the group's inability to make decisions or act together?
- What are people's assumptions about the constraints to the group's ability to develop and implement solutions together?
- What are the differences in people's sources of authority, and how might those influence the group's ability to move forward together?
- What structural conflicts (external forces) have contributed to or will contribute to the conflict?
- How can the group become aware of those dynamics and use an understanding of B/ART to handle them constructively?

VALUES CONFLICT

Provide opportunities to explore the source of values conflicts in the group and make choices about values.

- What are the ways in which differences about what people believe affect the group's ability to reach agreement and move forward together?
- Are there differences in approaches to practice and/or implementation?
- Are there differences in people's ideas about the purpose and meaning of the work the group is trying to do?
- Who or what inspires you to do the work you do?
- What are your values in this area of work?
- What are the differences in world view or assumptions that give you pause and make you wonder if the group can work together?
- What common values exist where people have a record of accomplishment together?
- What are your values about this particular situation?
- How will you be able to listen to people who hold different beliefs and assumptions than yours?
- What norms has the group developed, listed, and used as guidelines for its meetings?

STEP 3: MAKE DECISIONS ABOUT HOW TO RESOLVE CONFLICT

In Step 3 of applying the Circle of Conflict, you use insights from exploring the sources of conflict to work as a group to address the problem. When conflict arises, a B/ART analysis can reveal the conscious and unconscious roles people play. These roles may reflect group projections; for example, when the group perceives that someone has the authority to resolve a conflict that they may not have. Conversely, the roles may reflect self-authorization, such as when someone exercises authority that the group does not acknowledge that they have.

The group's ability to address conflict is enhanced by clarification of the roles that people play in the group and the roles that they might play. Bringing to the group's awareness each person's B/ART relative to the specific issues of the conflict can enable the group to act to resolve conflict.

In this process, the first step is for the group to become aware of and name the sources(s) of conflict. Once these are named, the group can see whose B/ART it is to resolve the conflict. With B/ART clarified, the group can decide how to address the conflict.

The following case study is an example of applying this three-step process for addressing and resolving conflict. In it, you will see how the examination of B/ART can identify the sources of conflict, generate hypotheses about what might resolve the conflict, and inform choices about what method to use to address the conflict.

Case Study: Scenario

A community multisector collaborative is committed to youth success in school and safety in the community (results). The youth engagement subcommittee has implemented a late-night basketball program using the city park's outdoor basketball courts. The program's purpose is to engage older youth, keep them safe, and connect them to youth counselors who encourage and support their success in school.

In response to noise concerns raised by neighbors, the board authorized an ad hoc task force co-led by the board's program subcommittee chair and the chair of the Youth Advisory Committee. The task force met with neighborhood representatives and developed recommendations to address the neighbor's concerns, continue the program, and establish an ongoing relationship between the program and the neighbors.

The ad hoc task force is presenting the recommendations at a special board meeting of the collaborative. To maximize attendance by the neighbors, the board meeting is held at a church next door to the city park courts used in the night basketball program.

The task force recommendation maintains the hours for the night basketball program from 7:00 p.m. to midnight. However, to address neighbors' concerns about noise, the program will move at 8:00 p.m. from the city park courts to the public high school's indoor courts. Buses will provide transportation for the youth from the outdoor city park courts to the high school indoor courts at 8:00 p.m. and back to their homes at midnight.

For the special meeting, the board works with a facilitator, and they have agreed to make decisions by consensus using PBDM.

MEETING PURPOSE:

To make decisions about the program based on the recommendations of the ad hoc task force.

MEETING RESULTS:

By the end of the meeting, the board will do the following:

- Decide on the night basketball program redesign.
- Identify what is needed to implement the redesign.
- Adopt a modification to the budget to finance the redesign.
- Make commitments as to who will do what when to implement the redesign.

ANALYSIS: SOURCES OF CONFLICT

DAY JOB	ROLE IN MEETING	SOURCES OF CONFLICT
Vice president, United Way	Board chair	No apparent conflict
Youth services coordinator, school district	Program committee chair	**Structural conflict**: Recommended program redesign entails youth being transported at 8:00 p.m. from outdoor City Parks and Recreation courts to the indoor high school courts, when there is no funding source for transportation.
Senior, public high school	Youth advisory board, chair	**Relationship conflict** with neighbor, a postal worker who lives next to the basketball court. The youth and the neighbor had an argument about noise. The youth felt the neighbor was making unreasonable demands and had no authority over the basketball court use.
President, PTA	Board vice chair	No apparent conflict
Counsel, law firm	Board treasurer	No apparent conflict
Program officer, local foundation	Board secretary	**Structural conflict**: Foundation is currently funding the program; however, its funding guidelines prohibit the foundation from paying for transportation due to liability issues. The ad hoc task force recommendation includes cost of transportation.

DAY JOB	ROLE IN MEETING	SOURCES OF CONFLICT
Chief operating officer, large business	Development committee chair	No apparent conflict
Executive director, collaborative	Executive director, collaborative	**Structural conflict**: The executive director finds the restrictions placed on how funds are spent by the foundation an ongoing frustration and a limitation to meeting the needs of youth.
Pastor of the church hosting the meeting	Board member	No apparent conflict
Retired postal worker, lives next door to the city parks basketball court	Neighbor	**Relationship conflict** with the chair of the youth advisory committee. The neighbor and the youth had an argument one night about the noise that was keeping the neighbor awake when he had to get up early for work the next morning. The neighbor thought the youth was disrespectful.
Small business owner	Neighbor	No apparent conflict
Freshman, public high school	Youth participating in program	**Interest conflict** with his mother. The youth wants an evening program so he can participate in after-school practice and an evening activity.
Night shift nurse local hospital	Mother of youth participating in program	**Interest conflict** with her son. The mother doesn't want her son out after 7:00 p.m. when she leaves for the night shift. Wants the program to be converted to an after-school program so youth are not on the streets late at night.
County Parks and Recreation employee and Boy Scout troop leader	Neighbor and referee for the program	**Structural conflict**: Under the current program design, the Parks and Recreation employee is paid overtime to referee the games played on the Parks and Recreation outdoor courts. The ad hoc task force recommends moving the games to indoor courts at the school. This might prevent the Parks and Recreation employee from being a paid referee.
Community police officer	Liaison between the police department and the collaborative board	**Interest conflict** with the mother of the youth; wants to continue funding evening program as part of anti-gang initiative.
Career counselor, local community college	Invited facilitator	No apparent conflict

The following chart uses the information from the scenario to provide an example of how the three-step process can inform facilitated discussions during the meeting, preparation activities before the meeting, and follow-up activities after the meeting.

STEP 1	STEP 2	STEP 3
Interest conflict: Different interests of night vs. afternoon program Parties: Youth program participant, mother of youth program participant, community police officer	Mother, youth, and community police officer all share an underlying interest that the youth be safe and productively engaged in the evening hours. *Options that maximized mutual gain:* All agreed that the youth would be home by 8:00 p.m. while still a freshman. The Parks and Recreation employee in referee role would remind youth of commitment to be home by 8:00 p.m., and the youth committed to phone mother at 8:00 p.m. The community police officer gave her cell number to the mother so she could call if she was worried about her son. The youth services coordinator committed to work with the youth so his schedule would include afternoon study hall to do homework before afternoon sports.	Interest-based negotiation to create mutual gain
Structural conflict: Foundation funding restrictions, Parks and Recreation volunteer policy Parties: Chair ad hoc task force, Parks and Recreation employee	The foundation program officer cannot change the funding policy, and the Parks and Recreation employee cannot change the overtime pay policy. *Short-term solution:* The community police officer can provide funding for transportation from the anti-gang initiative. The foundation program officer can pay a stipend to the Parks and Recreation employee to continue to referee at the high school indoor courts. *Long-term solution:* The board chair and the board development chair in their day jobs have a relationship with the president of the local foundation. They will request that the foundation consider easing the restrictions on how grants can be used.	Group members with influence take action to address structural barriers that are not within B/ART of group
Relationship conflict: negative feelings after argument Parties: Neighbor, youth advisory chair	The program committee chair has a good relationship with both the youth advisory chair and the neighbor and requests that they get together at the church before the meeting to offer and accept apologies.	Apologies offered and accepted to reconcile relationship

PRACTICE: USING THE THREE-STEP PROCESS TO RESOLVE CONFLICT

Consider a recent meeting you either facilitated or participated in where conflict was present, and that conflict is still unresolved. As a thought experiment, apply the three-step process.

- In your role, what insights do you have about how to address the conflict?
- What might you do at the next meeting to address conflict?

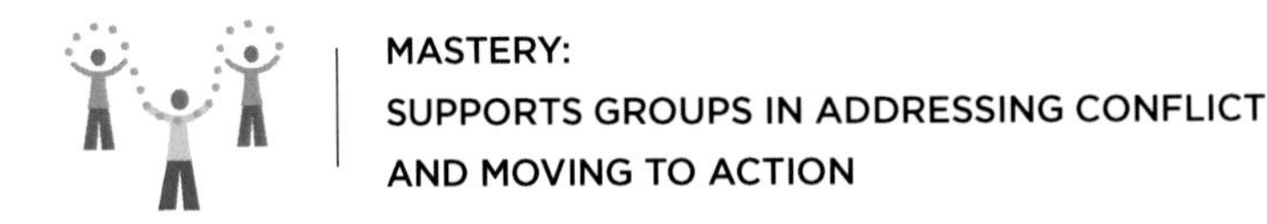

MASTERY:
SUPPORTS GROUPS IN ADDRESSING CONFLICT AND MOVING TO ACTION

You are demonstrating mastery of this skill when:

- *you use insights from MBTI and B/ART awareness to design conversations to address conflict.*
- *you integrate the application of the Circle of Conflict into PBDM.*

An awareness of MBTI preferences can be helpful to the group in understanding the sources of conflict and addressing them constructively. Research shows that the greatest areas for conflict exist between Thinking-Feeling and Judging-Perceiving. T and F preferences focus on different aspects of conflict. Thinkers take an information-driven approach, while Feelers focus on the people. Perceivers will seek input and exploration, while Judgers seek closure. These two preferences together provide insights into what might trigger a conflict and how the person might respond to conflict. A deeper understanding of these conflict pairs[24] can illuminate opportunities for conflict resolution.

Using conflict pairs raises awareness of the differential impact of the conflict sources and the desired outcomes. For example, within the T/F dichotomy, those with the F preference tend to focus most strongly on needs and values. For conversations about needs and values, their desired outcome is either intact relationships or respectful listening.

Insights from the J/P dichotomy would lead an FJ to be satisfied if there were no lingering bitterness and an FP to be satisfied when there was open exploration. In the participant or facilitator role, the conflict pairs framework can be explicitly introduced into discussions, and the group can also apply the conflict pairs to address the sources of conflict. The conflict pairs framework can be used to generate hypotheses that inform the design of conversations and meetings. The following shows the conflict-pair framework.

CONFLICT PAIR FRAMEWORK

CONFLICT PAIRS	WHAT TRIGGERS THE CONFLICT RESPONSE	DEALS WITH EMOTIONS BY	SATISFIED WHEN
TJ	Challenges to/of authority	Denying they exist	Conflict is over
TP	Challenges to/of trust	Excluding them	Outcome can subsequently be analyzed
FJ	Challenges to/of values	Including them	There is no lingering bitterness
FP	Challenges to/of belief	Accepting them	There is open exploration

PRACTICE: INSIGHTS FROM CONFLICT PAIRS

- How does your conflict pair illuminate what might be a common source of conflict for you?
- How might you use those insights in your participant role to resolve conflict?
- How might you use these insights in your facilitator role to support groups in addressing conflict?

PARTICIPANT PRACTICE GUIDE 5.7: ASSESS AND ADDRESS CONFLICT

The following guide presents ways to assess and address conflict as a participant.

AWARENESS	APPLICATION	MASTERY
No Risk Label your own orientation to conflict, and notice how it is similar to or different from others.	**Some Risk** Use the Circle of Conflict to identify the type(s) of conflict that might contribute to the group's inability to move forward. Invite others to share their observations about what types of conflict might be present.	**High Risk** Make a proposal to address a structural or values conflict that challenges the formal or informal authority relationships in the group.

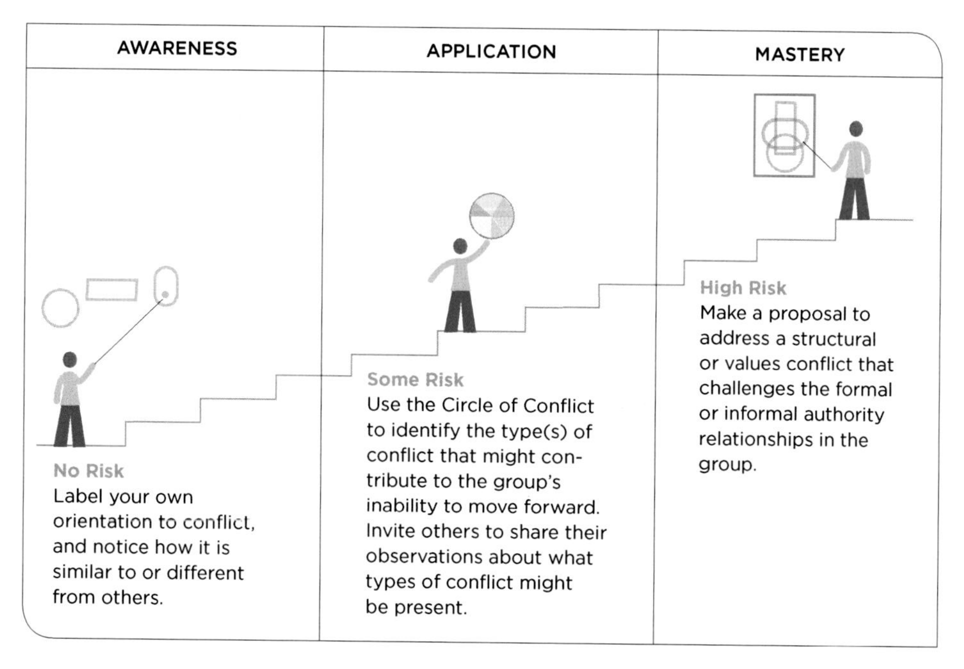

NOTES:

[1] Essinger. *Jacquard's Web: How a Handloom Led to the Birth of the Information Age.* Oxford University Press. 2004.

[2] http://en.wikipedia.org/wiki/Mental_model

[3] Young. *Mental Models: Aligning Design Strategy with Human Behavior.* Rosenfeld Media. 2008.

[4] Koerth-Baker. Crowds are not people my friends. *New York Times.* December 23, 2012.

[5] Peter Senge in *The Fifth Discipline* makes the distinction between inquiry and advocacy. PBDM is a formalized group process that operationalizes the concept of inquiry.

[6] Naming proposals as options creates a helpful link to the mental models of the Interest Based Negotiation method of achieving solutions that optimizes what everyone can gain from a negotiation and the MBTI-based Z model, which is a structured problem-solving approach that starts with facts and then develops options. Naming proposals as options also provides a bridge to using mental models in difficult or complex conversations.

[7] Pearman. *Introduction to Type and Emotional Intelligence.* Consulting Psychologists Press. 2002.

[8] The ladder of inference was developed by organizational psychologist Chris Argyris in the 1990s and popularized by Peter Senge in *The Fifth Discipline.*

[9] Joly. *Framing and the Maintenance of Stable Solitary Relationships.*

[10] Fisher, Ury and Patton. *Getting to Yes* (2nd Edition). Penguin Books. 1991.

[11] Krebs and Kummerow. *Type in Organizations.* Consulting Psychologists Press.

[12] www.myevt.com/teamdev/4-mbti-function-pairs Informed the Effective Questions used in the steps of the Z model.

[13] Bridges. *Managing Transitions: Making the Most of Change.* DeCapo Press. 2009.

[14] http://www.cellinteractive.com/ucla/physcian_ed/stages_change.html.

[15] Goddard-Truitt. School of Public Policy, University of Maryland at College Park. *Research Summary.* March 2011.

[16] Consulting Psychologists Press. *Using the Myers-Briggs Instrument with Lencioni's 5 Dysfunctions of Team Model.* www.cpp.com/pdfs/mbti-lencioni-guide.pdf.

[17] Plutchik. *Emotions and Life: Perspectives from Psychology, Biology and Evolution.* American Psychological Association. 2002.

[18] Killen and Murphy. *Introduction to Type and Conflict.* Consulting Psychologists Press. 2003.

[19] Heifetz and Linsky. Leadership on the line. *Harvard Business School Press.* 2002.

[20] Moore. *The Mediation Process: Practical Strategies for Resolving Conflict* (2nd Edition). Jossey-Bass. 1996.

[21] Lakoff. *Don't Think of an Elephant! Know Your Values and Frame the Debate.* White River Junction. 2004.

[22] Fisher, Ury and Patton. *Getting to Yes* (2nd Edition). Penguin Books. 1991.

[23] Arbitrators, unlike mediators, have the authority to make the decision.

[24] Killen and Murphy. *Introduction to Type and Conflict.* Consulting Psychologists Press. 2003.

HOLD ACTION AND RESULTS

COMPETENCY 6

DEFINITION: MAKE A DIFFERENCE IN PROGRAMS AND COMMUNITY POPULATIONS

NEVER DOUBT THAT A SMALL GROUP OF THOUGHTFUL, COMMITTED PEOPLE CAN CHANGE THE WORLD. INDEED, IT IS THE ONLY THING THAT EVER HAS.

- MARGARET MEAD

CONCEPTS IN THIS CHAPTER

FOUR KEY MEETING RESULTS TO ACHIEVE POPULATION RESULTS

SKILLS FOR THIS COMPETENCY

6.1 BE ACCOUNTABLE IN ROLE FOR CONTRIBUTIONS TO RESULTS

6.2 USE RBF SKILLS TO WORK COLLABORATIVELY TO ACCELERATE PROGRESS TOWARD RESULTS

The Hold Action and Results competency is the capacity to understand one's roles and leadership tasks to put results at the center of the work. The foundation skills plus the advanced competency of Hold Mental Models enable you as a participant or facilitator to move through the collaborative work cycle and, over time, contribute to making a measurable difference. The beneficial effect of using these competencies is more productive meetings and the development and implementation of more efficient, effective programs. The Hold Action and Results competency enables you to use your skills within role to contribute at the scope and scale necessary to make a measurable difference.

» **Results in the center:** using leadership roles to contribute to measurable improvements for populations

CONCEPTS IN THIS CHAPTER

The Hold Action and Results competency helps people work and walk through the collaborative work cycle to achieve population results and catalyze an emergent results-centered system. The Hold Action and Results competency provides the skill set to fully implement the three key elements of the Theory of Aligned Contributions. Therefore, the collaborative work cycle for population results starts with a "call to action" — e.g., an invitation for people to put a population result in the center of their work. People then have meetings specifically designed to create opportunities for everyone to join together and create and implement aligned strategies to make a measurable improvement in the result in a relatively short period of time.

The Population Result Collaborative Work Cycle illustrates how the Hold Action and Results competency enables people who respond to the call to action to have a robust container for their work and the capacity to collaborate effectively.

POPULATION RESULT COLLABORATIVE WORK CYCLE

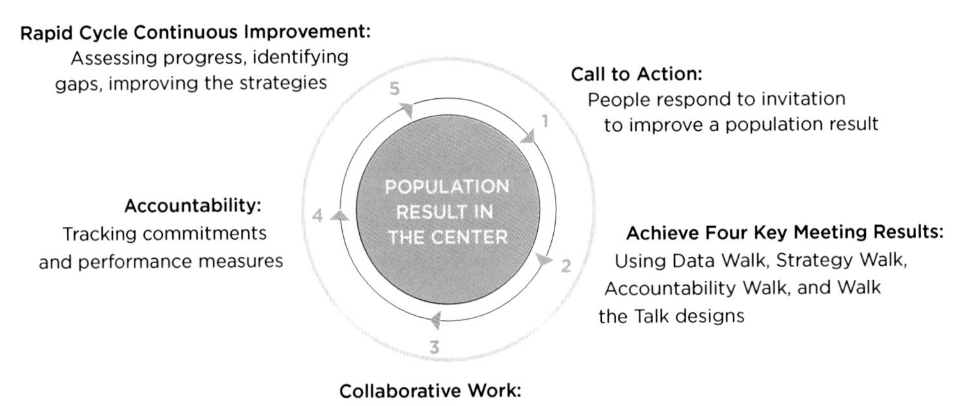

The competency works through a series of conversation/meeting designs that accomplish four important meeting results described below. The conversation/meeting designs are adapted to the nature of the convening and the time available. For example, in the Performance Partnership Summit, the four meeting results are accomplished in a day and a half. In LAP, the four meeting results are accomplished in the first few meetings over a period of months. In results-based leadership programs within organizations, the meeting results occur over two to four months.*

*For more information about these program examples, please see pages 21–28.

FOUR KEY MEETING RESULTS TO ACHIEVE POPULATION RESULTS

Those four meeting results are as follows:

1. Agree to work together and be accountable for making a measurable improvement in the result by a target date.

The target date is an essential component of public accountability. Dates are linked to improvement targets; for example, a 5 percent increase in all children entering school in Baltimore County by 2014. Action plans are built on strategies that are executed within that time frame.

2. Form strategy groups, and develop and implement strategies to achieve the result.

3. Hold accountability for making and keeping aligned action commitments to accelerate progress toward the result.

4. Continue moving through a collaborative work cycle together to implement and align strategies at a scope and scale needed to measurably improve the population-level result.

Four visual images (in the margin and on the next page) depict the designs that predictably produce these meeting results. One unifying theme is that people are highly engaged in participatory activities and get up and move — e.g., walk together, interact with each other and with the information in a dynamic way that achieves the four meeting results.

This approach of four linked designs, each emphasizing movement and decision making, is flexible and can be implemented in a shorter or longer time. For instance, in the Performance Partnership Summits, the first two meeting results are accomplished in a day and a half and the focus on action is high. Often, someone during the summit will make a call, send an email, or in some way take action and complete a commitment in real time.

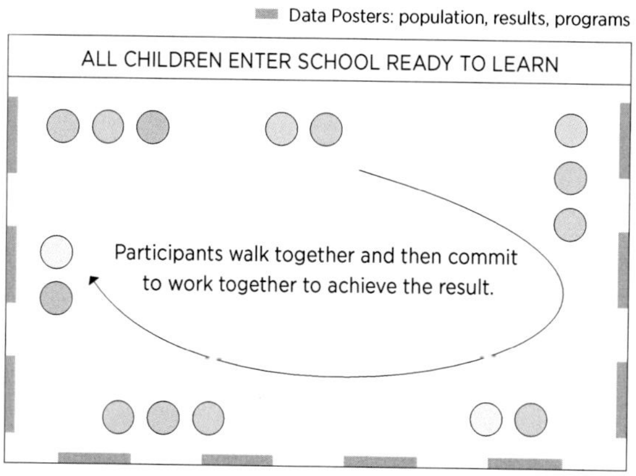

In each of the four diagrams, the circular arrow indicates the movement inherent in the design — where people walk and talk together as well as sit and work together. These designs are a sequential storyboard of activity, each building on the relationships, decisions, and commitments of the one before.

DATA WALK

Data Posters: population, results, programs

ALL CHILDREN ENTER SCHOOL READY TO LEARN

Participants walk together and then commit to work together to achieve the result.

#1. DATA WALK DESIGN

The Data Walk Design creates experiences and conversations that put the result in the center of a group's work and foster heterarchical relationships across sectors. The group walks and talks in pairs and trios, exploring, discussing, and reacting to the data on the wall. Based on that initial dialogue, the group decides to work together to make a measurable improvement in that result by a date certain. Setting a date certain by which a target will be reached provides a context for strategy development, implementation, and accountability.

STRATEGY ALIGNMENT WALK

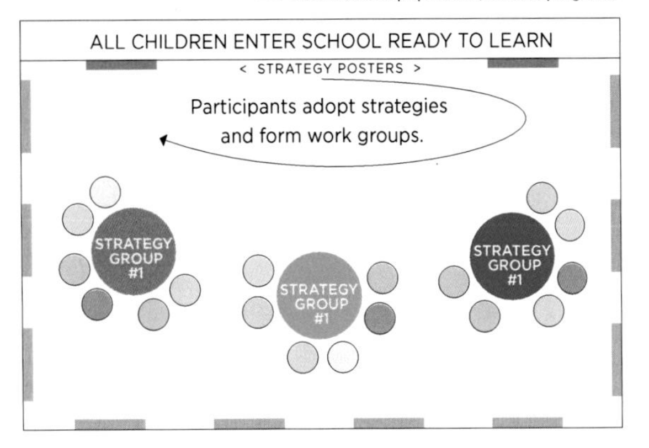

#2. STRATEGY ALIGNMENT WALK DESIGN

The Strategy Alignment Walk Design creates experiences and conversations that enable people to organize into subgroups to develop and implement strategies and create connections between subgroups to align action. After the data walk, and building on the decisions about population, result, indicator, and target with date, the group brainstorms what works. Using an affinity grouping process and proposal-based decision making, the group adopts a set of strategies. The strategies reflect what works and what people can contribute. Participants then self-organize and walk to the strategy tables to form work groups. The strategy groups work at their tables, visit other groups to provide feedback, discuss how best to align and leverage each other's work, and find ways to accelerate progress.

ACCOUNTABILITY WALK

At each session, participants are given RBF tools to help them do their work.

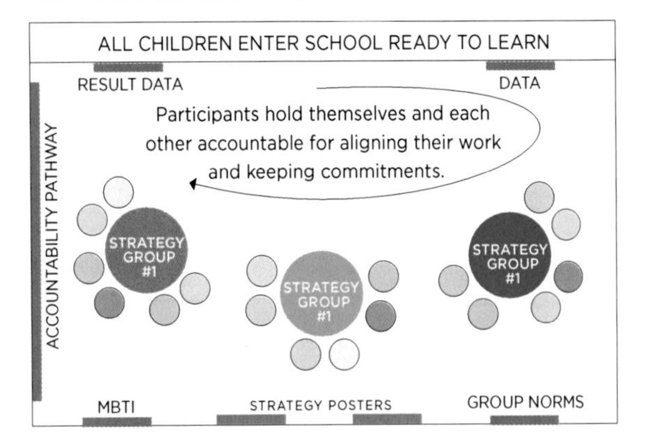

#3. ACCOUNTABILITY WALK DESIGN

The Accountability Walk Design creates experiences and conversations that enable people to hold accountability for aligned action. Building on their decisions and action commitments, the groups share progress, provide feedback, and hold accountability to address barriers to action and moving forward. The Accountability Pathway is a useful support to this design and a handy reference when posted on the wall, enabling people to walk together and have constructive problem-solving conversations.

WALK THE TALK

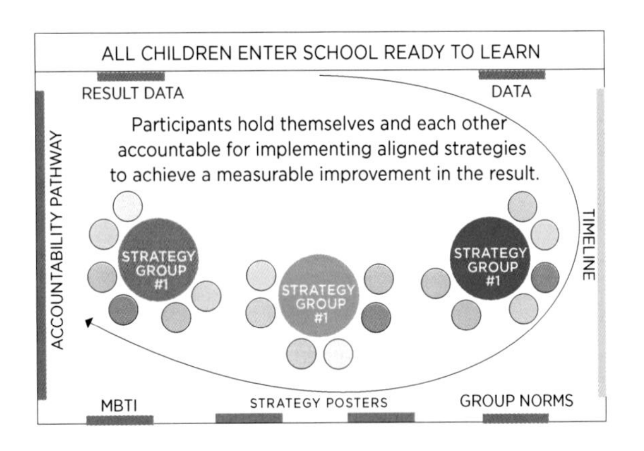

#4. WALK THE TALK DESIGN

The Walk the Talk Design creates experiences and conversations that support people in executing strategies at a scope and scale and with a timeline that makes measurable progress toward the result by the date certain. The group builds on the work of the subgroups and walks and talks to weave and integrate the subgroups into a timeline of aligned action. The timeline has measurable milestones for accountability and course correction. The design enables the people in the group to hold themselves accountable for making aligned contributions to results, to walk the talk of being a results-based leader in the emergent system they have created and in their home organizations.

Co-evolving Development: Individual Capacity and Collective Capacity to Align Contributions Accelerate Progress toward a Population Result

The two skills — *Be accountable in role for contributions to results* and *Use RBF skills to work collaboratively to accelerate progress toward results* — are developed through mutually reinforcing processes. The two co-evolve through the course of the progression to the four meeting results.

The evolution of individual skills benefits from and contributes to the evolution of the group's capacity to work toward results. The co-evolution is engendered by designs that intentionally focus on person-in-role development and role-in-system development.[1] In the Hold Action and Results competency, this development is co-occurring in multiple roles and systems. The pivot point is the individual's capacity to hold the competencies and skills in their roles, in their home organizations, and in the emergent results-centered system of collaboration.

In this chapter, the skill descriptions and practice methods for *"Be accountable in role for contributions to results"* start with the individual's perspective in his or her home organization. The approach is generic and can be implemented in a hierarchical environment or in a collaborative, heterarchical system.

The practice methods and designs that can be used in the home system and in collaborative systems are those described under the skill *"Use RBF skills to work collaboratively to accelerate progress toward results."* Included are examples of processes that engender the individual and collective development for both the results-based leadership programs and LAPs. In addition, these designs can be implemented without a leadership development component as is the case with Performance Partnership Summits.

SKILLS FOR THIS COMPETENCY

SKILL 6.1: BE ACCOUNTABLE IN ROLE FOR CONTRIBUTIONS TO RESULTS

The skill of being accountable for contributions to results, shown in the next table, enables people to understand their roles in relationship to results and determine what and how they can contribute to that result. That understanding is the foundation for working with others to ensure that contributions add up to a greater and more significant impact. When mastering this skill, people learn to hold themselves and others accountable for solving problems and overcoming barriers to making progress.

AWARENESS	APPLICATION	MASTERY
Makes contributions to a result • *Do I understand my potential contribution to the result in role and role-in-system?* • *Do I clarify and negotiate B/ART with others to contribute to the result?*	Is accountable for aligning contributions to a result • *Do I use performance measures to assess and improve my and others' contributions to the result?* • *Do I mobilize my own and others' resources to make progress toward population-level results?*	Addresses challenges and moves self and others into aligned action • *Do I work to strengthen action and alignment of contributions over time?* • *Do I comfortably exercise heterarchical and hierarchical authority in aligning my contributions with others?*
→	→	→

Most people, to be publicly accountable for a population result, need to reorient their role and stretch their acceptance of accountability to embrace the bigger whole. In the process they learn how to hold the role of a heterarchical leader in collaboration with other heterarchical leaders.

In developing the Hold Results and Action competency, the first step is to gain awareness at the person-in-role and role-in-system levels of the implications of putting the result at the center of your work.

PRACTICE: RESULT IN THE CENTER

- What is now in the center of your work?
- What bigger result does your work contribute to?
- What would be the impact of putting the bigger result in the center of your work?

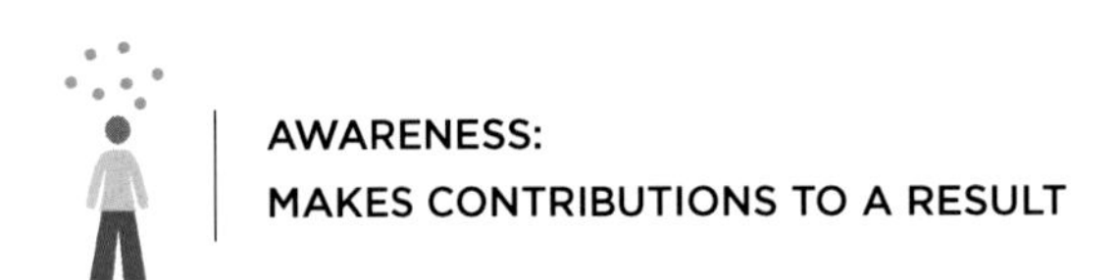

AWARENESS: MAKES CONTRIBUTIONS TO A RESULT

You are aware of this skill when:

- *you understand your potential contribution to the result in role and role-in-system.*
- *you clarify and negotiate B/ART with others to contribute to the result.*

To contribute to a result, you often have to shift your orientation putting a result at the center of your work, orienting yourself toward that result to understand your relationship to the result and others who contribute to result, and then using that new perspective to explore ways in which you can contribute to the result. Here is a four-step process that can be used to define and clarify what your contribution to a result might be.

1. Identify the population and the result you will put at the center of your work.
2. Map where you are in relation to the result and your potential partners.
3. Identify the others with whom you will align to make progress toward the result.
4. Define and clarify your potential contributions.

RESULT IN THE CENTER

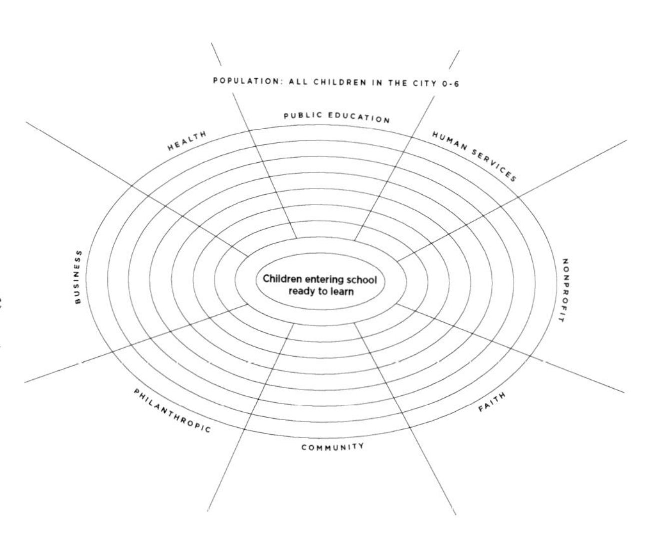

The *result-in-the-center* chart is a method to help groups move toward a population-level result and to help individuals clarify their contribution to a common result. Using the result-in-the-center chart shown on the right, the example below follows the four steps to define and clarify an individual's contribution to a result at the program level and make explicit the partners and connections needed for that contribution to have an impact at the community level.

Following the example is a result-in-the-center chart exercise that you can use to clarify your contribution in a collaboration.

Example – Using the Result-in-the-Center Charts

1. **Identify the population and the result and put them in the center. Identify your sector and other sectors that might contribute.**

In this example the desired result is that *all children in a city enter school ready to learn*. The first step is to clarify the age of the children. Children develop their ability to learn from birth until they enter school, and for this result, the focus is on children from birth to 6 years of age. The figure on the right illustrates that all children birth to 6 are a subpopulation of all children and adults within a city or a county. The city or county population of all children and adults is a subpopulation of a state and a nation.

POPULATION IN THE CENTER

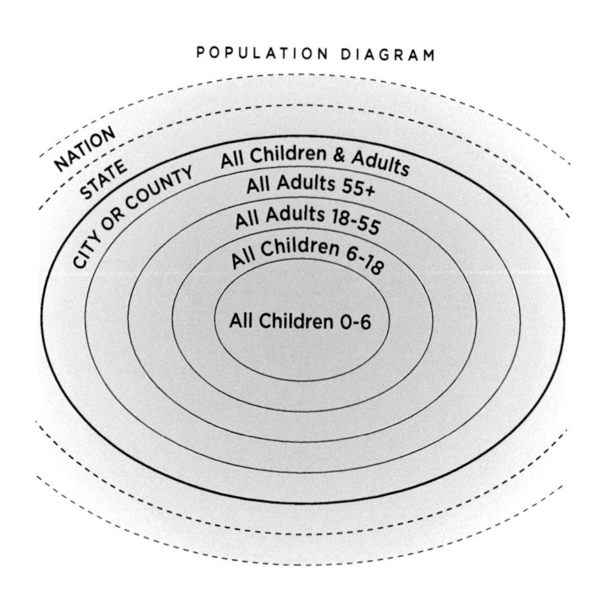

This level of specificity about desired result and population provide the context for further data gathering, disaggregation and analysis about the population, and the result that can bring attention to disparities.

Step 1 is complete when the desired result and population are clearly defined and you place that information in the result-in-the-center chart. As shown in the result-in-center chart on the previous page, the result and population are placed in the center of a set of nested ellipses. The center of the chart represents the actual children 0–6 in the city who will benefit from the contributions of many partners. The ellipses represent the people in many different roles and systems who can contribute to the result and represent how directly a person-in-role contributes to the result. Parents and family are in the first ellipse surrounding the children because their contribution is very direct. Teachers and caregivers who directly interact with the children are in the second ellipse. People who supervise, run programs, agencies, and systems are in the ellipses further away from the result, indicating their contributions are either indirect or through other people.

In order to clarify the multiple systems that can contribute to the result, the radiating lines that separate the ellipses into different sections serve to distinguish the sectors such as education, human services, business, philanthropy that can all contribute to the result. Sectors that have an impact on or contribute to school readiness are labeled.

YOUR ROLE IN SYSTEM

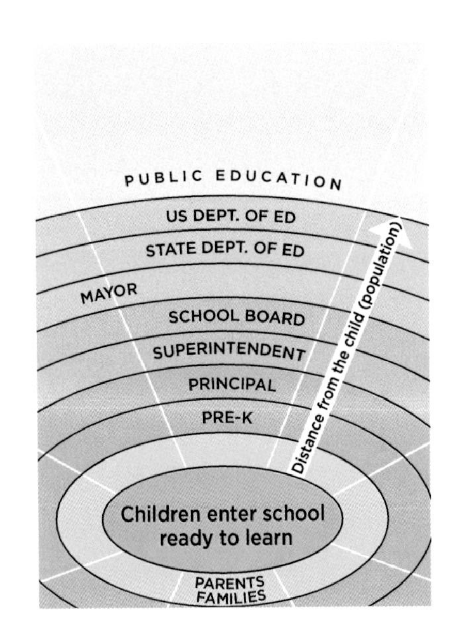

2. Map where you are in relation to both the result and potential partners within your sector.

Once the result, population, and sectors have been identified, place yourself and others in their roles and organizations.

The figure on the left is an example of where on the chart to place the principal of an elementary school with a pre-K program. The principal reports directly to the superintendent of schools and the superintendent to the school board. The school board works with the mayor in terms of budgets but is not accountable to the mayor, and therefore the mayor is not directly above the school board. The state Department of Education and U.S. Department of Education are in ellipses distant from the principal to represent their roles in the system.

3. Identify the others with whom you will align to make progress toward the result.

The figure on the following page shows a completed chart. Notice that not all levels (ellipse-sectors) for all partners are filled-in. For example, the philanthropic sector may be several ellipses removed from direct contact with the child. The Community Foundation might make grants to programs and agencies rather than having the foundation staff work directly with children.

4. Conceptualize your potential contributions.

Step 4 defines, aligns, and measures the contributions of different people in the system to illuminate the path to collective impact on the result.

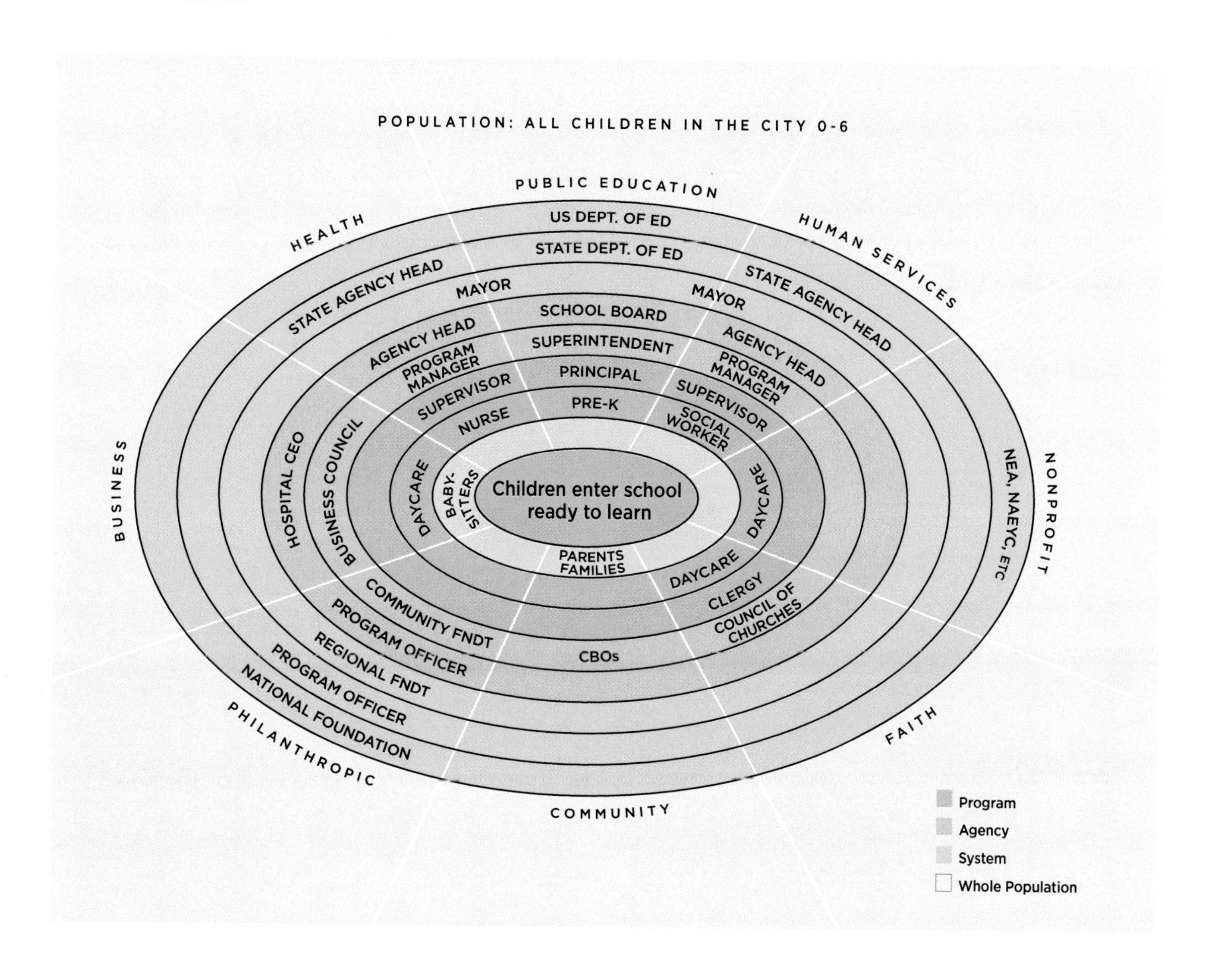

In the example, the Nurse Home Visiting Program serves children from birth to 6 who are at risk of abuse or neglect. In the past, the home visitors' primary focus was on the parenting skills needed to ensure the safety and well-being of these children. The program manager is in the city Department of Health, which in the figure on the following page is in the health sector.

The program manager decides to make a greater contribution to the result of children entering school ready to learn by implementing an evidence-based program through which the home visitors will also help the parents develop the language and literacy skills of their young children by increasing the frequency of verbal interaction.

In developing and executing this change to the tasks of the home visitors, the program manager disaggregates the population served by the home visitors to

PROGRAM POPULATION TO WHOLE POPULATION
Program- and Population-Level Result:
Children Enter School Ready to Learn

WHOLE POPULATION
All children 0-6 in the City DOH (20,000)

SYSTEM POPULATION
All children 0-6 served by City DHHS (5,000)

AGENCY POPULATION
All children 0-6 served by City DOH (2,500)

PROGRAM POPULATION
All children 0-1 served by DOH
Home Visiting Program (500)

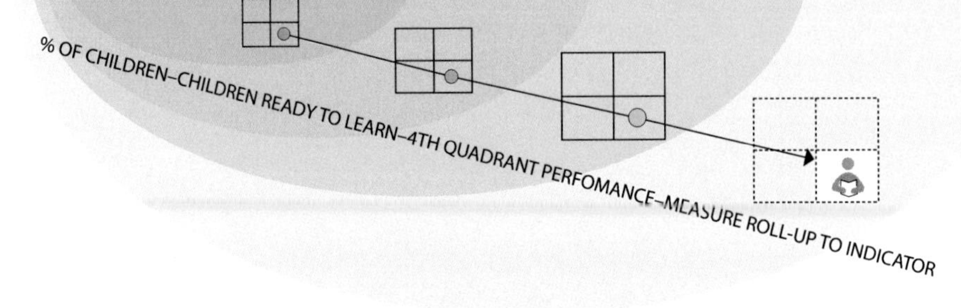

PROGRAM RESULT
Role: Program Manager Nurse Home Visiting Program
Result: Children Enter School Ready to Learn
Contribution: Help parents increase frequency of verbal interaction with their children

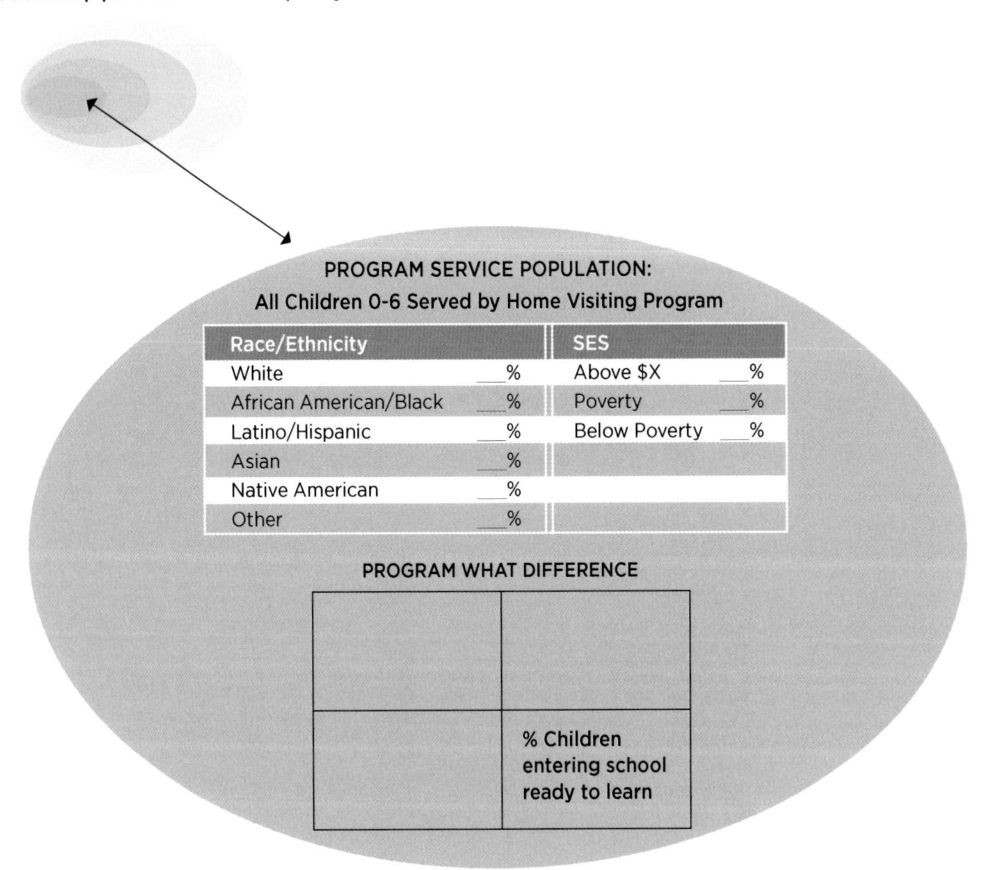

Race/Ethnicity		SES	
White	__%	Above $X	__%
African American/Black	__%	Poverty	__%
Latino/Hispanic	__%	Below Poverty	__%
Asian	__%		
Native American	__%		
Other	__%		

bring attention to and address disparities — see bottom figure on the previous page. The manager develops performance measures to guide the execution and the alignment of the contribution. Those performance measures might include the following criteria:

How much: Number of home visitors qualified in the method and provided with age-appropriate materials for each family they serve.

How well: Percent of families using the method and the materials.

What difference: Percent of children with age-appropriate language and literacy skills (i.e., entering school ready to learn).

In this example, the program manager's contribution and accountability are represented by the window graphic with the *what difference made* performance measure in the fourth quadrant.

The program manager's contribution of improving the number and percentage of the subpopulation of children under 6 in the Nurse Home Visiting Program becomes part of the larger collective impact when the leaders at every level of the system clarify and make contributions to the result. By attending to the number of children in each subpopulation, the contributions are understood in terms of the scope and scale needed to reach the result of children entering school ready to learn.

As shown in Program Population to Whole Population figure on the previous page, if leaders at every level clarify and align their contributions, the fourth quadrant program measures increase the probability that all the contributions roll-up to the whole-population result. Step 4 is complete when the contributions are conceptualized with specificity as to alignment, performance measures, and scope and scale.

PRACTICE: CONTRIBUTIONS TO A RESULT — USING THE RESULT-IN-THE-CENTER CHART

Step 1. Identify the population and the result you will put at the center of your work.

First think of a result for a population that you care about. Is there a contribution that you could make in role to the result? Once you have the result for a population in mind, consider the specific population you could contribute to. Unless you are choosing a global population, such as all children in the world, the population you are focusing on is a subset of a larger population. With the specific population in mind, think of an indicator that would let you know if

Practice continued on next page

POPULATION IN THE CENTER

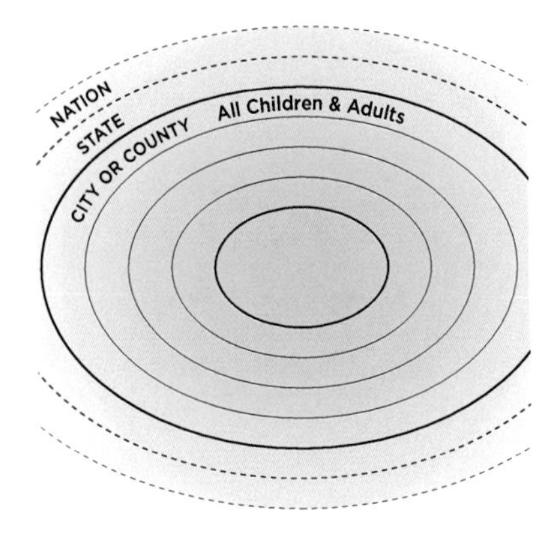

progress was being made toward the result. For example, the percentage of babies born at a healthy weight is often used as an indicator for babies born healthy. Mark Friedman's Results Accountability Framework gives examples and guidance on how to express results for populations and measure them.

The population diagram shows the whole population at the national, state, and local level that is the context for the subpopulation. Use the blank ellipses to identify your subpopulation within the context of the larger population. By specifically identifying the subpopulation, the result, and indicator, you can then gather information about the characteristics and demographics of the whole population and the subpopulation.

For example, you can compare the percentage of babies born healthy in the subpopulation to the larger whole population, bringing attention to any disparities that need to be addressed. Embedding the subpopulation within the larger population provides the data needed to compare progress in different populations or to illuminate areas for improvement. Making progress on the Hold Action and Results competency requires gathering population data disaggregated in ways that are meaningful to the result. Based on this analysis, put your population and result in the middle of the result-in-the-center chart shown in the figure below.

Step 2. Map where you are in relationship to both the result and potential partners.

SINGLE SECTOR

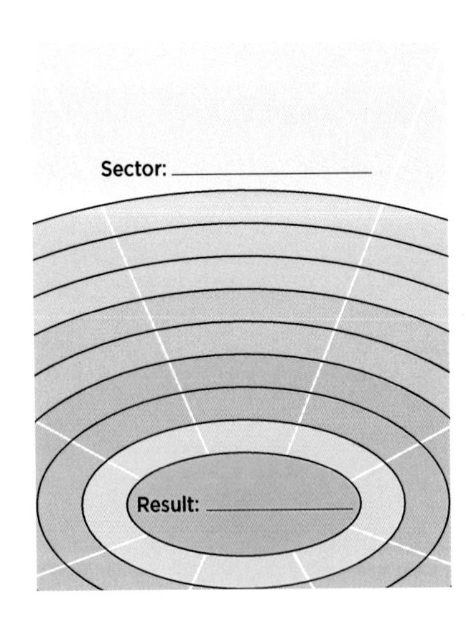

In the Single Sector figure, map where you are in relationship to the result. Label the sector you are in and, given your role in that sector, how direct your contribution is to the population.

Place yourself in the ellipse that represents how directly you contribute to the result in your role. Once you have mapped your own role and organization, take a moment to identify and map other individuals or organizations within your sector and place them in the ellipse that represents how direct their contribution is to the result.

Step 3. Identify the others with whom you will align to make progress toward the result.

With the population and result in mind, the next step is to determine who else is or could be involved in contributing to that result using the result-in-the-center chart on the next page. This is your opportunity to create a map or visual image of the complex system of interacting sectors, organizations, and agencies that contribute to the result. Label the sectors that are relevant, and add the people within those sectors into the ellipse that best represents the directness of their contribution to the result.

Practice continued on next page

As you do this mapping, you may discover that certain sectors are more fully involved or that you may not be as knowledgeable about some sectors as others. You may begin to perceive that you want to engage new partners and/or to work with current partners in a different way. The reflective practice below can help you better engage partners.

FILL IN THE ELLIPSES AND SECTORS

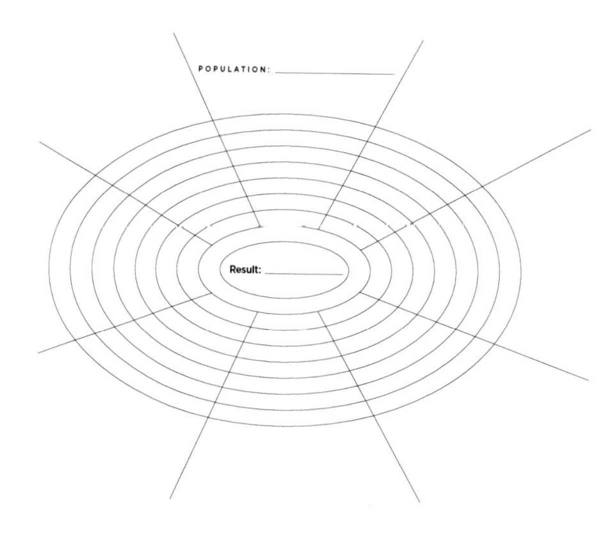

Step 4. Conceptualize your potential contributions.

Is there a contribution that you could make in role to the result?

What you might do in your role directly or indirectly to contribute to the result — directly, if you are close to the population, or indirectly, if you support those closer in. Once you have identified a potential way to contribute, ask yourself what actions you can take to make that contribution. The example questions below for the result of children entering school ready to learn may help you conceptualize contributions in role.

- As a business owner, what actions can I take to implement flex time for parents of young children?
- As an office manager in a pediatrician's office, what actions can I take to provide age-appropriate books to the parents of young children at annual check-ups?
- As a child welfare program director, what actions can I take to ensure foster parents have early childhood development training?
- As a school principal, what actions can I take to provide professional development to local daycare providers to support the quality of their programming?
- As a foundation program officer, what actions can I take to make grants that strengthen the capacity of grantees to be accountable for aligned contributions to results?

Identifying the actions you can take to make a contribution provides a general idea of your current or potential contribution. This general idea is clarified when you specify how much you will do, how well you will do it, and what difference you want to make. The answers to these questions are performance measures that can be displayed using the four-quadrant convention of Friedman's Results Accountability Framework. Use the Program Result figure on the next page to clarify your contribution.

Clarify the scope and scale of your contribution by using the Program Population to Whole Population figure on the next page to show your subpopulation within the context of the larger whole population.

Practice continued on next page

PROGRAM RESULT

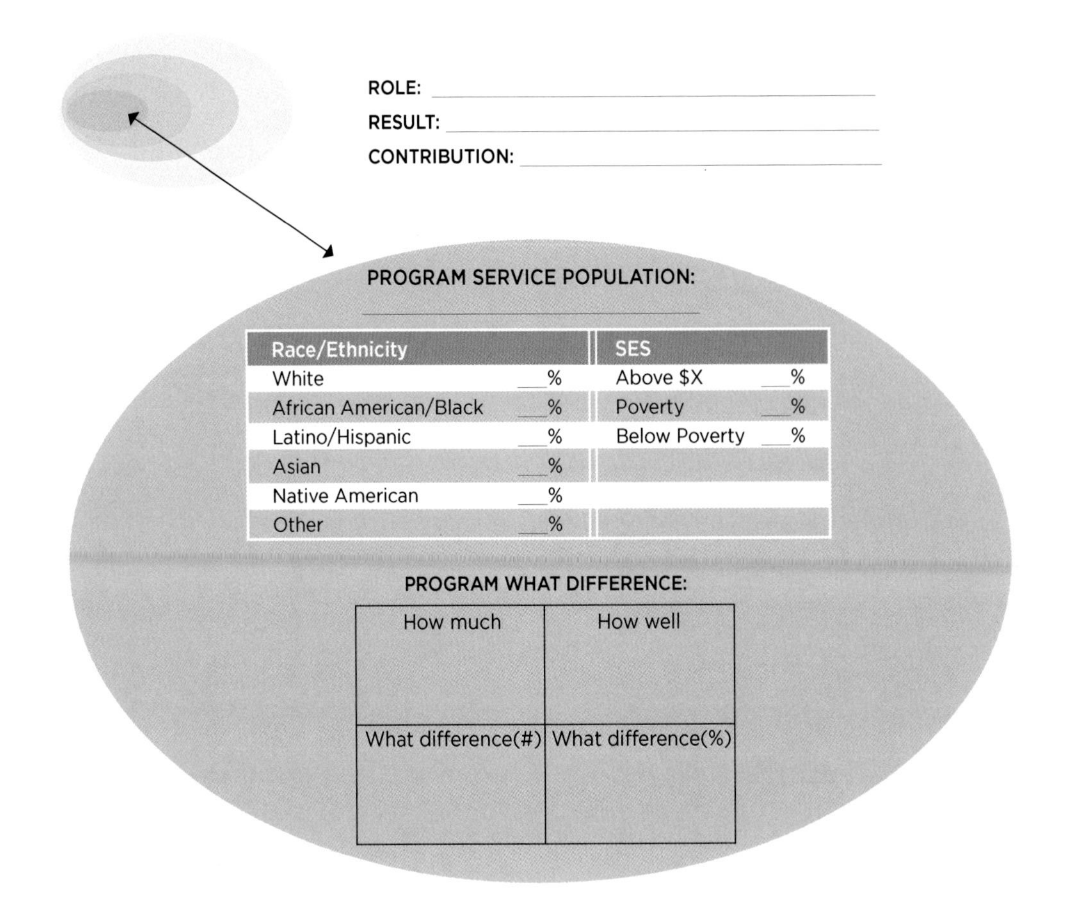

PROGRAM POPULATION TO WHOLE POPULATION

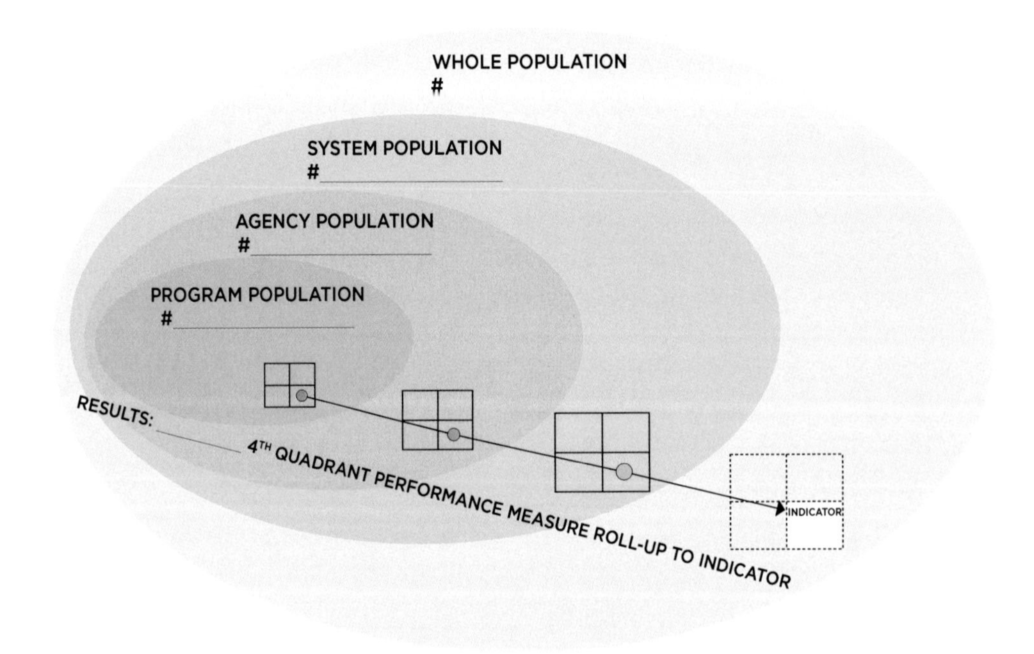

PRACTICE: BUILDING AWARENESS OF THE DIFFERENTIAL IMPACT OF SECTOR AND LEVEL

Consider the sector you are in and the other sectors you have identified that could or do contribute to the result in the center of your work.

- How does working in your sector influence how you understand the result in the center and your B/ART in relation to contributing to that result?
- How might that be different from current or potential partners in the other sectors?
- What do you think would be important to tell those partners in order to work together well?
- What might you want to hear from them?

Developing Population-Level Data

Beginning the work toward a result without accurate data may be difficult. Some things to consider when looking for population-level data are included in the tips below.

TIPS: FINDING POPULATION-LEVEL DATA

You can find information about the population from many sources, including Census data and data provided by many government and nonprofit organizations. For example, the Annie E. Casey Foundation's KIDS COUNT[2] data center provides disaggregated data for many results down to the county or city level.

The data on the result and population you are interested in may not be available. As Friedman suggests, take a pragmatic approach, commit to using the Best Available Data (B.A.D.), and work to make the data better.[3] For example, the LAP in DeKalb, Georgia, did not have consistent statewide data on children ready to learn in 2008.[4] In contrast, the LAPs in Maryland had more consistent and reliable data, a byproduct of the Maryland state Dept. of Education's decades-long investment in the Maryland Model for School Readiness. The first LAP in Maryland was statewide. It created the framework and support for the LAPs in local jurisdictions. Over the course of implementing the LAPs in Maryland, the data on children entering school ready to learn became more robust and reliable.

Similarly, the Marion County/Indianapolis LAP worked at the state and local levels to develop better data about ex-offenders successfully reintegrating into the community. The subsequent Indiana LAPs in Elkhart County and Wayne County had access to more timely and useful information. This example demonstrates how emergent results-centered systems take on the adaptive and technical challenges of using the data they have and working to make it better.

At a minimum ensure that you begin your work with the number of people in your population and at least one indicator or measure that lets you know, however imperfectly, how that population is doing in terms of the result.

PRACTICE: MAKING A MEASURABLE CONTRIBUTION TO A RESULT

Based on your answers in the prior exercise, answer the following question:

- What would it take for you to put the result at the center of your work and make a contribution in role to that result?

PRACTICE: CLARIFYING B/ART FOR YOUR CONTRIBUTION TO THE RESULT IN THE CENTER

Once you have considered your potential contribution to the result in the center, the opportunity exists to negotiate with others and establish clarity of the B/ART relative to the contributions you might make to the result.

System Questions

- Where do you exercise your primary leadership role?
- How does the sector you are in influence your role?
- How is success defined in your work?
- What is your sphere of influence and leverage? Who? How many? Where? What?

Synthesize how your influence and leverage can support your contributions in role.

Role Questions

- Is your role formal or informal?
- What is your title? How does your title describe what you do and what formal authority you have?
- What is your informal authority, and what is the source of your informal authority?
- Given your formal and informal authority in role, how might you use that authority to contribute to the result?
- How will that use of authority change your current B/ART?
- To use that authority to contribute to the result, who needs to be informed or consulted about your intention? Who needs to authorize the action?

List who needs to approve, be informed, or be consulted[5] about changes in your B/ART.

Person Questions

- How does your experience influence your ability to exercise leadership in the area of the result?
- How do your personal attributes influence how you exercise your leadership in role?
- Given your experiences and personal attributes, how might you work with those mentioned above to clarify the changes in B/ART needed for you to contribute to the result?

Describe your communication strategy for clarifying B/ART.

PRACTICE: IMPLEMENTING A ROLE SHIFT

> Based on your answers in the foregoing exercise, choose one area in which a shift in role will require a negotiation to clarify B/ART. For example, a school principal interested in partnering with daycare providers might need to *inform* the superintendent and the school district's Office of Early Childhood of the strategy and request support in sharing materials about best practices in early childhood. Conversely, an office manager in a pediatrician's office might need to get *approval* from a supervisor or materials from a central office may require a negotiation; you are taking on a new task that impacts your role and authority. For an area in which you are shifting role, consider these questions:
>
> - What is the role shift?
> - Who is affected by the shift or needs to know about the shift?
> - How might you engage them in an interest-based negotiation to shift to a win-win for everyone involved?

APPLICATION: IS ACCOUNTABLE FOR ALIGNING CONTRIBUTIONS TO A RESULT

You are applying this skill when:

- *you use performance measures to assess and improve your and others' contributions to the result.*
- *you mobilize your own and others' resources to make progress toward population-level results.*

Using information to make measurable progress is at the heart of the Hold Action and Results competency. The following scenario gives an example of how measures make alignment actionable.

Scenario: Measures Make Alignment Actionable

The result in the center is children entering school ready to learn. The scenario describes how six leaders in different sectors and at different levels of the system use performance measures to align their contributions and contribute to increasing the number and percentage of children entering school ready to learn. Two collaborative strategies are developed: one to improve the quality of early childhood curricula in daycare centers and another to ensure that children with developmental disabilities receive effective, early intervention. Both these strategies are implemented in partnership with the director of a local daycare center, strengthening the chances for all the children enrolled in that daycare center to enter school ready to learn. The following table shows a composition analysis of the six leaders in the scenario who partner to implement the two strategies.

PERSON-ROLE-SYSTEM FOR THE SCENARIO

PERSON		ROLE	SYSTEM
Name	**Background**	**Role/Organization**	**Sector**
Ms. Smith	Early childhood development	Director, Bright Futures Daycare Center	Bright Futures Daycare Center is a small, nonprofit in the early care and education sector, subject to licensure by the state and eligible to serve parents who have received vouchers from the state to pay for daycare. Ms. Smith is a member of the Daycare Directors Association. The association provides a representative to the Department. of Human Services Voucher Daycare Program Advisory Board.
Ms. Blue	Early childhood development	Manager, Program Quality, state Office of Early Education	The manager of Program Quality distributes curricula incorporating best practices for child development. In conjunction with the Daycare Directors Association, workshops are offered to center directors and their staff to support implementation of the curricula.
Dr. Jones	Education	Principal, Davis Elementary School	Davis Elementary School is a small school in a predominantly low-income neighborhood. Dr. Jones reports directly to the superintendent and is part of a citywide collaborative effort to ensure that all children enter school ready to learn.
Mr. Brown	Public administration	Director, Voucher Daycare Program, state Department of Human Services	The Voucher Daycare Program provides subsidies to low-income parents. The vouchers can be used as payment to licensed daycare providers. The program is federally funded and state administered.
Dr. Green	Nursing	Program Manager, Nurse Home Visiting Program, city Department of Public Health	The Nurse Home Visiting Program provides in-home support to children with developmental delays. The service is funded by both the state and city, and responds to referrals from a broad range of organizations in the city.
Mr. Thomas	Business administration	Executive Director, Daycare Directors Association	The membership of the Daycare Directors Association consists of daycare providers from across the state. The association provides a range of services and support to daycare directors and their staff and to advocates on issues of importance to their members.

Mr. Brown is the state-level manager responsible for ensuring that eligible parents have vouchers and that child care providers accept these vouchers. The voucher program is accountable to the federal government for the number of children in daycare paid for by vouchers, the timeliness and accuracy of payment, and documenting the level of unmet need indicated by, for example, the number children on a waiting list to receive vouchers. These measures provide information about the ability of parents to access daycare and the integrity of the payment system.

Mr. Brown is committed to the result and knows that the quality of the daycare program curricula can contribute to children's development. He partners with Ms. Blue, manager, Program Quality, state Office of Early Education, and Mr. Thomas, executive director of the Daycare Directors Association, to develop a strategy to ensure that all daycare providers who are part of the voucher program are using curricula that reflect the best practices in child development. Each makes his or her contribution. Mr. Brown and Mr. Thomas jointly implement a campaign to inform all daycare providers of the availability of the curricula. Ms. Blue provides the curricula, technical assistance, and workshops to the daycare centers. Local daycare directors such as Ms. Smith sign up as part of the campaign and use the curricula and the support from Ms. Blue's office.

Although each leader makes a separate contribution, they all hold themselves accountable for strategy implementation by sharing a common *how well* performance measure: the percentage of children in voucher programs using curricula that meet best practices standards. The partners also share a common *difference made* performance measure: the percentage of children from voucher programs entering school ready to learn. A common *difference made* performance measure ensures that the curricula are effective in supporting children's development.

Part of the strategy implementation includes the partners sharing these two performance measures and agreeing on how to collect and use the performance information to achieve alignment of efforts, how to ensure ongoing quality improvement for effectiveness in service delivery to program populations, and how to track progress in contributing to whole population collective impact. The next table summarizes the shared performance measures used by the partners for the first strategy.

Curricula alone cannot ensure that all children enter school ready to learn. Some children experience developmental delays. The second strategy — to have voucher daycare providers screen for developmental delays and make referrals to nurse home visiting programs — addresses this problem. This strategy includes a partnership with local elementary schools to ensure that the school is aware of the child's development plan and that he or she continues to receive the appropriate services.

SHARED PERFORMANCE MEASURES — STRATEGY 1

Strategy 1: Daycare providers who receive vouchers use curricula reflecting best practices in early childhood development.	
SHARED PERFORMANCE MEASURE	**PARTNERS**
% of children in voucher programs using curricula that meet best practices standards of child development (How well) % of children from voucher programs entering school ready to learn (What difference is made)	Mr. Brown, director, Voucher Daycare Program, state Department of Human Services Mr. Thomas, executive director, Daycare Directors Association Ms. Blue, manager, Program Quality, state Office of Early Education Ms. Smith, director, Bright Futures Daycare Center

The second strategy ensures that daycare providers who receive vouchers screen children for developmental delays and refer the children and their families to a nurse home visiting program to receive supportive services. The daycare provider has a role to play in encouraging and supporting families to use and benefit from the nurse home visiting services, as does the elementary school once the child has entered school. When all the partners share performance measures, they can work together to take aligned action to ensure that not only are screenings done, referrals made, and services offered and accepted, but that the children meet developmental milestones and enter school ready to learn. The shared performance measures for the second strategy are shown here.

SHARED PERFORMANCE MEASURES — STRATEGY 2

Strategy 2: Daycare providers partner with nurse home visiting programs.	
SHARED PERFORMANCE MEASURE	**PARTNERS**
% of children referred to nurse home visiting program who meet developmental milestones (What difference is made) % of children referred to nurse home visiting program who enter school ready to learn (What difference is made)	Dr. Green, program manager, Nurse Home Visiting Program, city Department of Public Health Ms. Smith, director, Bright Futures Daycare Center Mr. Brown, director, Voucher Daycare Program, state Department of Human Services Dr. Jones, principal, Davis Elementary School

When the voucher daycare provider and the nurse home visiting provider share performance measures to align the efforts of both programs, it is more likely that more children will enter school ready to learn. The following table provides examples of how the complementary performance measures held by the daycare provider and the nurse home visiting program support children in receiving timely services and how the shared performance measures support the child's developmental progress.

COMPLEMENTARY PERFORMANCE MEASURES

HOW MUCH	HOW WELL
# of referrals by daycare provider made to nurse home visiting program (daycare provider) # of referrals received from daycare provider by the nurse home visiting program (nurse home visiting program)	% of referrals to nurse home visiting program with complete documentation and preceded by a scheduling call (daycare provider) % of referrals receiving service delivery within 2 business days of referral (nurse home visiting program) % of children who have joint case management meetings involving the daycare teacher, the nurse home visiting service, and the parents (shared)
DIFFERENCE MADE	
% of children referred to nurse home visiting program who make developmental progress (shared) % of children referred from nurse home visiting program who enter school fully ready (shared)	

The figure on the next page highlights how, by forming these partnerships and adopting these measures, the voucher daycare program contributes to children entering school ready to learn. The arrows track the relationships and accountability that enable partners to use shared performance measures to increase the number and percentage of children from the improved voucher program entering school ready to learn. The children in the nurse home visiting program who still need support continue to receive services through a coordinated effort, bridging services from pre-K to kindergarten. This alignment and accountability could be strengthened by a set of shared performance measures among the nurse home visiting provider, Dr. Green, and Dr. Jones, the elementary school principal.

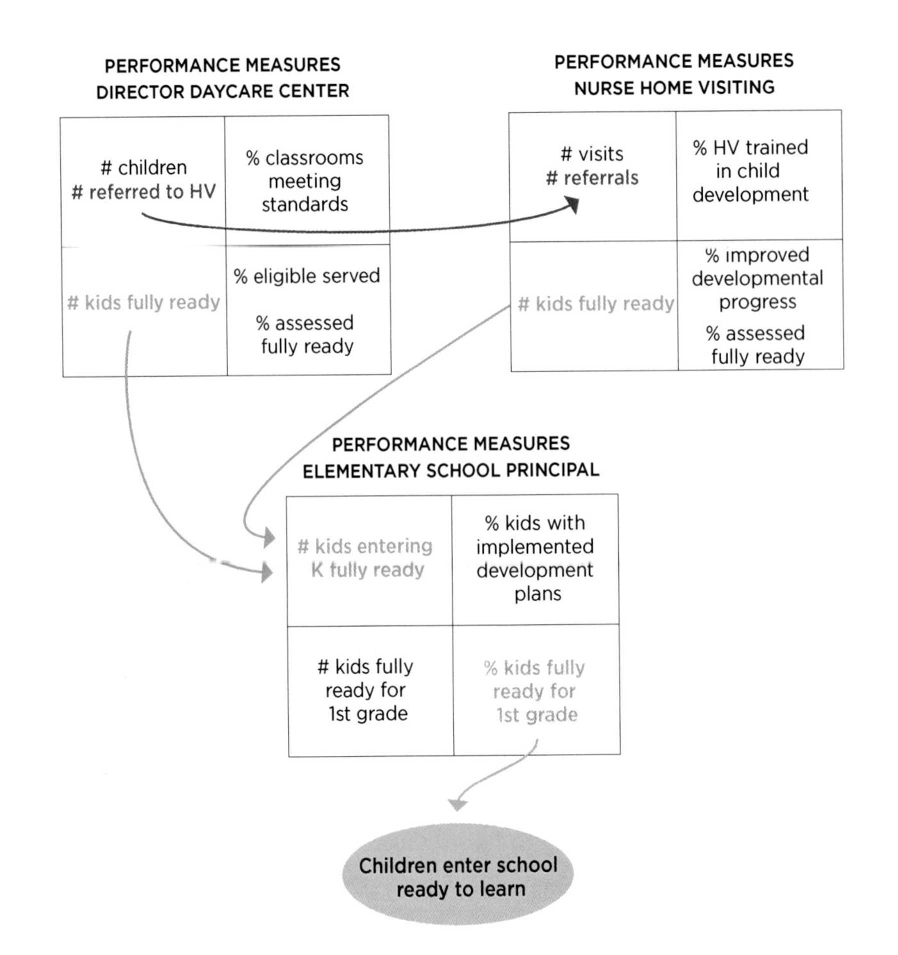

PRACTICE: USING DATA TO ALIGN ACTION

Use the chart below to identify partners you might work with to implement strategies to improve a result. Name performance measures that you would share with your partners to ensure aligned action.

WHO CAN CONTRIBUTE	WHAT STRATEGY WILL LEVERAGE THEIR CONTRIBUTION?	WHAT PERFORMANCE MEASURES CAN YOU SHARE TO CREATE ALIGNED ACTION?

PRACTICE: CREATING ALIGNMENT THROUGH SHARED PERFORMANCE MEASURES

Reflect on a partnership you currently have or one that you could have that can be strengthened by using shared performance measures.

- What are the technical and adaptive challenges in creating and using shared performance measures?
- How might you build a relationship with your current or prospective partners that would support accountability conversations?
- What steps can you take now to move forward with creating and using shared performance measures?

MASTERY:
ADDRESSES CHALLENGES AND MOVES SELF AND OTHERS INTO ALIGNED ACTION

You are demonstrating mastery of this skill when:

- *you strengthen action and alignment of contributions over time.*
- *you comfortably exercise heterarchical and hierarchical authority in working to align contributions.*

As you work to make your contribution to a result, you have a constant opportunity and challenge to work in alignment with others. The High Action/High Alignment Assessment is a method for determining the level of aligned action that you are achieving. When you find that you and others are not in high action and high alignment, you can design conversations to increase the level of aligned action.

Raj Chawla's *Ten Conversations*[6] is a helpful mental model for participating in or facilitating conversations that move people to high alignment and high action. It has been proven effective in developing mastery in the Hold Action and Results competency.

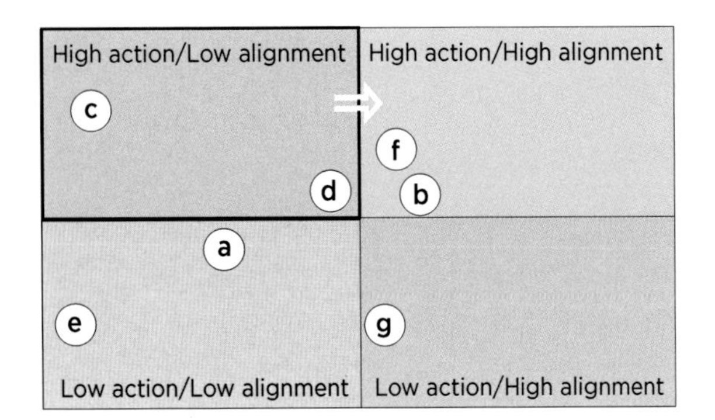

Strengthening Alignment

HIGH ACTION, LOW ALIGNMENT

After your initial assessment, you may notice someone who is in high action and acting independently, yet not aligning their contributions with yours. Or you notice that you yourself are in high action and not aligning with others. Lack of alignment can reflect a lack of shared values, interests, goals, or connectedness. In both situations, find an opportunity to explore the conversations and use the EQs in the following table to move from the upper left quadrant to the upper right as shown in the figure on the left.

CONVERSATIONS AND EQs TO MOVE FROM HIGH ACTION/LOW ALIGNMENT

CONVERSATION	EFFECTIVE QUESTIONS
Meaning	• This is what is important to me and what I want to do with you. What is important to you? What matters to you? What do you want to do together?
Relationship	• I'm not satisfied with our level of commitment. Can we talk about it? • I'd like to hear what you value about our working together. • How can we build a cohesive working relationship?
Success	• What is a successful outcome for each of us? What are our conditions of satisfaction for our work together?
Possibility	• What can we create together? What is possible? What are the different options? What is open to us? What is our true potential? What haven't we considered?

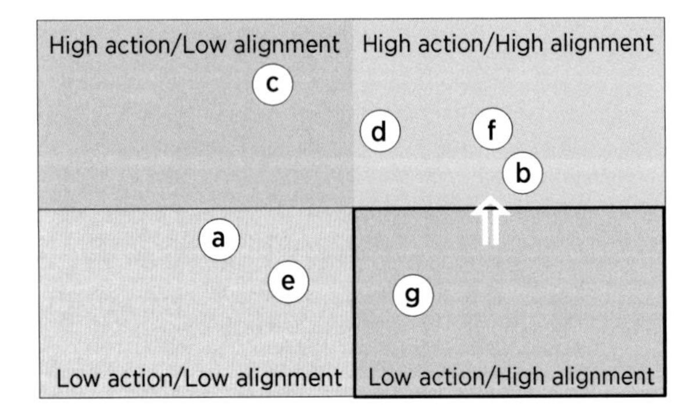

LOW ACTION, HIGH ALIGNMENT

You notice in yourself or others a sense of connection to a shared result that does not lead to you or others following through on commitments to action. Competing commitments, being unsure about how to move forward, or not valuing the results enough to take risks often leads to low action. The conversations and EQs in the next table can catalyze action. The figure on the left illustrates desired movement from low action/ high alignment.

CONVERSATIONS AND EQs TO MOVE FROM LOW ACTION/HIGH ALIGNMENT

CONVERSATION	EFFECTIVE QUESTIONS
Accountability	• This is what I am contributing. In what ways are you willing to contribute toward our success? • When are you willing to make the contribution? • What are you willing to say yes to? • What do you say no to? What are the consequences for each of us of taking this action? • What's required of us that no one has yet taken responsibility for?
Commitment and Promises	• What is your commitment to the results and the work so that we can meet our goals? What is your commitment to me so that I can be successful? • What commitment do you need from me so you can be successful? What has each of us promised to do?
Action	• How can we coordinate the timing and communication of our tasks to get this work done in time? • This is how I am progressing on my commitment. How are you progressing on yours? • Do you want my input? • Do you have any input for me? • What proposals do you have for who needs to do what when?
Results	• What outcome do we want to see? • How important is that result? • What are we willing to do, stop doing, not do, or change to achieve that result? • Is this bottom line reasonable? • What do others expect of us? • What do you expect as a result of our working together? • What do you expect that our work will produce? • Who will benefit from achieving the result? • How will we know if we have achieved the result? • What can other partners contribute?

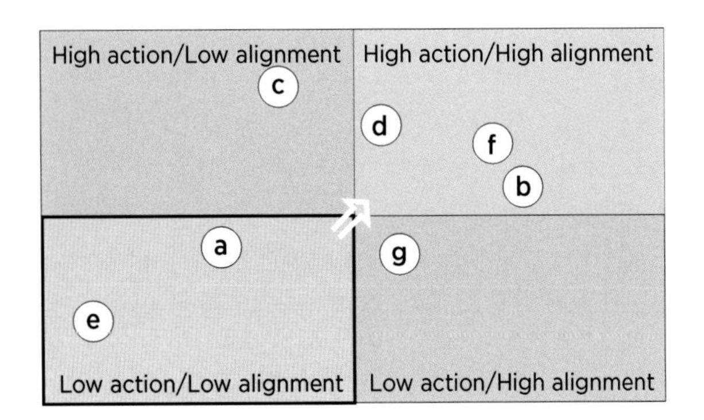

LOW ACTION, LOW ALIGNMENT

You or others may be neither aligned with the people and the work nor in action to contribute to the result. Have conversations using the EQs below that clarify choices to either more fully engage and contribute to the result or to leave the group. Making this choice often challenges people's assumptions about compliance — I am here because I have to, not because I want to — and calls them to use their personal power to use their time meaningfully. The movement from the lower left quadrant to the upper right is illustrated in the figure on the left.

CONVERSATIONS AND EQs TO MOVE FROM LOW ACTION/LOW ALIGNMENT

CONVERSATION	EFFECTIVE QUESTIONS
Personal Power	• If you could move forward on your own, what would you do? • What prevents you from exercising your power? • What are your sources of power — from your own unique gifts, talents and experience, and in your roles of both formal and informal authority in the systems you are part of? • If there were no constraints, how might you approach this? What do you need from those who support you? • What can you give yourself permission to do? • Is there risk you need to mitigate? If this is not a place you want to be, what can you do to make it meaningful? • What do you need to do to leave?

High action/Low alignment
High action/High alignment
c a b f d e g
Low action/Low alignment
Low action/High alignment

SUSTAINING HIGH ACTION AND HIGH ALIGNMENT

When you and others are in high action and high alignment together, as shown in the figure, take opportunities to reflect on the experience and use your insights to sustain the momentum of moving toward a result. Conversations and EQs to support this are given in the following table.

CONVERSATIONS AND EQs TO SUSTAIN HIGH ACTION/HIGH ALIGNMENT

CONVERSATION	EFFECTIVE QUESTIONS
Reflection	• What just happened? • What did we learn? • What should we do next time? • Were our working assumptions accurate when we started? • Isn't it time to stop and reflect? • Which of the conversations that got us here do we need to have again?

TIPS: ASSESSING LEVEL OF ALIGNMENT AND ACTION

Work with partners to assess the level of alignment and action.

Based on where you and others are, use the *Ten Conversations* EQs to move forward together.

Commit to check in with each other to see how your solutions are working and to sustain momentum.

TIPS: EXERCISING HETERARCHICAL AND HIERARCHICAL AUTHORITY TO HOLD ACCOUNTABILITY FOR RESULTS

The ability to exercise heterarchical and hierarchical authority in the pursuit of results can be enhanced by using data, making conscious choices about how you exercise authority, and, most of all, being transparent in hierarchical and heterarchical roles about your own accountability for results. The following tips support that transparency.

DO

- Provide timely performance measure tracking information about strategy implementation to those who report to you and to whom you report (hierarchical) and those you work with (heterarchical).
- Set clear performance standards for yourself and share your own performance data with superiors and subordinates (hierarchical) and peers (heterarchical).
- Use the Accountability Pathway to have conversations with superiors and subordinates (hierarchical) and peers (heterarchical) to accelerate progress toward results.
- Distinguish clearly the situations where you have the authority to direct activity and set standards (hierarchical) and the situations where you can negotiate, influence, or request activity (heterarchical).

DON'T

- Avoid conversations about meeting performance standards for fear of making yourself and others uncomfortable.
- Protect your own vulnerability while exposing others.
- Use blame and shame techniques to motivate performance.
- Behave as if you *have* authority to direct activities in heterarchical relationships or abdicate your authority to direct activities in hierarchical relationships.

PARTICIPANT PRACTICE GUIDE 6.1
BE ACCOUNTABLE IN ROLE FOR CONTRIBUTIONS TO RESULTS

As a participant, you can use these suggestions to be accountable for results.

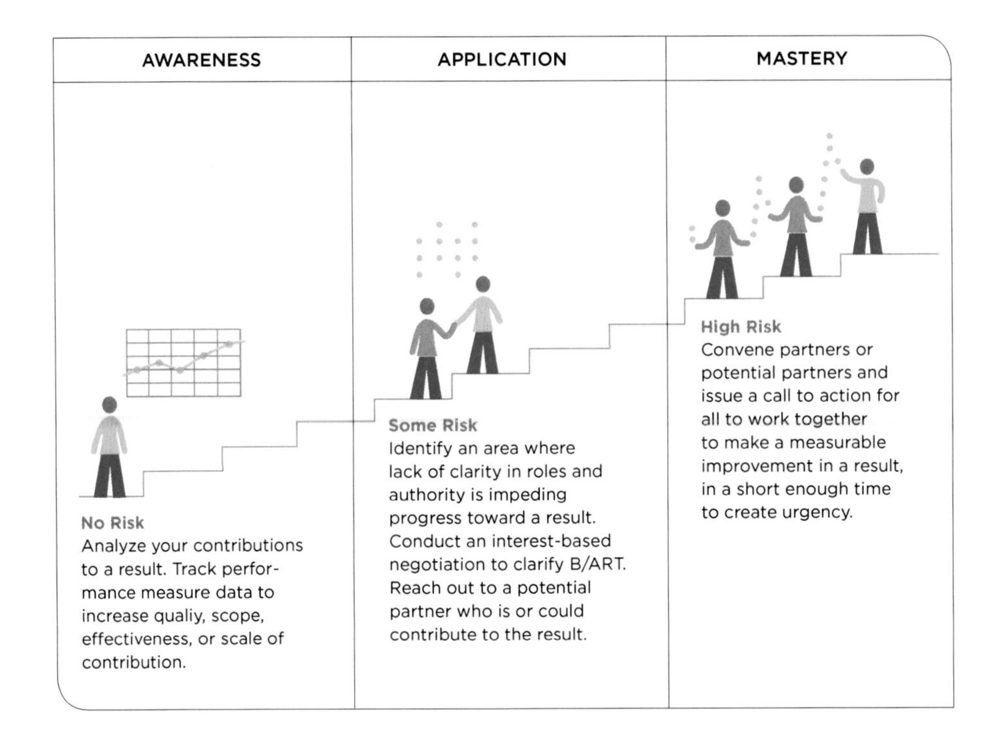

SKILL 6.2: USE RBF SKILLS TO WORK COLLABORATIVELY TO ACCELERATE PROGRESS TOWARD RESULTS

Using RBF skills to work collaboratively equips people to work in a number of roles that contribute to effective meetings. This skill, described at three levels in the following table, focuses on the role that conveners, designers, documenters, and facilitators can all play to design, execute, and follow up on meetings that catalyze groups to move from talk to action that contributes to the improvement of a result. The ability to use the set of four meeting designs discussed at the beginning of this chapter is integral to accelerating a group's progress through the collaborative work cycle.

AWARENESS	APPLICATION	MASTERY
Convenes, designs, documents, or facilitates meetings that put results in the center of the work • *Do I work as a member of a team to design and execute meetings that move groups to make aligned action commitments to a population-level result?* • *Do I contribute to creating a container for aligned contributions to a result?*	Convenes, designs, documents, or facilitates meetings where people are in high action and high alignment to make progress toward a result • *Do I ensure that there are 3R meetings that move partners from talk to action that produces results?* • *Do I facilitate conversations that support aligned action?*	Convenes, designs, documents, or facilitates meetings that sustain accountability for contributions at a scope and scale to accelerate progress toward a result • *Do I persist in the face of uncertainty, or slow or no progress, to implement what works to make population-level change?* • *Do I take risks to challenge others to put results in the center of their work and contribute to population-level change?*
→	→	→

Working consciously to align with others to contribute to population-level results is the highest level of mastery in using RBF skills. The Theory of Aligned Contributions posits that this work can occur when there is a *container* for the work, a call to action, and the capacity to collaborate. The call to action issued by a credible group invites people to join together to make a measurable difference in their community. The leaders do their work in a container, a space that is created where the leaders have the time, materials, and support to come together and build relationships, be vulnerable, and do the work of moving into accountable, aligned action.

THE BRIGHT LINE OF RESULTS

AND THE BRIGHT LINE PULLS US,
CENTERS US.

OUT FROM OUR SMALL PIECES OF
REALITY

TO A DIFFERENT WAY TO BE

THE BRIGHT LINE WE CREATE

OF RESULTS PAST, PRESENT, FUTURE

SAVES US FROM THE BLINDNESS OF

THE WAY THINGS SEEM TO BE.

— AUTHOR UNKNOWN

The Call to Action Is a Message that Convenes People and Joins Them to the Work by Specifying the Following:

- A population
- A big, community-wide result
- An indicator
- A time frame
- A forum for public accountability for working to make measurable progress

The following is the Baltimore City LAP call to action:

> *To make a measurable difference in the school readiness of Baltimore's children by November 2004.*
>
> *Right now in Baltimore City there are nearly 42,000 children, birth to age 5. More than 8,000 of them will enter kindergarten each year for the next five years. An average of 6,500 per year will become students of the Baltimore City Public Schools. Less than 30 percent enter ready to learn as measured by the Maryland Model for School Readiness-Work Sampling System.*

The Container Is a Data-Rich Environment That Supports the Work.

The container creates a physical space with visual cues that focus the group on the population, result, indicator, and factors that are important to consider when accelerating progress toward the result. In that environment, the group has the materials it needs to do the work, including flip charts, markers, laptops, printers, overhead displays, and other materials to support taking action together to produce a measurable improvement in the result. The next figure depicts the container of the Baltimore City LAP.

THE CONTAINER SETUP FOR THE DATA WALK

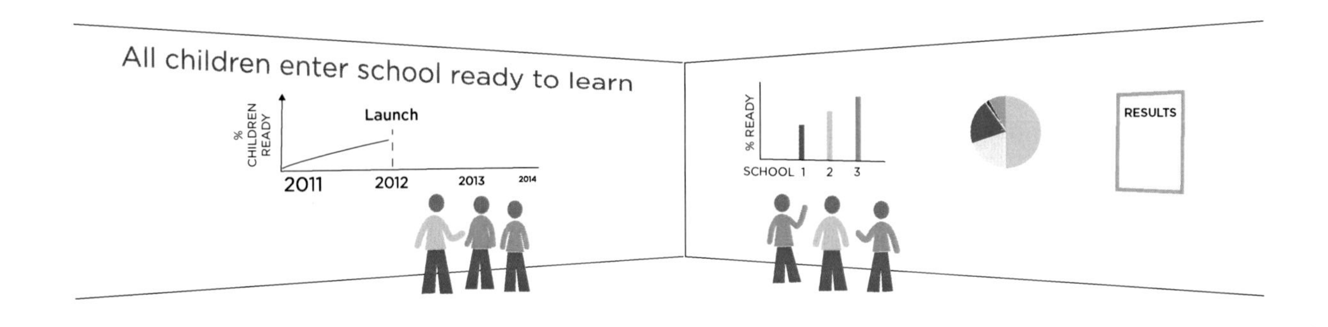

A Team Creates the Capacity to Collaborate.

This competency illuminates how a group of people working as a team can use RBF skills. By convening, designing, documenting, and facilitating meetings catalyzed by a call to action and operating within a container, the team enhances the group's capacity to collaborate.

A team with a specific set of roles is best positioned to implement meetings with the complexity and scale needed to focus on population-level results. Such meetings can be supported by four roles: convener, facilitator, co-facilitator, and documenter. These roles can be shared or split in many ways among the team members.

The team members can also use RBF skills as participants. In some instances, when there are resources and sponsorship for collaborative work toward results, the implementation team is contracted to do the work but is not part of the collaborative group. In other instances, the implementation team consists of authorized volunteers from the group. These volunteers can be meeting participants when not actively holding one of the support roles as members of the implementation team. An example of an implementation team and its roles, which reflects the approach used by LAPs and Performance Partnerships, is shown in the boxed text below.

CONVENER

Takes the lead by inviting people to join the work at the beginning of the meeting and authorizes the work of the facilitator/co-facilitator and documenter. The convener is authorized by either a sponsoring body or by the group.

FACILITATOR AND CO-FACILITATOR

Take the lead in helping the group to answer the questions needed to develop strategies and to translate those answers into an action plan by facilitating and charting conversations.

DOCUMENTER

Works closely with the facilitator and co-facilitator during the meeting to record decisions and commitments to action.

THE TEAM

Works together to design, prepare for, and execute meetings that move from talk to aligned action.

The team works together before the meeting to issue the call to action. The work begins when the team is clear about the population, result, and the indicator that measures the result for the population. Once these are clear, the team uses the figure on the following page to identify whom to invite to the meeting by looking at the different sectors and levels and identifying which organizations and individuals can contribute to improving the result.

Once the list of invitees is developed, the convener issues the call to action. The call to action can be done in person or by phone, letter, or email. The call sends a clear message emphasizing that the meeting purpose is to catalyze

ELLIPSES AND SECTORS CAN BE USED TO DETERMINE INVITEES

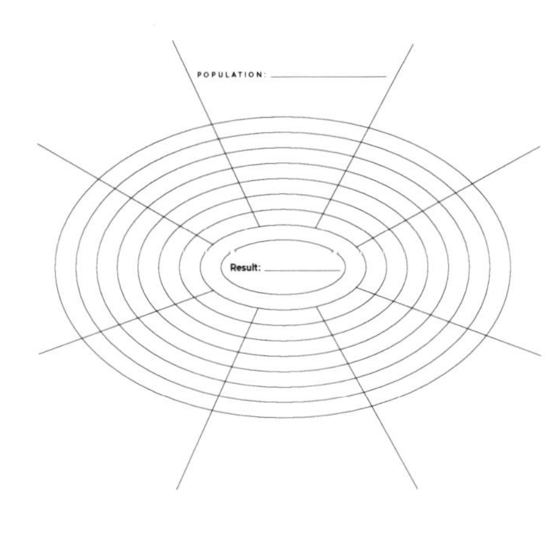

collaborative leadership committed to accelerating progress toward the result. The message can convey the purpose and approach in many ways. For example, the data and materials distributed to people in advance of or at the meeting can make a credible case for action and also appeal to people's altruism — reinforcing that the right thing to do is to contribute to the result.[7] The call to action message can also highlight that all invited will share accountability for making a difference in the result, and no one person, group, or organization can or will do it all.

Another useful context is to clarify that the work is not about getting grant money or funding. It is about people using what they have to make a bigger collective impact using low-cost or no-cost strategies that align and leverage their work. With this in mind, always encourage people to be prepared to bring resources of all kinds to the work (existing funding, expertise, influence, talent, energy, skill) and emphasize what's in it for them — an opportunity to make a measurable difference. The people called to action come together for one or more meetings at which they have the opportunity to put the result in the center of their work, to figure out their contributions and how to align them, and to be accountable for taking aligned action together to make measurable progress toward the result.

PRACTICE: CLARIFYING THE B/ART OF THE IMPLEMENTATION TEAM

Consider the four roles of the implementation team:

- Which roles would you be comfortable in?
- What would it take for you to be a convener, documenter, facilitator, or co-facilitator on a team?

In addition to issuing the call to action, the implementation team uses this competency to support a meeting or series of meetings that move the group from talk to accountable, aligned action for a result.

AWARENESS: CONVENES, DESIGNS, DOCUMENTS, OR FACILITATES MEETINGS THAT PUT RESULTS IN THE CENTER OF THE WORK

You are aware of this skill when:

- *you work as a team member to design and execute meetings that move the group to make aligned action commitments to a population-level result.*
- *you contribute to creating a container for aligned contributions to a result.*

PRACTICE: FORMING THE IMPLEMENTATION TEAM

Use the RBF skills to form an effective implementation team.

1. After each team member is clear about which role he or she will play, do a B/ART analysis of the roles so each member is clear about his or her tasks and authority.
2. Develop norms or ground rules for your team communication using the Z-Model.
3. Use the 3R meeting checklist to develop public and annotated agendas for the meetings and to develop project plans for preparation and follow-up.
4. Decide how your team will work together to develop the minimum elements for the container:
   - A statement of the result as either a banner or large flip chart to focus attention on the call to action and the purpose of the work
   - At least one graph of the indicator for the result — the most powerful image is of a trend over time to encourage people from the beginning to focus on their role in improving the trend
   - Information about the number of people in the population and some information about relevant population characteristics to support strategy development
   - Name tents, flip charts and markers, and a computer for the documenter

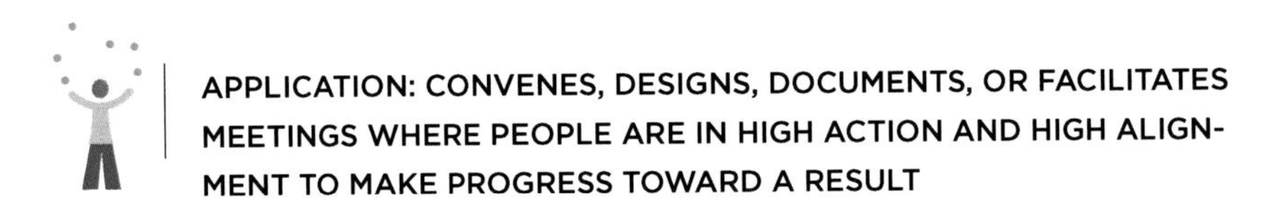

You are applying this skill when:

- *you ensure that 3R meetings move partners from talk to action that produces results.*
- *you facilitate conversations that support aligned action.*

Results-Based Meeting Designs for Population-Level Results

You can use the 3R approach to meeting design to achieve a range of meeting results. For example, a supervisor could use the 3Rs to design a meeting with subordinates to solve service delivery problems. Similarly, a business owner supported by the head of Human Resources could use the 3Rs to design a staff meeting celebrating a profitable year.

However, most people do not participate in RBF-designed and -facilitated meetings. The next table contrasts what people might experience in typical meetings intended to produce organizational or programmatic results. This *reality* of typical meetings is contrasted with an ideal 3R meeting design. The *ideal* design takes place within a container where people are gathered to the work by a call to action. It is designed and implemented by a team using RBF skills.

An ideal 3R meeting that accelerates progress toward population-level results can be achieved in several ways. The four meeting designs *(Data Walk Design, Strategy Alignment Walk Design, Accountability Walk Design,* and *Walk the Talk Design)* describe an ideal approach to achieving population-level results. When used sequentially either in a one-day Performance Partnership Summit or over a period of months in a series of meetings such as in the Leadership in Action Program, these four designs illuminate the Hold Action and Results competency.

Implementing the four designs and facilitating these conversations create a higher probability that the group will contribute to the measurable improvement of a population-level result. Creating environments where people have the opportunity and freedom to stand up and move reinforces through experience the underlying tenet of Results Based Facilitation — that results are accomplished when people *move* from talk to action.[8,9] As the following table illustrates, these ideal designs provide a contrast to the real meetings most people attend every day.

***REAL* MEETING COMPARED TO AN *IDEAL* POPULATION-RESULT MEETING**

MEETING CHARACTERISTICS	REAL MEETING	IDEAL MEETING
Meeting purpose and results	Varies by context	The explicit purpose is to work together to accelerate progress toward the improvement of a population-level result by a deadline. Meeting results always include joining through a check-in, making decisions, solving problems, resolving conflict, and leaving with commitments to action.
Meeting start	Initial welcome usually from convening authority; participants most often passive listeners	Initial joining includes participants walking and talking with each other, engaging in conversations that build relationships and connect people to the result. Initial check-in addresses meeting results, relationships, and resources, and leverages the initial interactive joining activity. People may be out of their comfort zone or encouraged to move beyond their habitual behavior from the moment they are greeted or the meeting starts.
Information transmission	One way only: from the experts to the participants.	Multiple directions — primarily among participants — leveraging the group's wisdom. Information offered in a way that enables the group to own its information processing.
Participation	Varies from passive to interactive; may not illuminate or address conflict or underlying tensions or challenge existing relationships.	Highly participatory — persistent use of reflection, paired discussion, small group and large group conversations to create engagement and ownership. Addresses conflict, relationships, and authority within group directly and moves to action commitment and accountability.
B/ART	Traditional authoritarian and/or undefined collaborative and/or unconscious or habitual roles; people intuitively or implicitly operate out of their assumptions about their own and other's formal and informal roles and authority.	Implementation team models role discipline and collaborative leadership by explicit use of RBF competencies. From the beginning, authority is with the group responding to the call to action. The design explicitly develops the individual and collective B/ART clarity necessary for people to align and move together toward the result.
Relationship building	Variable. Often the participants are all from one sector or organization; many participants may know each other or know of each other.	Intentional formation of relationships across sectors and organizational boundaries. From the beginning, people have opportunity to know themselves and others more clearly and in new ways. Some are known to each other or know of each other. Many are new to each other, and some are new to the traditional field that owns the result.
Documentation of meeting results	Variable. Sometimes minutes are kept.	Intentionally produces documentation that supports each meeting's decisions, actions, and insights. Documentation is designed to support action and accountability outside of or between meetings.
Meeting end	Concluding remarks by the authority or convener.	Check-out including all participants in some fashion addressing commitment to action and/or achievement of meeting results.

The following agendas show implementation notes for all four meeting designs. The designs are configured into two consecutive meetings — one a full day, the second a half-day, separated by at least 5–6 weeks to enable people to follow through on the action commitments made at the first meeting. The example is a hybrid of the LAP approach, where these conversations occur over the course of three meetings, and the Performance Partnership Approach, where the first two conversations occur in one day and later conversations occur through virtual check-ins.

Typical Day 1 Agenda: Data Walk and Strategy Alignment Walk Designs

9:00 am	Starting the Data Walk Meeting Result: People are joined to each other and the result
9:20 am	Where are we now? (Data Walk and Dialogue) Meeting Result: People affirm or adopt population, result, and indicator
10:30 am	Break
10:45 am	Where do we want to be? (Strategy Alignment Walk and Dialogue — Part 1) Meeting Result: People adopt target and form strategy groups
12:15 pm	Lunch
1:00 pm	How will we get there? (Strategy Alignment Walk and Dialogue — Part 2) Meeting Result: People develop action plans, align strategies, and adopt a timeline for execution
2:15 pm	Break
2:30 pm	Action Commitments and Next Steps (Check-out) Meeting Result: People commit to who will do what when to make progress by the next meeting. (Day 2)
3:30 pm	Adjourn

Typical Day 2 Agenda: Accountability Walk and Walk the Talk Designs

9:00 am	Check-in: Accountability Walk Meeting Result: People share progress on action commitments and problem solve to accelerate progress toward the target.
10:15 am	Break
10:30 am	Walking the Talk Meeting Result: People revise and align strategies to accelerate progress toward results.
11:30 am	Action Commitments and Next Steps Meeting Result: People commit to who will do what when to make progress by the next meeting.
12:30 pm	Adjourn

Conversation #1. The Data Walk Meeting Design: Putting the Results in the Center

Use this design to engage people in heterarchical relationships around the result and support them in putting the result in the center of their work. All LAPs and Performance Partnership Summits (PPS) launch the work with a group of leaders responding to the call to action. In LAPs and PPSs, this data walk design is the first activity that a group of leaders does together. It catalyzes experiential learning in conversations with peers and precedes and substitutes for more traditional ways to begin meetings, such as conveners or those with hierarchal authority speaking first and all participants listening.

DATA WALK: DESCRIPTION	
Purpose	The Data Walk creates the container and begins the process of putting the result in the center of the group's work. The Data Walk lays the foundation for the group to own population results, and it serves as a doorway to a set of new relationships formed around a common commitment to the result.
Results	Through the Data Walk, participants: › gain awareness about themselves; › build relationships with other participants by understanding similarities and differences in perceptions, experiences, and interpretations, and acknowledging the emotional impact of the information; › look at data to learn about the conditions of well-being of children and families through pictures, data charts, and stories; › better understand the use of data to connect the targeted result and the specific populations of children; › identify what data is needed and not yet available; › learn about resources available within the group through the relationship connection; and › experience the reality of having the best available data (B.A.D.). **Meeting Result: Affirm or adopt the population, result, and indicator.**
How to Use	› Prepare the room by displaying multiple poster-size data and photos such as children, families, child/teacher, etc. › Display data on poster-size graphs that show the trend line on such indicators as kindergarten assessment scores (by whole population and subpopulation, free and reduced-cost meal programs, etc.). Some data may also be displayed in tables. › Display banner in the front and center of the room with the result, population, and indicator expressed as statements — the abbreviated call to action.

Segments from a typical detailed agenda for the data walk are shown below.

9:00 AM STARTING THE DATA WALK

Action/Activity

1. The convener, facilitator, and co-facilitator welcome participants.
2. As they are welcomed, they are given a data walk guide handout and invited to find one or two people whom they don't know to go on the data walk together.
3. People are invited to look at the information, discuss what they see, and answer the questions together, writing their answers on the data walk guide handout.
4. Once people have gone on the data walk, they sit at tables.

Meeting Result: People are joined to each other and the result.

9:20 AM WHERE ARE WE NOW? (DATA WALK AND DIALOGUE)

1. People are welcomed by the convener, who reminds them of the call to action.
2. The facilitator uses the following check-in: (1) name and organization, (2) interest in the result, and (3) one observation from the data walk.
3. A large-group dialogue explores people's reactions to the data walk and what they learned from answering the questions on the data walk guide.
4. The dialogue serves to highlight themes in the conversation that people need to consider when they adopt the population, result, and indicator that establish where they are now. Affirming the population, result, and baseline measure is the foundation for setting an improvement target that will drive the action plan.
5. Proposal-based decision making is used to adopt population, result, and baseline measure.

Meeting Result: Affirm or adopt population, result, and baseline measure.

FACILITATOR NOTES

Listen For/Read Group

- Based on observations, decide when to transition from data walk to dialogue.
- Notice reactions to data; for example, what people are saying about which data engages them (spending the most time at a poster), energy level, emotion, voice tones.
- Map people and relationships: who is with whom, what are connections across pairs, etc.

Implementation Team Notes

- Room set-up with round tables. Two flip charts in the front of the room, and one flip chart available at each table.
- Markers (one each — black, blue, red, dark green) available at each flip chart.
- Results banner at the front of the room, large posters of indicator data on wall. Include the information from multiple sources about the result, indicators, and population.
- Population data disaggregated to inform insights and observations about the impact of race, class, culture, gender, language, geography, etc., on the result.
  - Posters of data sets spread out around room to accommodate free movement of pairs/trios.
  - Give thought to headers for data, data grouping, and data sequence — the tour can tell a story or convey a narrative.
- The conveners encourage and invite people to go on the data walk. Once a few people are up and moving, others are more willing to follow suit. Some may need gentle encouragement.
- Set a time for the data walk of 10–15 minutes; adapt to how much time people are taking, how energized they are, and how many data charts there are (up to 20 minutes).
- Have the pairs and trios sit together. Facilitate a large-group conversation or table conversation keying off the data walk guide questions.

THE DATA WALK GUIDE HANDOUT

1. Find two other people to form a trio.
2. Walk around the room together, look at the posted information, and answer the following questions:
   - What is the current state of the result?
   - How does the result for this population compare to other populations?[10]
   - What do you notice about the connections between the result and available resources? Demographics such as race, language, socio-economics, geography?
   - What data are missing? What would help you better understand the result?
   - How does what you see make you feel?
   - How central is the result to your daily work and life?
   - What experiences in your own life infuse your work in this area with passion?

TIPS: IMPLEMENTING A DATA WALK

- Keep an eye on the progress of the small groups and bring them back into a large group once they have made their rounds. (You can also set a time limit of 15–30 minutes, depending on the group's size and amount of data.)
- Each person needs the Data Walk Guide handout plus a pen or pencil.
- Leave enough space between the posters and graphs so people can work in groups of 2–3.
- Sharing observations — Most people do not make connections between the data and the results and between the data and the relationships. In the dialogue, use the answers from the questions of the data walk as the starting point. Select those that seem to resonate with the group or evoke interesting reactions and dynamics.
- Ask participants to share their observations and chart their responses, noting when the responses might be the items for the Data Development agenda. Go with the flow of the group, and insert the questions from the Data Walk Guide handout as appropriate.
- Listen for emotional reactions and tone.
- Give the work back to the group as you notice differences emerging that might separate people rather than join them. For example, an institutional authority figure at a table might be creating a distancing reaction from a community leader because of their differences about the work. Find a way to create a table conversation that allows people to find commonality or understand differences in a more appreciative way, and, from that appreciation, find their common interest in contributing to the population and result.

Conversation #2. Strategy Alignment Walk Design

After the group builds on the data walk and affirms the population, result, and baseline measure, the facilitator moves the group to the Strategy Alignment Walk Design, which creates the experiences and conversations enabling participants to organize into subgroups, develop and implement strategies, and connect with other subgroups to align action.

STRATEGY ALIGNMENT WALK DESIGN: DESCRIPTION PART 1 AND PART 2	
Purpose	The purpose of this design is to have the group first set a target for improvement and, based on what works and what people in the group can contribute, organize into strategy work groups and align the strategies to optimize progress toward the target. The design has two parts. Part 1 begins with setting the target and concludes when people self-select and walk to join their new strategy groups. Part 2 begins with the people in the newly formed strategy groups developing action plans. After these plans are developed, the members of the group walk together to review and discuss the plans. They provide feedback and recommendations to align the plans into one overall action agenda. The conversation ends with a public check-out of commitments to action and next steps. The public commitments to action and the strategy action plans become the foundation of the subsequent Accountability Walk Design. The purpose of the Part 1 conversation is to have the group answer the question: "Where do we want to be?" by setting a target for improvement in the baseline by a date certain. The process is a facilitated exploration of perspectives, development of options, and the use of proposal-based decision making. The purpose of Part 2 is to enable the small groups to further develop answers to "How will we get there?" by answering their strategy questions about who will do what when and with what impact. The impact of the strategies is captured by including how the strategy will be tracked — answering the question: "How do we know the strategy is successful?" The alignment of strategies occurs through the strategy walk process during which issues are identified and addressed to leverage, coordinate, or sequence strategies to optimize progress toward the target. The alignment is documented by producing an initial timeline for implementation.
Results	Through the Strategy Walk Parts 1 and 2, participants may › Set or affirm a time frame, such as the date certain by which they will make progress › Set or affirm a target for improvement — the measurable improvement you want to make by what date › Explore what works to make the improvement based on what works and the contributions people can make to the work **Meeting Result: People form into strategy work groups.** **Meeting Result: People develop action plans to move strategies forward.** **Meeting Result: People align the efforts of the strategy work groups and commit to action.**
How to Use	› People are seated at tables, each with their own flip charts to make proposals to the large group. › People have a record (handout or flip charts) of the decisions made during the data walk about the population, the result, and the indicator.

10:30 AM WHERE DO WE WANT TO BE?
(STRATEGY ALIGNMENT WALK DESIGN - PART 1)

Action/Activity

Step 1: At tables, agree on time frame(s) and a target to propose.

Step 2: Identify options for targets and time frames from the table proposals.

Step 3: Use proposal-based decision making to agree on targets and dates.

Step 4: At tables, brainstorm what works to make progress and what people can contribute. From a consideration of what works and what people can contribute, propose strategy groups to develop action plans to achieve the target.

Step 5: Using proposal-based decision making, agree on 5-7 strategies to work on to make progress toward the result.

Step 6: Identify tables for the strategy groups to gather and work together. People walk to the strategy group where they can make an active contribution.

Step 7: Join the strategy groups using a check-in to connect with each other and the work of the group.

Meeting Result: People form strategy work groups.

Facilitator Notes

Listen For/Read Group

- Clarify that the time frames can be both short and long term. Some people may want short-term time frames (next 3–6 months) and others long-term (2–3 years). Both can be accommodated.
- Be ready to explore people's assumptions about what is and is not possible as they discuss the pros and cons of the options.
- Invite people who are ready to set a target and date to share their assumptions with those who may not be ready. Help the group hear what the people who are not ready need to set a target and address their issues.
- Be ready to support the group if they struggle over their concerns that the data are inaccurate or not credible. Invite them to create a data development agenda if the data need to be strengthened.
- Listen for people who want to go deeper into what works and strategies. Put these themes on a separate "issues" chart to be addressed later and use it in the "How do we get there?" conversation.
- Listen for who in the group is ready to set a target and date using "best available data" and ask them to make a proposal.
- Use proposal-based decision making to reach agreement.
- Ask people to propose targets and dates. Listen for "options" of % increase, # increase, or reversing a decline, for example, as people consider setting a target.

Implementation Team Notes

- Provide each table a flip chart for writing out proposals.
- Arrange at least two flip charts in front to capture the dialogue.
- Ask each to provide a number or letter to label their proposal as an option.
- As people see similarities among the options, use a different color marker to highlight or circle the similar options.
- Be prepared to make a fresh, legible flip chart of the agreed-upon proposals and/or print and distribute copies and/or display on an overhead.

1:00 PM HOW WILL WE GET THERE (STRATEGY ALIGNMENT WALK — PART 2

Action/Activity

Step 1: Strategy groups develop action plans.

Step 2: Strategy groups record their work on flip charts and on the strategy development handout, or on computer at each table.

Step 3: People form small groups (each group comprising one member of each strategy group) and walk together to discuss each strategy group's action plan.

Step 4: People return to their original strategy groups and strengthen their work based on dialogue from the Strategy Alignment Walk.

Step 5: People agree on how the strategies fit together to form an overall action plan with an initial timeline of milestones for the strategies.

Step 6: People agree on how they will continue to work together.

Meeting Result: People develop action plans to move strategies forward.
Meeting Result: People align the efforts of the strategy work groups and commit to action.

Facilitator Notes

- Strategy work groups answer these questions:
  - Who will do what when and with what impact?
  - How will the progress be tracked (how will I know if the strategy is successful)?
  - What can other partners contribute and how do I enroll them?
- Once each strategy group develops an action plan, people form into mixed groups, comprising one representative from each strategy group. The mixed group walks together and visits each strategy group's posters of the strategy action plan. They review the flip chart, hear brief highlights of the strategy, and ask clarifying questions, and make suggestions to strengthen the strategy, including offers of resources — knowledge, connection, and access. As they walk and talk together, they begin to identify opportunities for synergy and connection among the groups.
- After the small groups have finished their strategy alignment walk, people return to their strategy groups to strengthen their strategies and engage in a large-group discussion to reach agreement about the following:
  - Priorities or sequence
  - Coordination among strategies
  - Timeline of who will do what when and with what desired impact
- Some areas of the action plan may require further discussion immediately after the meeting once people see the electronic copy of the combined action agenda.
- Prior to check-out, a final discussion addresses the execution and the next steps, exploring the following issues:
  - Roles of partners and contributions of all members to implement the action plan
  - Expanding the network
  - Communication: members make specific commitments for the next meeting, or calls are scheduled
  - Timeline of who will do what when and with what desired impact

Implementation Team Notes

- Using the format on the next page, each strategy group displays the results of its work on a flip chart or overhead.
- Strategy groups use an electronic template pre-loaded on computers to record their work. The action plan is developed in the form of an action commitment.

NAME	ACTION	WITH WHOM	WHEN	CONTRIBUTION TO THE RESULT	PROGRESS

Conversation #3. The Accountability Walk Meeting Design

After people have developed action plans and made public commitments, they will need time to execute and implement them. Use this Accountability Walk Meeting Design to help the group hold accountability for making progress toward the targets.

Accountability is intentionally explored at the person, the person-in-role, and the role-in-system levels. The design begins with a check-in that focuses on progress made in keeping commitments and taking next steps. The design incorporates the methods and approaches of the "be and help others be accountable for action commitments" skill.

ACCOUNTABILITY WALK: DESCRIPTION	
Purpose	The purpose of this design is to have the group share information on progress made on the action commitments and action plans developed in a prior session. The information from this design is used to solve problems, address conflict, and overcome barriers to forward progress.
Results	Through the accountability walk, participants may: › share progress made on keeping action commitments and executing group action plans; › learn about how to successfully keep action commitments and execute strategies; › identify strengths to build on and problems or barriers to be addressed; and › create a normalized atmosphere that allows learning and adaptation informed by both failures and successes. **Meeting Result: Use information to inform problem solving to sustain and accelerate progress toward the result in the Walk the Talk Design.**
How to Use	› People are seated at tables, each with its own flip chart, to update the strategy group work plan and their individual action commitments. › People have the overall action agenda with information on all the strategies. › If there is an external source of data for the trend lines that track progress (either performance measure or indicator), those data are updated and available to the whole group

9:00 AM ACCOUNTABILITY WALK DESIGN

Action/Activity

Step 1: Check in within the work groups and with the group as a whole about the progress in keeping commitments and implementing the action plan.

Step 2: Optional: If there are updated performance measure data or indicator data, the group walks together to review the data, similar to the initial data walk.

Step 3: Optional: After hearing progress from the check-in or walking to review new data, the group walks to the Accountability Pathway banner and explores where people are on the pathway.

Step 4: People hold a large-group dialogue to identify the strengths and challenges of holding accountability for their own action commitments, execution of strategy action plans, and overall progress toward the result.

Step 5: People agree on affinity groups and walk to where they can best develop strategies to keep commitments at the person, person-in-role, or role-in-system level.

Step 6: People hold a large-group dialogue to identify what to keep in mind as they transition to the Walk the Talk Design.

Facilitator Notes

- Strategy work groups update their action commitments using the same format as in the Strategy Alignment Walk Design.
- Affinity groups are formed by framing context statements that illuminate the most useful level for the conversation. For example, if the challenges are at the person level, the CS and EQ might be:
  - CS: It seems that a number of people are working on individual action commitments.
  - EQ: Who do you think/feel would be a good peer consultant for you in strengthening your ability to keep your individual action commitments? When you catch that person's eye, walk to him or her and spend time supporting each other.
- If the challenge is at person-in-role level, people might walk to affinity groups where people who share similar roles work together, or at the role-in-system level, people might walk to form affinity groups within sectors.
- In all instances, the affinity groups use the Accountability Pathway conversation to learn from the experience of trying to get things done. They identify issues or opportunities to take into the next step of the work.

Implementation Team Notes

- Display the Accountability Pathway banner on a wall to which the people can easily move.
- Make materials available to be updated on progress. These can include handouts, templates on table computers with capability for display, self-carbonized forms, or poster-size strategy action plan templates.

Conversation #4: Walk the Talk Design

The Walk the Talk Design creates a trajectory for execution with a timeline for aligned action at a scope and scale to make measurable progress toward the result. The container setup might look like that in the figure below.

WALK THE TALK DESIGN CONTAINER

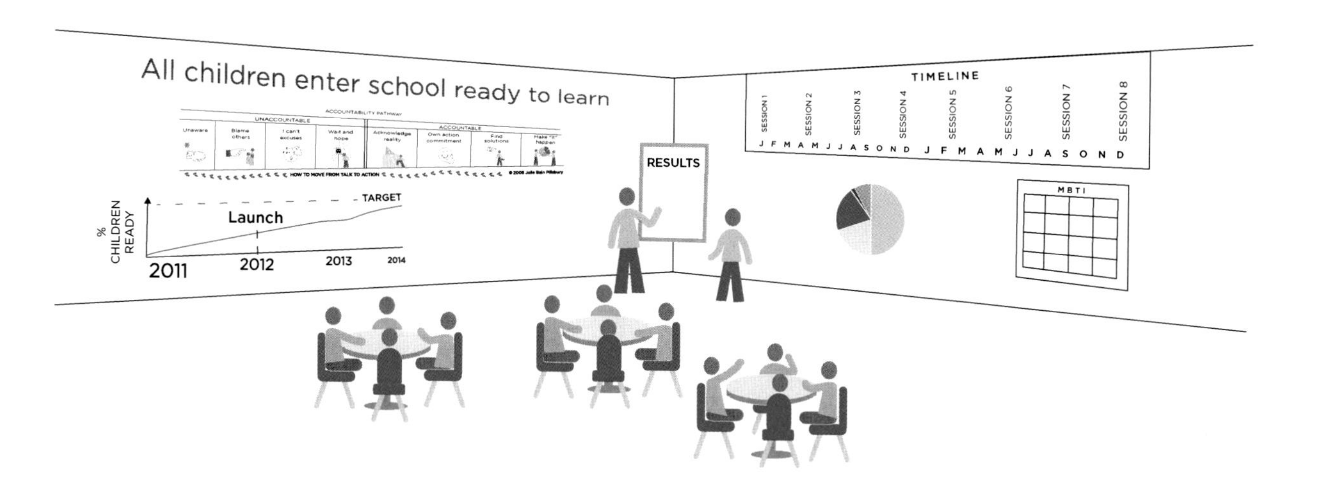

WALK THE TALK DESIGN: DESCRIPTION PART 1 AND PART 2	
Purpose	The purpose of this design is to develop an implementation timeline with performance measures for tracking progress and to make decisions about how the group can implement at a scope and scale to achieve the targets.
Results	Through the Walk the Talk Design, participants may: › develop and continuously update an implementation timeline with performance measures to document progress; › make decisions to ensure scope and scale and pace adequate to meet targets and dates; and › use information from the Accountability Walk Design and identify opportunities for course correction and alignment to accelerate progress. **Meeting Result: Hold each other accountable for execution at the person, person-in-role, and role-in-system levels to achieve the target.**
How to Use	› People are seated at strategy tables or with other groups to identify issues and problem solve. › People post updates on the timeline and walk together to assess progress and see opportunities for course correction and effective execution.

10:30 AM WALK THE TALK DESIGN

Action/Activity

Step 1: Strategy groups process their experience of the Accountability Walk Design. They walk to update the initial timeline or, if the timeline has not been created, create the timeline.

Step 2: The whole group walks to the timeline and assesses progress, opportunities for acceleration, and opportunities to implement at scope, scale, and pace to achieve targets.

Step 3: People return to their strategy groups and integrate information to revise strategy action plans and make individual commitments.

Step 4: The whole group dialogues to align strategies (may include the Strategy Alignment Walk Design).

Step 5: The group checks out with action commitments and next steps.

Facilitator Notes

- Strategy design builds on the work of the strategy groups. It focuses on the performance measures of each work group and how these performance measures contribute to the whole. The group's work is to create and implement action strategies using performance measures to execute and align contributions.
  - What performance measures will connect and align your strategy with that of the other work groups?
- Each work group answers the EQ in the following way:
  - Population addressed by the strategy: who, how many, important characteristics, etc.
  - Projected implementation for the next six months, using performance measures for how much will be done, how well it will be done, and what difference will be made for the population. Put the performance measures on sticky notes and post them on the timeline on the wall.
  - The table on the next page shows an example timeline. Strategies are listed in the far left column, and projected implementation dates are tracked using performance measures.
- The performance measures for the strategies are posted. People walk to the timeline and have two discussions:
  1. How strategies can be aligned: areas of coordination, sequencing, and joint action. Result of this conversation: action commitments to achieve the necessary alignment.
  2. The overall projected impact of all the strategies, assessing if the strategies are being implemented at a scope and scale to achieve the target. Result of this conversation: agreement that there is sufficient scope and scale or a commitment to increase the scope and scale if implementation will fall short of the target.

Implementation Team Notes

- Display the timeline banner on a wall to which people can easily move.
- Have sticky notes for people to use when posting and updating performance measures.
- Have computers for each strategy group and the capability to display information about scope and scale and progress along the timeline.

EXAMPLE TIMELINE

STRATEGY	MAR	APR	MAY	JUN	JULY	AUG	SEPT
Strategy 1:							
Strategy 2:							

The figure below shows the working slides that the Marion County/ Indianapolis LAP used to align strategies by constructing a timeline and assessing scope and scale.

MARION COUNTY DATA

Result: All ex-offenders in Marion County Successfully Reintegrate into the Community

POPULATION
- 55,000 ex-offenders residing in Marion County
- 5,800 offenders released to Marion County each year
  - 63% African American
  - 36% Caucasian
  - 1% Hipanic

TARGET IMPROVEMENT: 12% reduction in recidivism: 10% reduction in Marion County rearrest rate
SCOPE AND SCALE: 600 people successfully reentering: 500 people not rearrested

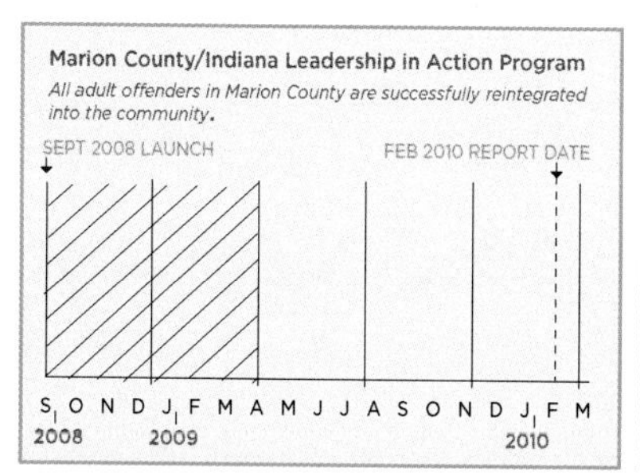

Scope and Scale

	12% Reduction in DOC one-year recidivism rate	10% Reduction in Marion County one-year rearrest rate
	600 PEOPLE	500 PEOPLE
EMPLOYMENT	250 Apollo 18-34 yo = 3,300	250 Apollo 18-34 yo = 3,300
EDUCATION	10,000	10,000
HEALTH	5,600	5,600
SPIRIT	5,600	5,600
POLICY	450	450
TOTAL		

MASTERY: CONVENES, DESIGNS, DOCUMENTS, OR FACILITATES MEETINGS THAT SUSTAIN ACCOUNTABILITY FOR CONTRIBUTIONS AT A SCOPE AND SCALE TO ACCELERATE PROGRESS TOWARD A RESULT

You are demonstrating mastery of this skill when:

- *you persist in the face of uncertainty, or slow or no progress, to make population-level change.*
- *you take risks to challenge others to put results in the center of their work and contribute to population-level change.*

Victoria Goddard-Truitt created a tool to assess and strengthen aligned contributions to results. The assessment tool reflects the research on aligned contributions and creates an effective feedback loop to inform ongoing quality improvement in the work of accelerating progress toward results. A summary of Dr. Goddard-Truitt's work is presented below.

Data Drive Leadership Efficacy

Emerging evidence indicates[11] that leaders who assess and track collaborative activities and engage in dialogue about the information are more likely to take action and align what they do to achieve a greater collective impact and measurable results. The engine driving action, alignment, and accountability is the ability of the group to keep moving through the collaborative work cycle, ending each meeting with every member making action commitments and beginning each meeting with an accountability conversation. In the context of the Accountability Pathway, the conversation enables the leaders to hold shared and mutual accountability to keep action commitments and to be in high alignment and high action together.

The ability of leaders to be in high alignment and high action is enhanced by using feedback data that allows the leaders to assess and improve their capacity to make progress. Leaders can use the assessment tool to improve the effectiveness of their work.

To achieve results, leaders commit to taking a course of action that will make a difference at the population level. These actions align with and leverage the actions of other leaders and partners who are working toward a shared result. Leaders who consistently and frequently act this way accelerate positive changes and build on and leverage the work of other leaders to make progress toward results. They move forward together by consistently answering the question, "Are we in high action and high alignment?"

Making a Powerful Commitment

Commitments are actions that an individual pledges to undertake. Powerful commitments are made with a conscious intent to get things done. The focus is on making one or two commitments that have the greatest potential to move the work forward, not on creating a long to-do list. Use the following questions to assess the power of a commitment:

- Is the commitment stated clearly? Does it describe what will be done by whom and when?
- Is the commitment observable and measurable?
- If the commitment is carried out well, will it support or leverage change that works toward a stated goal or benchmark, thereby driving the achievement of results?
- Is the commitment actionable? For example, can the person(s) making the commitment carry it out? Is the commitment written so that the person making the commitment is clear on how to engage those who need to be involved?
- Do the actions of the commitment stretch beyond the leader's everyday work? Does the commitment challenge the leader to address the adaptive challenges that are barriers to moving forward?

WEAK COMMITMENTS	POWERFUL COMMITMENTS
At the next staff meeting, I will share what we talked about in the leadership session.	I will meet with my reportees next week to review our trend line on adoptions and complete a factor analysis. This information will inform the next steps we will take to meet our targets.
I will talk with the director about the need to change policy and procedures to improve outcomes.	I will collect information and data to demonstrate what works and does not work, and link it to best practices. By the end of the month, I will make a policy implementation recommendation to the director.
I will design a job fair.	By next month, two key partners and I will attend two job fairs in the tri-state area to gather information. We will present our design recommendations at the next quarterly work group meeting.
I will use MBTI in my work.	I will review my MBTI preferences and reflect on a conflict occurring between my executive director and myself. Next week, I will observe his type preferences and implement a strategy to address our conflict.

The High Action/High Alignment Assessment Tool

The power of an action commitment is only realized when the commitment is implemented. Leaders who hold themselves accountable for performance are more likely to complete action commitments.[12,13] Completion rates increase when action commitments are written, shared publicly with the team or work group, and reviewed and discussed regularly to improve execution and efficacy.[14]

Action commitments are assessed along a continuum of action and alignment. Collaborative groups spend a great deal of time collecting information and planning but often lose momentum and fail to execute at a scope and scale that will make a difference. The following assessment tool allows leaders to assess whether they are in high action and high alignment. Imagine a rowing team with each member rowing in a different direction — lots of action but no forward movement! When in high alignment, collaborative groups are linking goals and objectives to focus on a common result, with each leader making a contribution.

The assessment tool has two separate ratings for the levels of action and alignment, as shown in the following tables. Each table has a rating scale from 0–4 and an explanation of the level.

RATING THE LEVEL OF ACTION

NO ACTION (0)	ASSESSING/PRE-PLANING (1)	PLANNING/ PREPARING (2)	EXECUTION (3)	INCREASING SCOPE/SCALE (4)
No action commitment is made that focuses on • Outcomes, benchmarks • Actors (direct reports or peers, program recipients, superiors, or external partners) • Personal leadership development	The action commitment focuses on the collection or sharing of information, including • Collecting baseline information and data • Understanding underlying issues and factors • Sharing general information to increase awareness of the problem but without the expectation of influencing the outcomes/result • Developing personal leadership skills	The action commitment focuses on the preparatory phase required for successful execution, including • Developing strategies or structured activities • Preparing people, materials, or products required for execution • Meeting with others to leverage contributions to achieving results • Joining strategic partners who will make a direct contribution • Collecting information or data to assess the needs of a population or to strengthen strategies	The action commitment focuses on implementation of strategies/activities/ tactics. This involves action that has a direct impact • Implementing activities to improve the well-being of a population • Preparing strategic partners to make a direct contribution • Using information to assess the effectiveness of strategies • Providing information to target populations for their use	The action commitment focuses on strengthening actions or taking actions to scale. These commitments might include • Restructuring strategies for better impact • Expanding the scope or scale within the group, agency, or community • Expanding the scope or scale to broaden reach across agencies or communities

RATING THE LEVEL OF ALIGNMENT

NO ALIGNMENT (0)	LOW ALIGNMENT (1)	MODERATE	HIGH ALIGNMENT (3)	ALIGNMENT WITH OTHERS OUTSIDE OF ORIGINAL SCOPE (4)
Actions are not connected to • Results • Goals • Strategies • Interests of other leaders • Development needs of leaders	Actions are aligned with • Meeting development needs of leaders • Supporting the structure of a team • Building basic understanding of agreed-upon results • Connecting with individuals to build familiarity • Joining new people without specifying role and contributions • Gaining deeper understanding of other leaders' perspectives, values, resources, and interests	Actions are aligned with • A broad vision and strategic direction • The need to build capacity in self and others • Agreed-upon preliminary actions • Strengthening relationships and resolving conflicts • Accepting the distribution of work to accomplish strategies based on common agreements	Actions are aligned with • Agreed-upon strategies and actions • An assessment of the impact of actions and performance to inform decisions and accelerate results • Leveraging relationships on behalf of results, strategy, or performance • Leaders holding themselves and others accountable for commitments • Holding a part/ whole mental model	Actions are taken to link and connect • The actions of others for greater impact • The trust and the resilience of relationships to support taking the risks necessary to make the changes to execute effective strategies

Getting and Staying in High Alignment and High Action

Once leaders have used the High Action/High Alignment Assessment Tool to assess their own level of action and alignment and/or given feedback to other leaders, the ratings can be displayed to indicate progress and identify opportunities for more leaders to be in high action and high alignment. The table below shows an example of how the rating is applied to an action commitment; in this case, to implement a shared strategy between the elementary school and the Daycare Association to improve the quality of educational activities in daycare centers.

EXAMPLE RATINGS OF ACTION AND ALIGNMENT

MEETING #2	MAY 2013
Action Commitment Made By	Joe P., elementary school principal, in cooperation with Riva S., director, Daycare Association
Action Commitment	Five daycare providers will be enrolled by the end of next month into the pre-K quality instructional program offered by the school district. Program completion includes workshop and follow-up mentoring to support implementation of best practices.
Rating	Alignment rating: High (3); Action rating: High (3)
Progress Update	After two months, all five daycare providers attended the workshop and are receiving follow-up mentoring. Best practices have been implemented in 60 percent of all pre-K classrooms.
Performance Measures Used to Track Contribution to Result	Performance measure progress at two months: How much: 100 percent of daycare providers completing program How well: 60 percent of classrooms implementing best practices What difference: % children entering school ready to learn — to be assessed in six months when children enter kindergarten.

An Excel-based tool, based on research lead by Dr. Victoria Goddard-Truitt and developed for use by participants by Dr. Robert D. Pillsbury, can be used to capture the action commitment ratings and to display the ratings in a way that supports problem solving, accountability, and increased collaborative leadership efficacy.[15]

The figures on pages 176–177 are examples from Marion County Indianapolis of the data displays produced by using the High Action/High Alignment Assessment Tool. The information was presented to the LAP participants at each session. Using RBF and the other results-based leadership competencies, LAP members used the data to strengthen their action and alignment to implement strategies.

PRACTICE: INTRODUCING AND USING HIGH ACTION/HIGH ALIGNMENT ASSESSMENT TOOL

- What do the data tell you about the progress toward high action/high alignment?
- How might you use this information to strengthen what you do, how you do it, and with whom you do it?
- What will you do next?
- What might you see in the data a month from now that will let you know if you are improving in your ability to be in high alignment and high action?

The displays present information on the number of commitments made by session for trend line analysis; the percentage of action commitments kept (pie charts) enabling the comparison of two points in time; the ratings by session of the strength of action and the strength of alignment for each session; and a bubble graph showing the relative scale of the number of action commitments at different levels of action and alignment.

This information was generated by the Automatic Action Commitment Rating Tool, which can be incorporated into the Accountability Walk Meeting Design and Walk the Talk Meeting Design to give participants useful information about the opportunities to strengthen their work together.

MARION COUNTY ACTION COMMITMENTS DATA DISPLAYS

NUMBER OF ACTION COMMITMENTS (HOW MUCH)

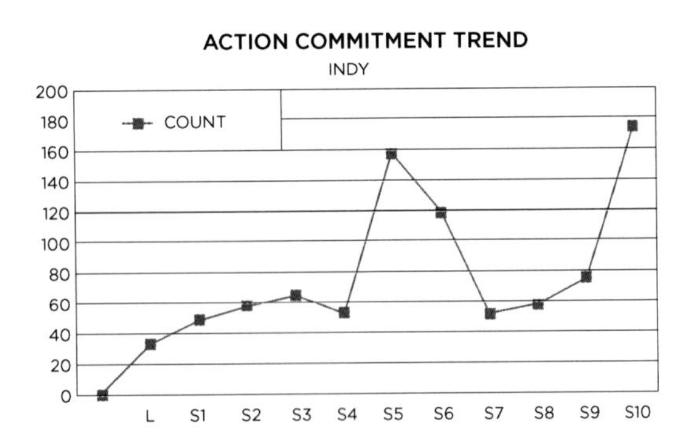

PERCENTAGE OF ACTION COMMITMENTS KEPT (HOW WELL)

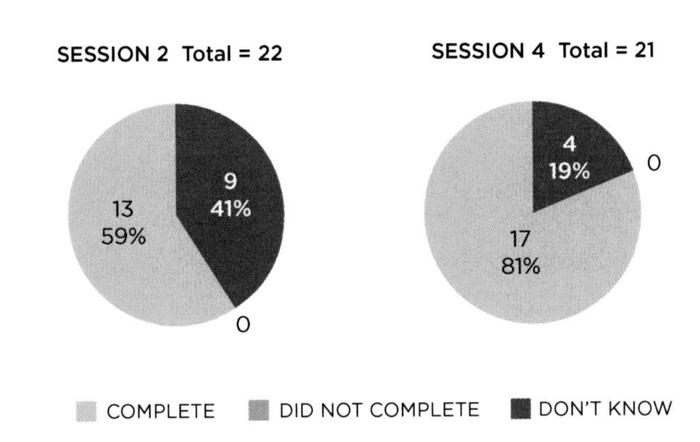

MARION COUNTY HIGH ACTION/HIGH ALIGNMENT DATA DISPLAYS

TREND OVER TIME STRENGTH OF ACTION
(HOW WELL)

ACTION RATING BY SESSION

INDY

200
150
100
50
0

L S1 S2 S3 S4 S5 S6 S7 S8 S9 S10

■ HIGHEST
■ HIGH
■ MEDIUM
■ LOW

TREND OVER TIME STRENGTH OF ALIGNMENT
(HOW WELL)

ALIGNMENT RATING BY SESSION

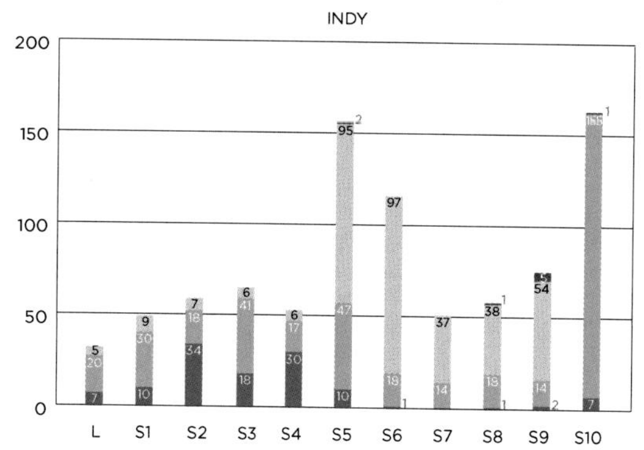

POINT-IN-TIME COMMITMENTS AT DIFFERENT
LEVELS OF ACTION AND ALIGNMENT

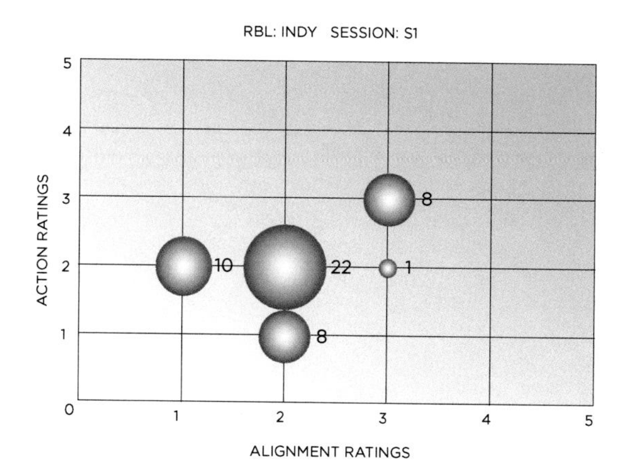

PARTICIPANT PRACTICE GUIDE 6.2: USE RBF SKILLS TO WORK COLLABORATIVELY TO ACCELERATE PROGRESS TOWARD RESULTS

As a participant, you can use all the RBF competencies and skills to work in collaboration to accelerate the progress toward population-level results. This table presents a range of things you can do as a participant.

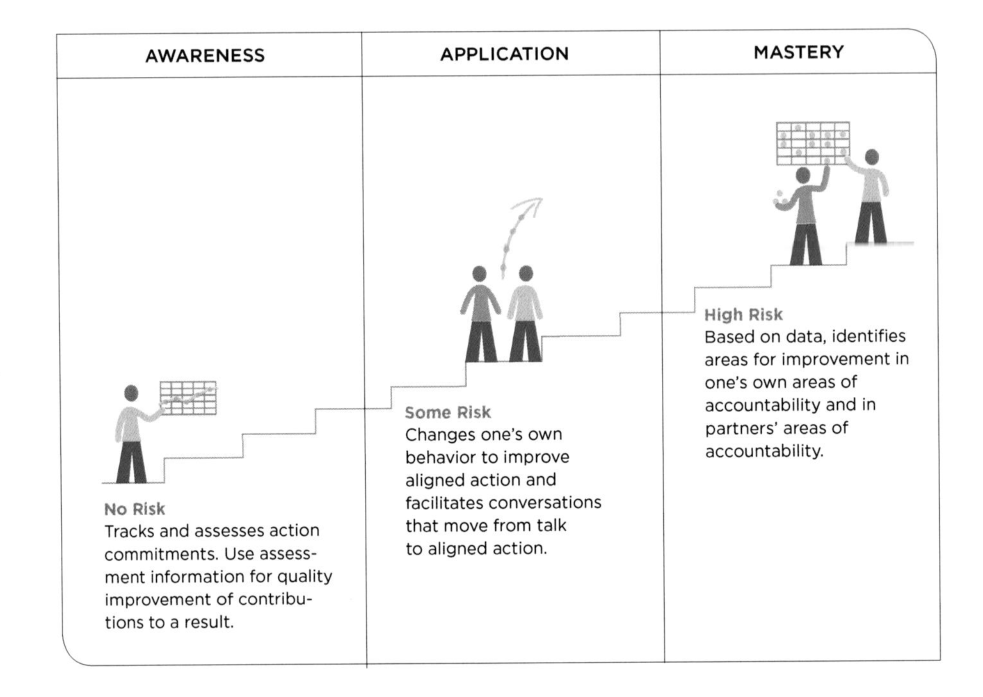

NOTES:

[1] Jones. *Major Growth Processes in Groups*. Pfieffer Library. Vol. 13, 2nd edition. Jossey-Bass/ Pfieffer. 1998.

[2] http://www.datacenter.kidscount.org

[3] Friedman (2009). *Trying Hard Is Not Good Enough: How to Produce Measurable Results for Customers and Communities.*

[4] The Annie E. Casey Foundation. *Improving School Readiness in DeKalb. County, Georgia*. 2010. Retrieved from www.aecf.org.

[5] Responsibility charting clarifies accountability and authority in role by classifying for specific decisions whether a person in that role is responsible for a decision, is informed of a decision, is consulted on a decision or approves a decision. *Introduction to Responsibility Charting*. Center for Applied Research (CFAR). 2006.

[6] Chawla. *Ten Conversations*. The OCL Group. www.tenconversations.com.

[7] Revell and Meriwether. The Performance Partnership Model to smoking cessation: Lessons learned by the Smoking Cessation Leadership Center. *Health Promotion Practice*. Vol. 12, No. 6, Supplement 2. 2011.

[8] There is a growing body of literature correlating physical movement with improved cognition and reduced stress. Ratey and Loehr. The positive impact of physical activity on cognition during adulthood. *Review of Neuroscience*. Vol. 22. 2011.

[9] Other designs that incorporate movement include Open Space Technology and Future Search.

[10] From the beginning it is important to have information that puts the population in context, e.g., county population compared to state population or state population compared to national population.

[11] Pillsbury, Goddard-Truitt, and Littlefield. *Cross-Sector Performance Accountability: Making Aligned Contributions to Improve Community Wellbeing*. Panel presentation at the American Society for Public Administration Conference. Miami. 2009.

[12] Littlefield and O'Brien. *Policymaking Through Collaborative Networks: Issues of Accountability and Performance*. Poster presented at the annual conference for the Association for Public Policy Analysis and Management. Boston. 2010.

[13] Pillsbury, Goddard-Truitt, and Littlefield. *Cross-Sector Performance Accountability.*

[14] O'Brien, Littlefield, and Goddard-Truitt. A matter of leadership: Connecting a grantmaker's investments in collaborative leadership development to community results. *The Foundation Review*. Vol. 5, No. 1. 2013.

[15] Rating data can be easily displayed and analyzed using the Excel HA/HA Assessment Tool found at www.rbl-apps.com.

USING DATA TO IMPROVE PRACTICE

CONCEPTS IN THIS CHAPTER

USING DATA TO INFORM YOUR OWN PRACTICE

DATA-INFORMED RBF COACHING

Using RBF advanced skills with mastery opens up many possibilities for further development, innovation and creativity. It also allows groups to work by design, consciously and intentionally moving to results. This work is continuous, however, and demands continuous improvement for results to be achieved. This final section will equip you with ways to improve your practice with data and to hone your skills as an RBF coach so that you can help improve the practice of others.

> **Continuous improvement:** using data in ongoing efforts to achieve effective practice

CONCEPTS IN THIS CHAPTER

Used well, RBF's 22 skills, organized into six competencies with a scaffolded development path, create consciously shared mental models, behaviors, and values that move groups from talk to action and produce results together. At the mastery level, the skills are held with unconscious competence and fluidity of practice. This makes what once was complex and difficult simple to do. At that level of internalized competence, there is a freedom that further contributes to a cycle of learning, growth, and adaptation.

The melding of discipline and freedom may seem paradoxical; however, as Jeanne Carbonetti observed, mastery is based on the premise that one is "learning what you can do so deeply that you develop automatic responses. Thus one is free to expand in any number of ways. Playfulness, then, is the ability to respond with the newness of a child's wonder and the skills of a practiced adult."[1]

Achieving mastery of the RBF advanced skills requires using data to improve your own practice and working to improve the practice of others as an RBF coach.

USING DATA TO INFORM YOUR OWN PRACTICE

In today's world of explosive knowledge growth across increasingly interdisciplinary fields, it is a major challenge to practice skills with fidelity and achieve predictable, desired outcomes at the scale of population well-being. For example, in the health care sector, hospitals strive to do simple things well and consistently, like hand washing, and complex things consistently well, like hip replacements. Positive health outcomes require all who touch and support patients to do both the simple and the complex tasks to practice standards. Failure to practice with fidelity contributes to health problems and complications caused by the medical treatment, including elevated death rates. However, the development and use of meaningful data and the commitment by all involved to practice with fidelity and continuously improve are contributing to better outcomes in some settings.

EVERYTHING SHOULD BE AS SIMPLE AS IT CAN BE, BUT NOT SIMPLER.

— ALBERT EINSTEIN

Medicine is a mature field, benefiting from an enormous investment in developing, testing, and refining the use of data to improve practice. Facilitation in general, and Results Based Facilitation in particular, is at best an emergent field, where data-informed practice is in its infancy. However, due to RBF's design, anyone practicing Results Based Facilitation has the opportunity to gather and use information to improve the quality of practice and contribute more effectively to achieving results.

RBF is intentionally designed as a fractal — a common structure of information at every level, from meeting results, to program or neighborhood results, to community population results. As a practitioner, you can gather information that enables you to track consistent data sets that can be used to improve practice. For example, using the competencies in meeting preparation and design produces information about the percentage of meetings that achieve meeting results, the percentage of action commitments that are made and kept, the percentage of action commitments that are high alignment/high action, the percentage of programs that are making a difference for their populations, and whether the scope and scale of program implementation is sufficient to make a measurable difference in a community population result. Collecting, tracking, and analyzing this information make it possible to determine what RBF practices contribute to people's capacity to make progress.

IF YOU DO IT, YOU CAN;
IF YOU DON'T, YOU CAN'T.

- SHINAGAWA TETSUZAN

RBF has benefited and continues to benefit from being implemented within organizations as part of results-based leadership programs and in multisector environments involving many organizations, as part of Leadership in Action Programs and Performance Partnership Summits. This decades-long experience with implementation provides examples of how information can be used to improve practice. The information collected during implementation illuminates the connection between the skill levels of teams and individuals and their capacity to execute strategies successfully. This type of data-informed practice and quality improvement increases the probability that the work of groups contributes to measurably improved results.

The measures are the byproducts of implementing the practice method. For example, during implementation, information is generated about skill levels as people assess and develop skills. Information about meeting results and assessing whether results are accomplished are part of the design and execution of meetings. Making action commitments, tracking completion of action commitments, and assessing the quality of action commitments (high action/high alignment) are part of the group's work. Identifying and tracking performance measures ensure strategy execution and efficacy are contributing to improved outcomes. Using population-level information on results to connect strategy execution and results achievement is at the heart of the RBF method. Because data generation is a byproduct of the work, data collection and analysis can be accomplished at no or low cost, using a straightforward format such as Excel analysis templates.

To collect and use the data, you must document and track meeting results and action commitments.[2] Using that information in combination with the best available data on program performance and community-population results provides a context for continuous quality improvement of RBF practice and the execution of strategies that work. The following table illustrates how data informs practice.

PRACTICE: USING DATA FOR IMPROVEMENT

- List some opportunities to use data at each level (meeting, group, strategy execution, population result) to improve practice.
- What is the simplest step you can take now to use data at any one of these levels?

HOW DATA INFORMS PRACTICE

EXAMPLE: A Teachable Method for Changing Unhealthy Behavior (Small Business Innovation Research Grant, 2007)	
DESCRIPTION	**DATA USE TO INFORM PRACTICE**
Research on the effectiveness of developing the skills of an implementation team to convene and facilitate Performance Partnership Summits (PPS)	Research demonstrated that people in teams could learn RBF skills and use them to convene Performance Partnership Summits for smoking cessation. Most of the teams were able to successfully conduct summits that produced action plans. The action plans were executed, and the teams tracked how their strategies contributed to an increase in referrals to the telephone quit line. Referrals to the quit line are positively correlated with successful quit attempts, and that measure was used as a leading indicator of contribution to the population result of reducing smoking prevalence. The skill development methods and the PPS design can be used in a wide range of settings. The data produced from the skill development, the execution of the summit, and the execution of action plan strategies provide a robust data set for practice improvement.
EXAMPLE: Leadership in Action Programs	
Research on the effectiveness of the implementation team and the participants using RBF as part of a collaborative leadership competency	Research findings support the hypothesis that RBF-supported groups and LAP implementation contribute to population-level results. The research findings identified the practices that make a difference (such as holding transparent conversations about accountability) and validated the importance of making and keeping action commitments. The research also indicates that the use of the skills by the implementation team and the participants is positively correlated with the group's capacity to produce results and sustain its efforts. The LAP design and modifications are used in a wide range of settings. The Maryland State Department of Education, in partnership with the Annie E. Casey Foundation, has worked to develop the RBF skills of implementation teams in every jurisdiction in the state as one of several strategies to measurably improve the number and percentage of children entering school ready to learn.

EXAMPLE: Results-Based Leadership Programs within Organizations	
DESCRIPTION	**DATA USE TO INFORM PRACTICE**
Descriptive information and program performance data indicate that using RBF skills as part of a broader implementation of results-based leadership competencies equips leadership teams to develop and execute strategies	The Baltimore City Department of Social Services participated in an Annie E. Casey Foundation results-based leadership program for a number of years. The executive team has applied many of the elements of the advanced skills — including making and tracking action commitments, using the Accountability Pathway, and using MBTI insights — to inform an understanding of how to build leadership skills at the person, person-in-role, and role-in-system levels. The participants in the program perceived it to support their ability to implement the strategies that have led to a dramatic and measurable improvement in child well-being measures for the child welfare system population. The results-based leadership program designs, including the implementation team's and the participants' use of RBF, were well received and perceived to contribute to the organization's enhanced ability to make measurable improvements in program performance measures. One critical success factor has been the willingness and commitment of the most senior leadership to adopt, model, practice, and coach the skills within their organizations.

You can use the methods and approaches like these in your own practice. The transferability of the methods and approaches depends on your role in your own system and your level of mastery of RBF and other leadership competencies. To gain the benefit of data-informed practice, analyze your daily activities and identify opportunities where — in role — you can develop and use data to continuously improve your ability to contribute to results.

DATA-INFORMED RBF COACHING

As you practice the advanced skills, you may find yourself coaching others in developing their skills. Using observational and assessment data in a coaching role contributes to your own development and the development of others. The data used in RBF coaching come from three sources: a self-assessment of RBF skills done by the coachee, assessment of RBF skills by the coach based on observation of the coachee during practice sessions or actual facilitations, and review of the documentation developed by the coachee in the design, preparation, execution, and follow-up of meetings.

In RBF coaching, the RBF Competency Assessment (in either the electronic version found at www.rbl-apps.com or the paper version found in this book) is first done by the coachee as a self-assessment. The coach then discusses the self-assessment and shares his or her coach's assessment based on observational data. During that discussion, the coach and the coachee use data to develop a common perspective on the current skill level of the coachee and the practice methods that the coachee will use to build skills. The commitments to practice are included in the coachee's Individual Development Plan. As the coachee implements the development plan, he or she and the coach bring data from observation and documentation to gauge progress toward mastery and further inform practice methods.

Continuously focusing on the data that can inform practice is central to the success of the RBF coaching approach. The following are some tips for using data in the RBF coaching role.

TIPS: DEPLOYING RBF SKILLS IN THE COACHING ROLE

- Always get permission to coach.
- Introduce SBI, and coach people to use SBI with integrity and consistency. SBI is an effective tool for building the foundation competency of Hold Roles and a primary source of data for improved practice.
- Model and label the use of skills in role to provide experiential data to improve practice.
- Resist the urge to teach and tell. Consistently model and label, giving work back to the group.
- Provide skill-focused feedback using the competency assessments for each skill in the sequence of skill development: Hold Roles, Hold Conversations, Hold Groups, Hold 3R Meetings, Hold Mental Models, and Hold Action and Results.
- Encourage others to do self-assessments of skills and to use that information to create an Individual Development Plan. Use your coaching role to support that development plan.

COACHING PRACTICES AT EVERY LEVEL OF DEVELOPMENT

In a coaching role, you can enhance the deployment of RBF skills by paying attention and providing data to calibrate the developmental level of those you are coaching. The coaching practices that support RBF skill development at each level of mastery are shown in the next table.

RBF COACHING PRACTICES

STEPS TO MASTERY	COACH'S ROLE
AWARENESS	See and accurately assess the skill level of coachees using the RBF Competency Assessment. Provide data using SBI to illuminate the differential impact of a coachee's current behavior or choices. Identify alternate choices regarding use of the skill, knowledge application, or behavior. Provide data to inform a coachee's understanding of what might be standing in the way of making the behavior changes necessary to improve skill. Provide support so that coachees have an increased capacity to take risks and try something new.
APPLICATION	Encourage the conscious use of skills by modeling and labeling. Support self-assessment and do a coach's skill assessment to provide feedback on a coachee's skill level. Ensure that coachees are using SBI to refine their use of the skill. Enhance their use of self-reflection and journaling to identify practice options. Provide direction in use of the skill informed by the coachees' MBTI preferences. Invite coachees to replicate the coach's modeling of the skill. Generate a hypothesis about what might be preventing coachees from changing their attitudes or behaviors necessary for skill mastery. Share your hypothesis. Structure the work to ensure that coachees commit to repetitive practice. Provide coachees with methods for daily, deliberate practice to sustain skills.
MASTERY	Provide learning opportunities to integrate skills into their repertoire of responses. Encourage them to use RBF skills in the participant role to accelerate their ability to access the skills rapidly in real time. Support the coachees in tracking progress toward meeting results as a source of information for continued development. Expand their awareness of opportunities for further development.

PRACTICE: THE COACH'S ROLE

Use this three-step process and EQs to practice the coaching role.
When you see a skill gap in someone you are working with, ask permission to coach. • May I coach you?
Coach using EQs so people can see the gap between their current skill level and the skill level needed to achieve the meeting result. • What are you experiencing now? • How is what you are doing now working for you? • What is the skill that can help you now?
Coach so people say what they will do to close the gap. • What will help you use that skill? • What might you do?

COMPETENCY ASSESSMENT OF RBF SKILLS

Using data to improve practice and coaching of RBF skills is helpful in attaining mastery, especially if done in the context of your own skill assessment and development. Take the time to self-assess your skill level for each of the 22 RBF skills in this table and then develop your own Individual Development Plan.

COMPETENCY ASSESSMENT OF RESULTS BASED FACILITATION SKILLS

RBF COMPETENCIES AND SKILLS	SKILL LEVEL/CONTINUUM		
	AWARENESS	APPLICATION	MASTERY
HOLD ROLES: *Be aware of and make choices about roles that contribute to achieving results.*			
Use B/ART to define and differentiate roles as they relate to meeting results			
Use B/ART to understand group dynamics and achieve meeting results			
Hold neutral facilitator role			
Give the work back to the group			
HOLD CONVERSATIONS: *Listen with openness, curiosity, and attentiveness to frame dialogues that achieve meeting results.*			
Demonstrate appreciative openness			
Use Context Statements, Effective Questions, and Listen Fors			
HOLD GROUPS: *Support groups in having focused conversations that move to results.*			
Use flip chart to display the group's work			
Sequence			
Summarize			
Synthesize			
Check in and check out			
HOLD 3R MEETINGS: *Use the 3R framework to design and facilitate meetings that move groups from talk to action.*			
Use the 3Rs to design the meeting			
Use the 3Rs in the meeting to achieve results			
HOLD MENTAL MODELS: *Use a repertoire of perspectives that contribute to achieving meeting results.*			
Use proposal-based decision making to move from talk to action			
Use conversations to develop convergence			
Name and address barriers to convergence			
Make and help others make action commitments			
Be and help others be accountable for action commitments			
Observe and respond to group dynamics			
Assess and address conflict			
HOLD ACTION AND RESULTS: *Make a difference in programs and community populations.*			
Be accountable in role for contributions to results			
Use RBF skills to work collaboratively to accelerate progress toward results			

PRACTICE: ANALYZING OPPORTUNITIES TO SUSTAIN MASTERY

1. Look at your assessment of all six competencies and 22 skills in the Competency Assessment. Are there any skills where you are not at the mastery level? If so, focus on those skills in your Individual Development Plan.
2. Where in your daily work can you deploy RBF skills in a variety of roles? Identify roles where you can use data to inform practice and to experiment with the RBF coaching role.
3. Use the format of the IDP (see below) to identify the skill(s) you want to develop and, specifically, where you might use data or pick up the coach's role to continue on your path to mastery.
4. Pay attention to the quality of your practice and identify what works for you in sustaining and growing mastery. Review your IDP frequently (weekly or monthly) to record and note the impact of your practice and incorporate the principles of deliberative practice into what you do.

INDIVIDUAL DEVELOPMENT PLAN: SUSTAINING MASTERY

Based on your assessment of all the RBF skills and your interest in using data and coaching to sustain your growth, you have an opportunity to create an IDP for sustaining mastery.

Skill/Present level	What will I practice to build skill?	Where and how will I practice daily?	What is the desired impact of improving the skill?

PRACTICE: IMPLEMENTING THE INDIVIDUAL DEVELOPMENT PLAN

Review your IDP and reflect on the following questions to increase the likelihood that you will move forward and implement your plan:

- What strengths will support you in following through on this plan?
- Who can support and challenge you to be accountable for continuing your development and sustaining mastery?
- How can you notice the benefits of your practice and sustain your motivation to practice?
- What do you need to do to use data to inform your practice?
- Where are the opportunities to practice RBF skills in the coach's role?

RESOURCES FOR CONTINUED LEARNING

You can find Book One and Book Two, other materials, and tools at www.rbl-apps.com. Many of the agendas, templates, and worksheets from the examples, practices, and tips have been posted on the website.

In addition, support for the practice and development of the foundation and advanced skills can be found through the Results Based Facilitation Network. The network's mission is to support the application and integration of RBF skills. Connect to this network at www.rbfnetwork.com.

NOTES:

[1] Carbonetti. *The Tao of Watercolor, A revolutionary Approach to the Practice of Painting*. Watson-Guptil Publications. 1998.

[2] The checklists for conveners, facilitators, and participants found in *Results Based Facilitation: Book One — Foundation Skills* (pp. 154–155) generate the data on meetings useful for skill development and quality improvement.

COMPETENCY ASSESSMENTS AND IDPS

An IDP is included after each of the competency self-assessments to support you in designing skill-focused practice for each skill.

Hold Roles: Be aware of and make choices about roles that contribute to achieving results.

SKILL 1.1: USE B/ART TO DEFINE AND DIFFERENTIATE ROLES

AWARENESS	APPLICATION	MASTERY
Understands the concept of B/ART • *Do I understand the Person-Role-System framework?* • *Do I know and can I name my own B/ART in my daily work and in meetings?* →	Consciously establishes role in groups • *Do I comfortably name my role in meetings?* • *Do I understand the differences in my various roles?* →	Uses awareness of B/ART to contribute to meeting results and move from talk to action • *Do I consciously make choices to hold my stated role during a meeting?* • *Do I use my understanding of B/ART to align my actions with others to achieve results?* →

SKILL 1.2: USE B/ART TO UNDERSTAND GROUP DYNAMICS AND ACHIEVE MEETING RESULTS

AWARENESS	APPLICATION	MASTERY
Applies the concept of B/ART to understand group dynamics • *Do I use the Person-Role-System framework to assess the B/ART of meeting participants and consider how their B/ART will affect their participation?* →	Applies B/ART insights to assist groups in identifying and achieving meeting results • *Do I clarify or help the group clarify the alignment of meeting results with the B/ART of the participants?* • *Do I model awareness of B/ART in meetings?* →	Accurately identifies B/ART issues and brings these issues to the group's awareness • *Do I see how B/ART is affecting the group's work and then use labeling, inquiry, or hypotheses to illuminate the issues for the group?* • *Do I map who in the group holds the B/ART to address issues, make decisions, and move to action?* →

SKILL 1.3: HOLD NEUTRAL FACILITATOR ROLE

AWARENESS	APPLICATION	MASTERY
Knows the role of neutral facilitator and is aware of what it takes not to seek one's own personal agenda • *Do I employ specific practices to maintain the neutral facilitator role and not use the authority of the facilitator to pursue my own agenda?*	Holds the neutral role most of the time • *Do I refrain from using my expertise or authority to influence group decisions?* • *Do I recognize when I am not holding the neutral facilitator role?*	Consistently holds the neutral role • *Do I have a repertoire of practices to acknowledge lapses and return to neutral?*
→	→	→

SKILL 1.4: GIVE THE WORK BACK TO THE GROUP

AWARENESS	APPLICATION	MASTERY
Understands the role of the facilitator in giving the work back to the group • *Do I refer questions about the work back to the group?* • *Do I patiently hold the neutral facilitator role while the group takes time to find its own solutions and make its own decisions?*	Applies a repertoire of methods to give the work back to the group • *Do I recognize pivotal moments when to give the work back to the group?* • *Do I go to the balcony to invite group awareness and insights for forward movement?*	Consistently gives the work back to the group • *Do I use observation, inquiry, and reflective practice to invite the group to move forward?* • *Do I use humor, physical activity, intuition, spiritual awareness, and analytical insights to illuminate the group's capacity to do its hardest work?*
→	→	→

IDP: HOLD ROLES

SKILL/ PRESENT LEVEL	WHAT WILL I PRACTICE TO BUILD SKILL?	WHERE AND HOW WILL I PRACTICE DAILY?	WHAT IS THE DESIRED IMPACT OF IMPROVING THE SKILL?

Hold Conversations: Listen with openness, curiosity, and attentiveness to frame dialogues that achieve meeting results.

SKILL 2.1: DEMONSTRATE APPRECIATIVE OPENNESS

AWARENESS	APPLICATION	MASTERY
Understands the primacy of listening as a skill; is aware of and monitors own listening behavior • *Am I genuinely curious about the conversation and what is being said?* • *Am I aware of when I am consciously listening and when I am not?* • *Do I make conscious choices about when to speak and when to listen?*	Attends to participants to ensure all ideas and voices are heard • *Am I aware of filters that may influence what is heard and not heard for myself and others?* • *Do I use strategies to remain open, appreciative, and in the moment?* • *Do I use nonverbal cues of attentiveness and interest?* • *Do I ask Effective Questions (EQs) to gain insight into assumptions, facts, and points of view and verify understanding of what was said?*	Consistently demonstrates interest in conversations of others throughout the meeting • *Do I keep my own interests and interpretations in check (be neutral) when I am listening?* • *Do I use a variety of strategies to engage the speaker (e.g., silence, non-verbal, EQs)?* • *Do I quickly notice lack of listening, acknowledge the lack, and self-correct?* • *Do I maintain focused listening for the duration of a meeting?*
→	→	→

SKILL 2.2: USE CONTEXT STATEMENTS, EFFECTIVE QUESTIONS, AND LISTEN FORS

AWARENESS	APPLICATION	MASTERY
Understands and uses CS, EQs, LFs as a core technique for facilitating • *Do I set a context to focus a conversation on a meeting result?* • *Do I prepare EQs in advance to engage people, focus discussion, and move conversations forward toward meeting results?* • *Do I integrate a CS with an EQ and link it to an LF?*	Frames the work (purpose, focus, boundary) with a CS, EQ, and LF in the moment • *Do I use EQs (open ended, inquisitive) to engage people, focus conversations, and move conversations forward toward meeting results?* • *Do I listen for responses and incorporate them into the group's work by setting another CS and linked EQ?*	Regularly uses CS, EQs, and LFs to accelerate a group's ability to achieve meeting results • *Do I use CS, EQs, LFs to understand the group's experience of pace and adjust the pace to sustain maximum engagement?* • *Do I use awareness of differential impact (as informed by MBTI and B/ART) in CS, EQs, LFs?* • *Do I flexibly modify or change a CS, EQs, LFs in the moment based on my reading of the group?*
→	→	→

IDP: HOLD CONVERSATIONS

SKILL/ PRESENT LEVEL	WHAT WILL I PRACTICE TO BUILD SKILL?	WHERE AND HOW WILL I PRACTICE DAILY?	WHAT IS THE DESIRED IMPACT OF IMPROVING THE SKILL?

Hold Groups: Support groups in having focused conversations that move to results.

SKILL 3.1: USE FLIP CHART TO DISPLAY THE GROUP'S WORK

AWARENESS	APPLICATION	MASTERY
Displays group's work accurately • *Do people read what is captured? Is it accurate?* • *Do I use the Context Statement, Effective Questions and Listen Fors to inform what is captured?* • *Does the speaker recognize what was said in what I captured?* • *Do I easily capture parallel conversations and accurately record decisions?*	Displays group's work to focus on meeting results • *Do my charts serve as a tool to recap work for summary?* • *Do I use techniques (color, underlining, symbols, spacing, lines) to highlight, track, and distinguish conversations?* • *Do people who were not in the conversation know its content from what is charted?* • *Do group members look at and refer to my charts?*	Displays group's work to accelerate progress toward achieving meeting results • *Do my charts support the building of proposals and making decisions?* • *Does my charting support synthesis and movement toward meeting results?* • *Do my charts support accountability for action during and after the meeting?*
→	→	→

SKILL 3.2: SEQUENCE

AWARENESS	APPLICATION	MASTERY
Understands and practices sequencing speakers • *Do I establish who speaks when in a way that is clear to the group and enables participants to relax and listen?*	Understands and practices sequencing topics or ideas • *Do I recognize different topics or conversations, label them, and invite the group to choose which conversation to have when?*	Understands and practices sequencing the work of meetings and meeting results • *Do I recognize opportunities for proposals, decisions, and commitments to action and invite the group to sequence them during the meeting to accomplish meeting results?*
→	→	→

SKILL 3.3: SUMMARIZE

AWARENESS	APPLICATION	MASTERY
Remembers and can list ideas from short conversations • *Do I have a way to practice hearing, accurately remembering, and restating a list of ideas that emerges from a conversation?*	Remembers and can list categories of topics from medium to long conversations • *Do I concisely and accurately describe the content of conversations?* • *Do my summaries move a group forward toward the meeting results?*	Remembers and can briefly list process description or meeting results from a whole meeting • *Do I mentally review and then concisely state what has occurred in the meeting and the results achieved?*
→	→	→

SKILL 3.4: SYNTHESIZE

AWARENESS	APPLICATION	MASTERY
Briefly states the meaning of short conversations • *Do I listen for the central meaning of the conversation and state that concisely?* • *Do I use basic methods of synthesis (comparison, themes, part/whole connections) in listening for and concisely stating where the group is in their work?*	Integrates and briefly states the meaning of a number of conversations or longer conversations • *Does the group affirm my synthesis and use it to move forward to meeting results?* • *Do I use images and symbolism to help the group own the results of a whole meeting?*	Integrates and briefly states the meaning for a whole meeting • *Does my synthesis accelerate the group's work?* • *Does the group use my synthesis to move to action?*
→	→	→

SKILL 3.5: CHECK IN AND CHECK OUT

AWARENESS	APPLICATION	MASTERY
Understands and uses check-in and check-out • *Does my check-in establish a foundation for the group to own the achievement of meeting results?* • *Do my check-outs assess meeting results and move people to action?*	Connects group members to each other and the meeting results • *Do I consider the relationships of the people to each other and the work in framing the check-in and check-out?* • *Do my check-ins and check-outs illuminate B/ART and make it more likely that members will contribute their resources to the meeting results?* • *Do my check-outs address whether meeting results were achieved and elicit how group members felt about the meeting experience?*	Reads group to inform check-in and check-out • *Do I use the technique of checking in and out flexibly during a series of conversations, or do I facilitate transitions from one meeting result to another?* • *Do I use check-in or check-out to explore hypotheses about group dynamics or make the group aware of group dynamics?* • *Do my check-ins and check-outs at the beginning and end of meetings and the beginning and end of conversations move a group to action?*
→	→	→

IDP: HOLD GROUPS

SKILL/ PRESENT LEVEL	WHAT WILL I PRACTICE TO BUILD SKILL?	WHERE AND HOW WILL I PRACTICE DAILY?	WHAT IS THE DESIRED IMPACT OF IMPROVING THE SKILL?

Hold 3R Meetings: Use the 3R framework to design and facilitate meetings that move groups from talk to action.

SKILL 4.1: USE THE 3Rs TO DESIGN THE MEETING

AWARENESS	APPLICATION	MASTERY
Understands the interrelationship and use of the 3Rs as they relate to the design of a meeting agenda • *Do I clearly articulate the results for meetings (specific, observable, measurable)?* • *Do the proposed meeting results contribute to a program or organizational result?*	Uses EQs and LFs to elicit what the group wants to accomplish, who is and needs to be involved, and what people have and can bring to achieve the desired results • *Do I use B/ART in analyzing the composition of groups to explore who might be invited to contribute to meeting results?* • *Do I assess if those invited can accomplish the meeting results with their relationships and resources?*	Designs the meeting agenda and environment for the group to own its work by applying the 3Rs • *Do I align meeting preparation and design with the desired results?* • *Do I ensure that the required resources are accessible at the meeting?* • *Do I recognize and encourage people aligning their resources to achieve results?*
→	→	→

SKILL 4.2: USE THE 3Rs IN THE MEETING TO ACHIEVE RESULTS

AWARENESS	APPLICATION	MASTERY
Understands the interrelationships and use of the 3Rs to help groups achieve results • *Do the meeting results align with the meeting purpose?* • *Do all meeting results add up to the purpose?*	Uses EQs and LFs with the group to elicit 3Rs during the meeting • *Do the CS, EQs, and LFs achieve the meeting result?*	Creates an environment for the group to own its work by applying the 3Rs. Captures decisions, commitments, etc., in a 3R framework • *Do I use the 3R framework to follow up on meetings to move from talk to action?* • *Do I capture decisions and commitments in terms of who will do what when, how, and with whom, and with what resources?*
→	→	→

IDP: HOLD 3R MEETINGS

SKILL/ PRESENT LEVEL	WHAT WILL I PRACTICE TO BUILD SKILL?	WHERE AND HOW WILL I PRACTICE DAILY?	WHAT IS THE DESIRED IMPACT OF IMPROVING THE SKILL?

Hold Mental Models: Use a repertoire of perspectives that contribute to achieving meeting results.

SKILL 5.1: USE PROPOSAL-BASED DECISION MAKING TO MOVE FROM TALK TO ACTION

AWARENESS	APPLICATION	MASTERY
Understands and uses proposal-based decision making • *Do I make proposals and build on proposals?* • *Do I set a context and ask an Effective Question to elicit proposals?* • *Do I use the rule of thumb to scan levels of support?*	Synthesizes proposals and gives the work back to the group • *Do I concisely introduce the concept of PBDM?* • *Do I label proposals as options?*	Helps groups stay in the hard work of decision making • *Do I attend to pace to support engagement?* • *Do I recognize when a group is not moving forward in decision making?*
→	→	→

SKILL 5.2: USE CONVERSATIONS TO DEVELOP CONVERGENCE

AWARENESS	APPLICATION	MASTERY
Frames conversations that move people toward convergence • *Does my synthesis of the group's work support movement toward convergence?* • *Do I set a context so the group can work with emotion-laden proposals?*	Labels where the group is in the process of convergence and supports forward movement • *Do I share observations about the group and invite others to share theirs?* • *Can I use Effective Questions to move the group forward toward convergence?*	Recognizes, labels, and synthesizes conversations to support the group's ability to make choices about what to do next • *Can I support the group in making choices about the process of decision making?* • *Do I regularly and quickly help groups choose the conversation that will move them forward?*
→	→	→

SKILL 5.3: NAME AND ADDRESS BARRIERS TO CONVERGENCE

AWARENESS	APPLICATION	MASTERY
Names divergent mental models • *Do I label my own mental models and listen for the mental models expressed by group members?* • *Can I use the ladder of inference or the 5Fs (Feelings, Frames, Filters, Facts, Findings) to listen for other people's mental models?* →	Uses mental models to develop solutions and make decisions • *Do I apply the underlying concepts of interest-based negotiation to help the group develop solutions?* • *Do I use the MBTI communication preferences Z model to sequence discussions and move groups toward decisions?* →	Uses a repertoire of mental models to address barriers • *Do I readily identify and shift to another mental model to address barriers?* • *Can I use mental models that do not represent my own world view or values?* →

SKILL 5.4: MAKE AND HELP OTHERS MAKE ACTION COMMITMENTS

AWARENESS	APPLICATION	MASTERY
Understands the intent and form of effective action commitments • *Do I set a context for making public action commitments?* • *Do I Listen For action commitments with a disciplined focus on who, what, and when?* • *Do I support the group in documenting action commitments for future reference?* →	Helps groups commit to action • *Do I help groups manage the change process associated with moving to action?* →	Helps groups align action commitments • *Do I use MBTI awareness to support people making action commitments?* • *Can I use the High Action/High Alignment framework?* →

SKILL 5.5: BE AND HELP OTHERS BE ACCOUNTABLE FOR ACTION COMMITMENTS

AWARENESS	APPLICATION	MASTERY
Understands and uses the Accountability Pathway • *Do I introduce the Accountability Pathway as a method for people to keep commitments to action?* • *Am I comfortable and do I help others become comfortable holding genuine accountability conversations?*	Helps groups hold accountability for action commitments • *Do I use EQs that make it easy for me and others to assess progress along the Accountability Pathway, move to owning action commitments, and make them happen?*	Strengthens the group's capacity to be accountable for action • *Do I label the emotional reactions of myself and others and use EQs to support the group in making and keeping commitments to action?* • *Do I use MBTI awareness to support groups in holding accountability for action?*
→	→	→

SKILL 5.6: OBSERVE AND RESPOND TO GROUP DYNAMICS

AWARENESS	APPLICATION	MASTERY
Maps who is saying what and what role he or she plays in the group • *Do I notice and remember who is saying what when? Their affect? Their body language?* • *Do I see, label, and generate hypotheses about patterns in the group?* • *Do I consistently use the five-step process to create engagement?*	Observes, understands, and responds to patterns of behavior in groups • *Do I respond to group behaviors in ways that give the work back to the group?* • *Do I observe pace and know when to slow down and when to speed up?*	Helps groups move through difficult conversations • *Do I make in-the-moment observations about the group that enable it to move forward?* • *Do I invite group members to make observations about facts and feelings, generate hypotheses, and respond to what they observe in group?*
→	→	→

SKILL 5.7: ASSESS AND ADDRESS CONFLICT

AWARENESS	APPLICATION	MASTERY
Understands own and others' orientation toward conflict • *Do I understand my own and others' orientation toward conflict?* • *Do I accept that conflict is a fact of life that can be addressed and resolved?*	Introduces and applies the Circle of Conflict • *Can I apply the Circle of Conflict to identify sources of conflict?* • *Can I frame conversations that engage people in addressing the sources of conflict?*	Supports groups in addressing conflict and moving to action • *Do I use insights from MBTI awareness to design conversations to address conflict?* • *Do I integrate the application of the Circle of Conflict into PBDM?*
→	→	→

IDP: HOLD MENTAL MODELS

SKILL/ PRESENT LEVEL	WHAT WILL I PRACTICE TO BUILD SKILL?	WHERE AND HOW WILL I PRACTICE DAILY?	WHAT IS THE DESIRED IMPACT OF IMPROVING THE SKILL?

Hold Action and Results: Make a difference in programs and community populations.

SKILL 6.1: BE ACCOUNTABLE IN ROLE FOR CONTRIBUTIONS TO RESULTS

AWARENESS	APPLICATION	MASTERY
Makes contributions to a result • *Do I understand my potential contribution to the result in role and role-in-system?* • *Do I clarify and negotiate B/ART with others to contribute to the result?* →	Is accountable for aligning contributions to a result • *Do I use performance measures to assess and improve my and others' contributions to the result?* • *Do I mobilize my own and others' resources to make progress toward population-level results?* →	Addresses challenges and moves self and others into aligned action • *Do I work to strengthen action and alignment of contributions over time?* • *Do I comfortably exercise heterarchical and hierarchical authority in aligning my contributions with others?* →

SKILL 6.2: USE RBF SKILLS TO WORK COLLABORATIVELY TO ACCELERATE PROGRESS TOWARD RESULTS

AWARENESS	APPLICATION	MASTERY
Convenes, designs, documents, or facilitates meetings that put results in the center of the work • *Do I work as a member of a team to design and execute meetings that move groups to make aligned action commitments to a population-level result?* • *Do I contribute to creating a container for aligned contributions to a result?* →	Convenes, designs, documents, or facilitates meetings where people are in high action and high alignment to make progress toward a result • *Do I ensure that there are 3R meetings that move partners from talk to action that produces results?* • *Do I facilitate conversations that support aligned action?* →	Convenes, designs, documents, or facilitates meetings that sustain accountability for contributions at a scope and scale to accelerate progress toward a result • *Do I persist in the face of uncertainty, or slow or no progress, to implement what works to make population-level change?* • *Do I take risks to challenge others to put results in the center of their work and contribute to population-level change?* →

IDP: HOLD ACTION AND RESULTS

SKILL/ PRESENT LEVEL	WHAT WILL I PRACTICE TO BUILD SKILL?	WHERE AND HOW WILL I PRACTICE DAILY?	WHAT IS THE DESIRED IMPACT OF IMPROVING THE SKILL?

LIST OF PARTICIPANT PRACTICE GUIDES

Each of the skills can be used in the participant role. For easy reference, the following is a list of all Participant Practice Guides.

LIST OF PRACTICES

The following is a list of the practices provided to support skill development. Not every skill in each competency has a practice.

LIST OF TIPS

In addition to practices, for many skills, tips are provided to support your application and use of the skills. As with the exercises, not all skills have tips.

APPENDIX C

TERM	DEFINITION
3Rs (Relationships, Resources, and Results)	Results Based Facilitation's underlying mental model for designing and executing meetings that produce results in programs, organizations, and communities.
5Fs	Feelings, Frames, Filters, Facts, Findings
Accountability Pathway	A mental model for helping people strengthen their ability to keep the commitments they make.
Acknowledge, Rephrase, and Explore (ARE)	A method to give the work back to the group through listening, providing empathetic responses, and asking open-ended questions.
Action Commitment Form	A template for recording and updating what people commit to do to improve a result. The format enables the assessment of both action and alignment and the tracking of completion.
Action Plan	A document to guide the implementation of and accountability for aligned actions to achieve a measurable improvement in a population-level results. The Action Plan contains the following elements: • population, result, indicator, and target for indicator improvement • factor analysis, strategies, performance measures for strategies and performance measure targets, and the action commitments with targets and timeline to implement the Action Plan
Adaptive Challenges	Heifetz term describing changes in behavior, beliefs, habits, or values.
Aligned Action	Complementary, supportive actions that people take together to make measurable progress toward a result.
Balanced Scorecard	A strategic planning and management system developed by Kaplan and Norton to align business activities to the vision and monitor organization performance against strategic goals.

TERM	DEFINITION
Best Alternative to a Negotiated Agreement (BATNA)	An articulation of how a party's interests might be met in the absence of reaching a negotiated agreement.
Boundaries of Authority, Role, and Task (B/ART)	The defined parameters that circumscribe and illuminate who is responsible (authority) for what activity (task) in what capacity in relationship to others and their activities (role).
Check-In	A process to facilitate connections to a person or people and a task. When checked in, people are ready to work together.
Check-Out	A process to facilitate the closing of a meeting or a conversation so people are committed to the next steps, ready to move on, and aware of the progress made toward their own results and the meeting results.
Circle of Conflict	A mental model developed by Christopher W. Moore to assess and address conflict by identifying categories of conflict.
Collaborative Work Cycle	A mental model of how to use meetings to move from talk to accountable, aligned action between meetings.
Composition Analysis	Information about the person, the person-in-role and his or her role in system. The information is used to clarify B/ART and inform hypotheses about group dynamics before, after, and during conversations and meetings.
Context Statement (CS)	A brief phrase or short sentence introducing a conversation that lets people know what the conversation is about.
Differential Impact	The varied reactions people have to a common experience.
Effective Questions (EQs)	Open-ended queries that convey curiosity and an invitation to share focused information relevant to the conversation.
Experiential Learning Cycle	Skill development grounded in a process that allows people to discover and learn what they need and want by reflecting on their own practice experiences, by seeing what their colleagues are doing, by using skills they want to learn, and by receiving feedback and coaching.
Friedman's Results Accountability Framework	Developed by Mark Friedman, a framework for defining and achieving conditions of well-being for programs and whole populations.

TERM	DEFINITION
Going to the Balcony	A mental stance described by Heifetz wherein a person gains perspective by imagining being on a balcony above the situation and looking down at the group dynamics to see one's own role and that of others.
Heterarchy	A system of organization characterized by overlap, multiplicity, mixed ascendancy, and/or divergent-but-coexistent patterns of relation.
High Action/High Alignment (HA/HA)	Action Commitments that are aligned to achieve greater impact for a common result. Groups are in high action and high alignment when each leader is making an impactful contribution that connects and strengthens the contributions of others to accelerate progress toward population results.
Hold 3R Meetings	The competency of using the 3R framework to design and facilitate meetings that move groups from talk to action.
Hold Action and Results	The competency to make a difference in programs and community populations.
Hold Conversations	The competency of listening with openness, curiosity, and attentiveness to frame dialogues that achieve meeting results.
Hold Groups	The competency of supporting groups in having focused conversations that move to results.
Hold Mental Models	The competency of using a repertoire of perspectives that contribute to achieving meeting results.
Hold Roles	The competency of being aware of and making choices about roles that contribute to achieving meeting results.
Individual Development Plan (IDP)	A template used to focus skill practice and competency development.
Interest-Based Negotiation (IBN)	Fisher and Ury's approach to negotiation where people listen to each other to find common ground and build win-win solutions.
Ladder of Inference	Argyris originated and Senge popularized this concept that illuminates connections and interactions between actions, beliefs, conclusions, assumptions, meaning, data, and experiences.
Leadership in Action Program (LAP)	A collaborative leadership development program where multisector leaders work together to make a measurable improvement in community well-being.
Listen Fors (LFs)	The ability to consciously focus on hearing clearly the specific content areas of a conversation.

TERM	DEFINITION
Mnemonic	A short phrase to help people remember and apply skills and practices in their daily work.
Myers-Briggs Type Indicator (MBTI)	A personality inventory of psychological types reflecting people's preferences for gaining energy, taking in information, making decisions, and organizing their lives.
Performance Partnership Summit (PPS)	One and a half day meetings implemented with RBF skills at which leaders create and commit to implement strategies to reduce smoking prevalence in their communities.
Person-Role-System (PRS)	A framework for understanding the interrelationship of a person's unique characteristics and qualities and the roles they play (consciously and unconsciously) in different systems.
Proposal-Based Decision Making (PBDM)	A mental model and a practice for collaborative decision making.
RBF Hypotheses	The three hypotheses that inform the theory and practice of Results Based Facilitation.
RBL-APPs	Results Based Leadership Applications — resources available on the *www.rbl-apps.com* website to implement RBF designs and support the development of results based leadership.
Result in the Center and Results in the Chart	An orientation when a population result is the center of one's work enabling an understanding of your relationship to the result, your contribution to the result, and your relationship to others who can or do contribute to the result. This orientation supports accountability for aligned action to make measurable improvement in population-level results. The Results in the Center chart is a template for mapping your and others' relationship to a result in the context of sector and role. This tool is useful in developing an awareness of the B/ART and leveraging contributions across sectors into aligned strategies.
Results Based Facilitation (RBF)	A competency-based approach to participating in and facilitating meetings that get results.
Results Based Leadership (RBL)	A competency-based approach to leadership that equips leaders to make contributions in role to a measurable improvement in programs or whole populations.
Robert's Rules of Order (model of advocacy and majority rule)	A method of formal decision making in which people debate each other and as advocates present arguments to convince others to support their idea. The idea is expressed as a motion, and a decision is made when debate is concluded and a majority of people vote in favor of a motion.

TERM	DEFINITION
Role	The function assumed or part played by a person in a particular situation.
Role Clarity	Conscious awareness and choice about the role in conversations, meetings, and groups with an understanding of the boundaries of authority, role, and task for that role in that time and place.
Scaffolding	An intentional sequencing of learning to support competency development.
Sequence	The skill of ordering people speaking in conversations, topics and/or meeting results.
Situation, Behavior, Impact (SBI)	A method of feedback on the impact of using RBF skills that describes the situation where the facilitation was experienced, the behavior of the facilitator, and the impact of the facilitation on the participant.
Stages of Change Model (Prochaska and DiClemente)	A mental model that illuminates six stages in the behavioral change process.
Summarize	The skill of listing the content of conversations or meetings.
Synthesize	The skill of bringing parts into a meaningful whole.
Theory of Aligned Contributions (TOAC)	People practicing a specific skill set can be in high alignment and high action toward a common result. Alignment means that people's actions are coordinated, leveraged, and sequenced to accelerate progress toward the measurable improvement in organizational and community conditions.
Wheel of Emotions (Plutchik)	A classification scheme developed by Plutchik to categorize and name a nuanced range of emotions.
Z model	Based on MBTI, a structured problem-solving approach that starts with facts, then develops options.

ABOUT THE AUTHOR

Jolie Bain Pillsbury, Ph.D., President of Sherbrooke Consulting, Inc., is the author of the two book set on Results Based Facilitation. Ms. Pillsbury is a cofounder of the Results Based Facilitation Network and the Results Based Leadership Consortium, and she is a founding co-director of the Results Based Leadership Collaborative at the University of Maryland School of Public Policy.

As a developer and practitioner of Results Based Leadership, she has authored the *Theory of Aligned Contributions,* which serves as the foundation for research and basis for continuous improvement in the effectiveness of results based leadership practice.

For more information visit, *www.sherbrookeconsulting.com*, *www.rbl-apps.com*, *www.rbfnetwork.com*, and *www.rblconsortium.com*.

Made in the USA
Middletown, DE
21 June 2019